the pages of ANATOMY OF A HIT. Here too are the hard facts of money spent and money lost or earned.

Many of the facts are indeed noteworthy. During the first weeks of the Broadway production of Abie's Irish Rose, the auditorium was half empty, but it established a six-year record; Tobacco Road almost flopped during the first month, but it finally closed after a staggering eight-year run; The Ladder ran two years and yet was the greatest failure in the New York theater with losses estimated at over one million dollars; and plays as dissimilar as Mary, Mary and Who's Afraid of Virginia Woolf? have packed audiences in during the same year.

Mr. Laufe analyzes the play-doctoring of "The John Golden Play Factory," of Eddie Dowling, Elia Kazan, Joshua Logan and George Abbott. He evaluates the contributions of stars like Helen Hayes, Henry Fonda, Laurette Taylor and Ralph Bellamy. He examines the effect on the box office of timeliness, sordidness, sensationalism and literary merit.

ANATOMY OF A HIT is for everyone who loves the theater. It is an exciting history and an important reference work, including photographs of the original productions, an appendix of vital statistics and a complete index.

Anatomy

of a

HIT

Anatomy

Long-Run Plays on Broadway

HAWTHORN BOOKS, INC.

ABE LAUFE

of a HIT

from 1900 to the Present Day

INTRODUCTION BY

JACK GAVER

PUBLISHERS, NEW YORK CITY

First Edition, March, 1966

Photographs: Wide World and UPI

To Anna and Ben

FOREWORD

IF the subject of this book were such as to justify the title *Anatomy of an Igloo* or *Anatomy of a Cheesecake,* it would be reasonable to expect that the reader of same would acquire sufficient facts to enable him to construct his own ice palace or whip up a dairy dessert.

Goodness knows, there are enough facts in this book, *Anatomy of a Hit*—facts nostalgic, illuminating, entertaining—to—well, to fill a book, as Mr. Laufe has done so ably. But the reading of it isn't going to enable anyone to use these facts as a blueprint to produce a hit show on the Broadway stage.

There are dozens of examples in this book, with full and authentic details, of how various shows achieved financial success. Some of the examples may seem similar—Ah! A pattern; so that's the way it's done! But be not deceived. For in the Broadway theater, nothing is ever, ever the same.

Well, you might reasonably observe, if the book gives no certain formula for ensuring a hit show, possibly one can deduce, conversely, a set of rules showing what NOT to do and thus avoid producing a flop. Forget it. The same elements that make one show a failure might very well combine for a successful miracle in the case of another.

The commercial American theater is, in short, a morass of perversities, a labyrinth of contradictions, a bottomless well of intangibles. Nothing is that might not have been; what there is not well could have been.

Anything else, including such steadfast verities as AT&T and mother love, would sicken and quickly expire if similarly afflicted, but that Fabulous Invalid, the theater, seems to be kept alive by its miseries.

Mr. Laufe's book is, of course, more than a mere record of those productions that achieved long and prosperous runs. Into his account of these has been woven a pattern of the whole American professional stage of more than half a century. It will be appreciated by theater buffs of all ages. It will remind the oldsters anew of memories they cherish or things they have forgotten and are happy to have recalled for them. The younger set will find in it a liberal and entertaining education in matters outside their own experience.

It might even encourage many persons to try to write plays, hoping to pan some of that Broadway gold. This might not do the Invalid any good, but it would help the paper and typewriter manufacturers.

JACK GAVER

I want to express my thanks to Judge Florence Perlow Shientag and Mr. Julian S. Bach, Jr., whose encouragement helped me to complete this book; to Dr. Ralph Ware, whose sage advice helped me organize the material in Parts I and II; to Dr. and Mrs. Ford Curtis, who made available all resources of the Curtis Drama Collection; and to Mr. George Caldwell and Mr. Fred Kerner for their kindness and patience in helping me overcome many problems in preparing the manuscript.

I particularly want to thank Miss Hannah E. Bechtel for her invaluable technical assistance.

ABE LAUFE

CONTENTS

ILLUSTRATIONS

What
Makes
Drama
Run?

Introduction

In the early 1900s, Broadway productions, after ending successful runs, made road tours; plays established in New York had second and third companies on tour; and new plays had extensive out-of-town tryouts prior to New York premières. In New York City, the acknowledged focal point of theatrical activities, the number of productions increased steadily from 130 in the 1910–1911 theatrical season to approximately 270 in the 1927–1928 season.

In the 1930s, as the popularity of talking motion pictures increased, legitimate theaters converted to film entertainment, rising production and transportation costs caused fewer productions to be sent on tour, and the scope of the theater shrank until it became centered within a small radius of several city blocks in New York. Even in that small area, the theater contracted. All theaters on the once famous 42nd Street became motion picture houses, and television producers leased theaters in the section between 42nd Street and Central Park. The number of productions decreased steadily from 190 in the 1930–1931 season to approximately 50 in the 1961–1962 season.

To most people, the legitimate theater in America today signifies Broadway because theatrical activities have become concentrated in New York. Paradoxically, as the number of productions has decreased, the number of long-running plays on Broadway has increased. In the early 1900s, theatrical producers considered any play which ran 100 performances or more a success. In the 1960s, any play which runs only 100 performances is likely to be an outright failure. Very often a run of six months, or approximately 250 performances, is not long enough to recoup the original production costs.

In the history of Broadway's most popular plays, *Lightnin'* was a theatrical phenomenon in 1922 with its record of 1,291 consecutive performances. *Abie's Irish Rose,* produced in 1922, started uncertainly, developed into a commercial success, and established a new record in 1928 with a total of 2,327 performances. In 1933 when *Tobacco Road* opened, no one would have predicted that it would be a record breaker. The first few performances were not successful commercially, and actors took salary cuts to keep the play running. Then Burns Mantle helped the box office receipts by writing a second review in which he called the play a sociological study. Theatergoers began talking about the not-so-sociological, lurid angles of the play, and word-of-mouth advertising helped catapult the drama into a success. The management cut the price of admission and found that the larger audiences kept the gross receipts from falling. The long run on Broadway helped draw audiences on the road where *Tobacco Road* played extensive runs in larger cities and one-night stands in smaller communities which had not seen a stage production for almost twenty years. At the same time, the advertising on the road helped keep up attendance in New York. *Tobacco Road* finally closed in 1941 with a staggering total of 3,182 performances. Skeptics doubted that this record would ever be broken.

In 1939, *Life with Father* opened with little or no fanfare. After the production ran five years without a losing week, however, the producers were confident they could approximate the record set by *Tobacco Road.* They rented a theater for an entire season and scheduled Sunday performances, since the comedy drew its largest audiences on the weekends. Toward the end of the run, when the motion picture version was ready for release, the play operated at a loss. The producers brought the original leading actors back for several weeks, moved to a larger theater, lowered the admission prices, and kept the play running. After the final curtain of the

3,183rd performance, on June 14, 1947, the management held a special *Life with Father* party to celebrate the play's new record as the longest run in the history of the New York theater. A few weeks later, *Life with Father* closed with a total of 3,224 performances.

It would be foolhardy to speculate whether any production will ever top the record of *Life with Father*. At this writing, there is no production which has run long enough to be considered a rival, for any production must run at least six years to surpass *Abie's Irish Rose,* or eight years to surpass *Tobacco Road* and *Life with Father*.

For anyone interested in statistics, the list of plays and the number of performances offer ample opportunity for carping. Statistics for *Abie's Irish Rose* vary from 2,327 to 2,532 performances. The records for *White Cargo* are even more confusing, with total number of performances ranging from 686 to 864. *Peg o' My Heart* is listed in some books as having run 603 performances; in others, the total is 692. To quibble over the number of performances, therefore, is an easy matter, depending entirely upon which source of information the reader picks.

In discussing Broadway's most popular plays, the importance does not lie in the actual number of performances for any one production so much as in the fact that all plays with five hundred or more consecutive performances have run at least fifteen months on Broadway. To keep some standard of uniformity when there are variances in numbers of performances, the figures used in this book are those found in the majority of sources checked.

Authors and
Play Doctors

WHAT makes plays run five hundred or more performances on Broadway? Analysts who believe improved national economy influenced the long list of popular plays overlook the fact that the second longest running attraction, *Tobacco Road,* started during the height of the depression years. If economists argue that *Tobacco Road* operated at cut rates, they overlook another factor. Many plays running in the 1960s, including *Come Blow Your Horn, Never Too Late,* and *Mary, Mary,* operated toward the end of their runs on a two-tickets-for-the-price-of-one basis (twofers). The steady increase in admission prices would indicate that the number of long runs might be cut by such top prices as $7.50 per ticket for nonmusical productions, but even the reputed high premium prices of $20 and $25 per ticket bought from under-the-counter speculators didn't seem to affect recent hit dramas.

An author's reputation might logically explain a play's popularity, but if reputation means recognition from critics, then the list of authors who have written long-running plays presents some curious omissions. Eugene O'Neill heads the list of prize-winning American dramatists with four Pulitzer Prizes, one Critics' Circle Award, and the Nobel Prize for literature. Robert E. Sherwood ranks second with four Pulitzer Prizes, one for biography and three for drama. Yet not one play written by O'Neill or Sherwood ever reached the five-hundred-performance record. There aren't any long-running plays written by such prize-winning dramatists as Maxwell Anderson, Clifford Odets, Rachel Crothers, Thornton Wilder, William Inge, John Steinbeck, or William Saroyan.

My Fair Lady, based on George Bernard Shaw's *Pygmalion,* established a record as the longest-running American musical comedy. Ferenc Molnár's *Liliom* became the Rodgers and Hammerstein musical *Carousel;* S. N. Behrman adapted the book for the musical *Fanny* from a trilogy by Marcel Pagnol; and Frank Loesser used Sidney Howard's *They Knew What They Wanted* as the basis for his musical *The Most Happy Fella.* Yet none of the plays written by Shaw, Molnár, Behrman, or Sidney Howard ever ran five hundred performances.

If authors who wrote long-running successes continued to write popular plays, it would be logical to assume that their reputations as dramatists had box-office drawing power and that New York audiences were author-conscious. The production records for many authors, however, indicate that the dramatist alone is not responsible for the commercial success of a play. After winning both the Pulitzer Prize and the Critics' Circle Award for *Death of a Salesman,* Arthur Miller next wrote an adaptation of Henrik Ibsen's *An Enemy of the People* which ran only a few months. In 1934, Sidney Kingsley won a Pulitzer Prize for *Men in White. Dead End,* produced the following year, ran 687 performances. Kingsley followed this success with *Ten Million Ghosts,* a failure, as was his next play, *The World We Make,* produced in 1939, which closed after 80 performances. The first Tennessee Williams play produced on Broadway, *The Glass Menagerie,* a Critics' Circle winner, ran 581 performances. His second play, *You Touched Me,* written in collaboration with Donald Windham, closed after 109. Williams balanced two more long runs, *A Streetcar Named Desire* and *Cat on a Hot Tin Roof,* with two failures, *Orpheus Descending* (68 performances) and *Camino Real* (60 performances). After winning public approval for *The Show-Off* and the Pulitzer Prize for *Craig's Wife,* George Kelly wrote *Daisy Mayme* and *Behold the Bridegroom,* both failures. Mary Chase followed the prize-winning *Harvey* (1,775 performances) with *The Next Half Hour* (8 performances).

While Howard Lindsay and Russel Crouse were breaking records with *Life with Father,* their comedy, *Strip for Action,* produced during the run of *Life with Father,* failed. Their next play, *State of the Union,* ran two years and won the Pulitzer Prize. Showmen predicted, therefore, that *Life with Mother* would be another popular success. Lindsay and Crouse had already written two long-running plays; they had produced a third, Joseph Kesselring's *Arsenic and Old Lace;* and they had written a sequel to the most popular play on Broadway. Audiences definitely should have been conscious of the reputations of Lindsay and Crouse. Yet *Life with Mother* failed, with a reputed loss of about forty thousand dollars.

Jack Kirkland's *Tobacco Road* ran over 3,000 performances; *Tortilla Flat,* which Kirkland later adapted from the Steinbeck novel, ran 5. Garson Kanin's *Born Yesterday* ran 1,642 performances; his next play, *The Smile of the World,* 5. After two long-running successes, *I Remember Mama* and *The Voice of the Turtle,* John Van Druten's next play, *The Mermaids Singing,* which George Jean Nathan cited as "the best new comedy" for 1945–1946, should have been a popular hit. It closed after 53 performances.

The following tabulation proves even further that an author's reputation is unimportant to New York audiences:

AUTHOR	AUTHOR'S LONG RUNS	NO. OF PERF.	RECENT PLAYS	NO. OF PERF.
Robert Anderson	*Tea and Sympathy*	712	*All Summer Long*	44
			Silent Night,	
			Lonely Night	124
Jerome Lawrence	*Inherit the Wind*	806	*The Gang's*	
and Robert E. Lee	*Auntie Mame*	639	*All Here*	132
			Only in America	28
Ketti Frings	*Look Homeward, Angel*	564	*The Long Dream*	5
John Patrick	*The Teahouse of the August Moon*	1,027	*Good as Gold*	4
Dore Schary	*Sunrise at Campobello*	556	*The Highest Tree*	21
Carson McCullers	*Member of the Wedding*	501	*Square Root of Wonderful*	45
Elmer Rice	*Street Scene*	601	*The Winner*	30
Howard Teichman	*Solid Gold Cadillac*	526	*Miss Lonelyhearts*	12

AUTHOR	AUTHOR'S LONG RUNS	NO. OF PERF.	RECENT PLAYS	NO. OF PERF.
Noel Coward	*Blithe Spirit*	657	*Look after Lulu*	39
John Van Druten	*Voice of the Turtle*	1,557	*I've Got Sixpence*	23

Another complication is that the dramatist listed in the program is not always responsible for the final script which may well include the work of the director, the collaborator, the adaptor, or the unprogramed collaborator known as the play doctor. For most long-running productions which have been adaptations, the original authors are usually named in theater programs.

To the critics, authorship credits for most adaptations are a problem of evaluating, a problem of determining just how much the dramatist is indebted to his original source material. It is not surprising, therefore, that critics, fully aware that Lillian Hellman found the inspiration for *The Children's Hour* in "The Great Drumsheugh Case," a famous criminal court trial in the Scottish courts, either disregard or else briefly dismiss the primary source. They credit the merits in characterization or the flaws in dramatic construction solely to Miss Hellman. *I Remember Mama* is based on Kathryn Forbes's book, *Mama's Bank Account,* and Miss Forbes is listed in the credits, but critics always point out that John Van Druten reshaped and gave the isolated stories the dramatic unity and suspense which made the play a popular success. Similarly, no one fails to mention Clarence Day's sketches from which Howard Lindsay and Russel Crouse adapted *Life with Father,* but critics agree that Lindsay and Crouse deserve full credit for converting the sketches into America's longest-running play.

Double authorship credits present another problem—that of determining just how much each collaborator worked on a play or whether one author contributed the original idea and the second author revised or re-edited the first draft. Winchell Smith and Frank Bacon are credited as collaborators on *Lightnin',* which some critics have called a Winchell Smith "fixed" play. Smith's reputation as a play doctor is well enough established to assume that Smith probably rewrote and revised *Lightnin'* rather than collaborated on the original draft.

There is more conclusive evidence that two of George Abbott's collaborations were revisions of completed scripts. Philip Dunning wrote *Bright Lights,* later called *The Roaring Forties,* but before the play opened in New York, Abbott worked on the script, the play acquired a new title, *Broadway,* and Abbott and Dunning received equal billing as collaborators. Several producers had rejected the second play, a John Cecil Holm comedy, before Abbott read the script and agreed to revise it. By the time the play reached Broadway, the title had changed from *Hobby Horse* to *Three Men on a Horse,* and the program carried Abbott's name as collaborator.

Joshua Logan had no intention of being a collaborator when he started working on the dramatic adaptation of *Mister Roberts* with Thomas Heggen, author of the book, but Heggen insisted that Logan get credit for his invaluable contributions to the play. Since Logan started working on the production as a play doctor, it is logical to assume that other writers who have not received recognition have worked on productions in the long-running list ascribed to single authorship.

Dramatic criticisms and the written history of the American theater seldom reveal the work of play doctors. The extent of their revisions varies. The unofficial play doctor may be a director, producer, or actor who offers suggestions for rewriting or who helps reshape a play. The official play doctor is often an established dramatist who is called to revise, to rewrite, to suggest new scenes, or to make deletions. In general, however, the play doctor's contribution is omitted from discussions of plays. Several books have included brief items acknowledging reputations as play doctors for Winchell Smith, Max Marcin, John Hayden, and Harry Wagstaff Gribble, but the information is usually vague with little or no specific reference to the extent of their work.

Information about conditions under which the play doctor works or the nature of his revisions is even less specific. Inferences, insinuations, and obscure references about play doctors creep into newspaper columns and magazine articles dealing with popular plays, but any speculation on the basis of this evidence usually leads only to confusion. To know the complete story of who actually wrote a play, it is necessary to know the successive drafts, the conversations of authors and play doctors, and the suggestions of the actors and directors. The impossibility of finding such records is obvious. It would take a modern James Boswell to give a complete production record for any play unless the author himself has written a book about the production, as William Gibson did in *The Seesaw Log,* a factual account of the production of *Two for the Seesaw,* or as Frank D. Gilroy did in *About Those Roses,* a diary explaining the production problems of *The Subject Was Roses.*

Of all the drama critics, George Jean Nathan provided the most conclusive evidence to prove that an author is not always responsible for the success of a play and that authors often neglect to acknowledge the work of the play doctors. Eric Bentley, another eminent critic, commended Nathan for this "debunking." Critics who have not read the original script do not know who is responsible for writing the final draft of a play and, as a result, often make guesses about the indirect authorship. When Moss Hart and George S. Kaufman directed popular plays, critics frequently speculated on the Hart and Kaufman contributions to final drafts. They knew, for example, that Kaufman, in addition to being a collaborator, often worked as a play doctor and received a share of the author's royalties for plays which did not list him as collaborator. When he staged the Joseph Fields-Jerome Chodorov comedy, *My Sister Eileen,* New Yorkers insisted Kaufman had helped with the rewriting, but Kaufman denied it and credited full authorship to Fields and Chodorov. The same speculations and denials arose when Moss Hart directed another Fields-Chodorov comedy, *Junior Miss.* Yet denials did not convince critics that their speculations were unjustified.

Other producers and directors have also denied charges of play doctoring. When Howard Lindsay and Russel Crouse produced Joseph Kesselring's *Arsenic and Old Lace,* several reviewers credited them either for rewriting the play or else for elaborating on the original script, which Kesselring had called *Bodies in Our Cellar.* One critic explained that Kesselring had written the play as a serious drama but Lindsay and Crouse had converted it into a comedy. Other critics felt the producers' humorous touches were responsible for the play's immense popularity. Lindsay and Crouse denied everything and gave Kesselring full credit. The denials or lack of acknowledgments proved nothing to the reviewers, who retaliated that Kesselring had not written another popular play.

Rumors indicate that George Abbott doctored scripts which did not carry his name as collaborator, but comments about some of his doctoring are merely references to changes or suggestions he made for such plays as Clifford Goldsmith's *What a Life*. In *Best Plays of 1949–1950,* John Chapman revealed that it was Samuel Taylor, author of *The Happy Time,* who had rewritten *What a Life* for George Abbott's production. Other Abbott-directed popular plays described as "heavily doctored" include *Boy Meets Girl* and *Brother Rat.*

Both Brock Pemberton and his associate, Antoinette Perry, have been linked with play doctoring. As producers, they may have revised the Josephine Bentham-Herschel Williams comedy, *Janie,* or Lawrence Riley's *Personal Appearance,* but apparently they never disclosed whether they asked for or made any changes in the scripts. Probably the authors of these two plays were more cooperative than Preston Sturges, who wrote *Strictly Dishonorable*. Sturges agreed to revise the script if Pemberton and Perry would give the leading role to an actress he had chosen for the part rather than to Muriel Kirkland, whom Antoinette Perry wanted to play it. Pemberton refused and threatened to cancel the production. Sturges stopped arguing about the casting but did not make all the changes the producers wanted. When the play opened out of town and Sturges discovered Pemberton and Perry had changed lines and added new dialogue, he openly expressed his indignation, but evidently he calmed down when the New York critics gave *Strictly Dishonorable* excellent reviews.

Brock Pemberton and Antoinette Perry were also associated with *The Ladder,* which Pemberton produced and in which Miss Perry appeared as the leading lady. The play was written by J. Frank Davis but Edward Knoblock revised it before the New York première. Sometime during the run, Murdock Pemberton, brother of the producer, made further revisions, but apparently none of the doctoring helped the drama, nor did any of the play doctors seem anxious to get acknowledgment for their work.

John Golden was another producer who often doctored scripts but never asked for author credit when a play came through what he called "the Golden Play Factory." It is difficult to estimate, therefore, whether Golden did much or any doctoring on Frank Craven's *The First Year* or on the Winchell Smith–Frank Bacon comedy, *Lightnin'*. On the other hand, in discussing Austin Strong's *Seventh Heaven,* Percy Hammond revealed how much Golden had contributed to the play. According to Hammond, Golden had written a stack of revisions "three feet high" and had changed Strong's heroine, Diane, from a prostitute to a pickpocket. The uninformed critic cannot be blamed for speculating whether *Lightnin'* and *The First Year* underwent the same type of play doctoring in "the Golden Play Factory."

Discussions of *Abie's Irish Rose* usually include arguments about the popular appeal and the merit or lack of merit in the play but never about the author credit given to Anne Nichols. Oliver Morosco, who first produced *Abie's Irish Rose* in Los Angeles although not the final version in New York, reported in his autobiography, *Oracle on Broadway,* that he contributed a great deal to the structure and characters of *Abie's Irish Rose,* originally called *Marriage in Triplicate.* In the first draft, Miss Nichols had three changes of scene in the first act. Morosco explained that he speeded up the act and eliminated the scene shifting by adding two new characters, Mr. and Mrs. Cohen, who helped pull the play together as well as add laughs. Morosco further reported that Miss Nichols was delighted with the revisions.

Morosco also stated that he made an important revision of *Peg o' My Heart.* According to Morosco, J. Hartley Manners, the author, objected to any changes which would detract from Peg, played by his wife, Laurette Taylor. In order to get the changes, Morosco said he got Manners drunk, took him back to the hotel room, and then dictated the new scene he wanted. Morosco did not explain whether Manners and Miss Taylor were satisfied with the revision or why they permitted the revised scene to remain in the play.

Philip Yordan's *Anna Lucasta* underwent extensive doctoring at least twice. Yordan wrote the play, which he called *Anna Lukaska,* about a Polish family. Abram Hill, founder of the American Negro Theatre, agreed to produce it uptown and, at the suggestion of Yordan's agent, had it rewritten for his theater group to tell the story of a Negro family. In his review, George Jean Nathan named Philip Yordan as author and Harry Wagstaff Gribble and Abram Hill as adaptors. John Wildberg then decided to produce the play on Broadway and, once again, Harry Wagstaff Gribble readapted the script. Frederick O'Neal, a member of the cast, who discussed these revisions when the show played in London, said Gribble had rewritten the play extensively. The exact nature of the revisions has never been fully explained, and the only concrete proof is the

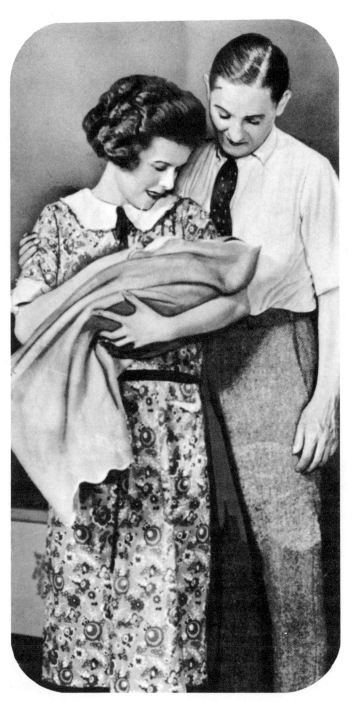

Abie's Irish Rose, the original Rosemary and Abie

credit given to the adaptors, although Yordan's name is usually listed as sole author.

There is more specific information about Tennessee Williams' *The Glass Menagerie,* for George Jean Nathan persistently made references to the contributions of Eddie Dowling, the director and producer, and Laurette Taylor, the star. When the play opened, the critics praised Laurette Taylor's performance as the mother and Eddie Dowling's excellent direction. After the New York opening, Mr. Williams, in an interview, said no lines were changed after he made the final draft and that only one scene suggested by Dowling had been inserted but that Williams himself had written the scene. Williams did admit that Dowling had written the last line, "There my memory ends—and your imagination begins." In *The Theater Book of 1945–46,* George Jean Nathan, who had advised Dowling to cast Laurette Taylor as the mother, said Williams had rewritten the one scene he mentioned in the interview, the drunk scene, at least four times until Dowling was satisfied, and that both Laurette Taylor and Eddie Dowling in acting their roles had kept the thought of the lines but had changed words or phrasing to suit their needs. The following year in *The Theater Book of 1946–47,* Nathan further elaborated on the importance of Miss Taylor's contribution to the play, explaining that she changed her performance from night to night, deliberately ad-libbing to give the audience a remarkable portrayal of the mother.

When Nathan first reviewed the play, he credited Dowling with its success because the original script included such trick devices as silent motion picture titles flashed on a screen. It was Dowling, according to Nathan, who gave the final production its simplicity and imaginative qualities. Williams edited the first published text of the play and explained in the production notes that the one major difference in the original and in the acting version was the exclusion of the screen titles and lantern device which he still included in the printed text. Curiously enough, more recent texts have eliminated the screen titles. In a later reference to *The Glass Menagerie,* Nathan again emphasized that Dowling had cut the screen titles and had also contributed more than the drunk scene, for he had invented the scene on the fire escape. Without it, Laurette Taylor would not have had time to make the costume change Williams specified in the script.

Controversy over the play seemed to die down when Williams' *A Streetcar Named Desire* opened. Some critics suggested the credit for tightening the play should go to Elia Kazan, the director. George Jean Nathan, in contrast to his many long explanations of contributions to *The Glass Menagerie,* merely indicated that he was not certain whether the play, as the audience saw it, was the original script or whether it included changes by Kazan. Nathan added that Williams admitted Kazan had helped the play, "so," Nathan concluded, "I remain in the dark." Perhaps if Williams had denied getting any help, Nathan might have probed for more precise information.

Williams' *Cat on a Hot Tin Roof* shows more concretely changes made in production. In the printed text, Williams included two third acts: first, the act as performed on Broadway and which Williams said he was required to write, and second, the last act as he wrote it originally and which he preferred.

When the scattered inferences and references to play doctoring are sketchily assembled, as they are here, the theatergoer becomes troubled. It is futile to evaluate an author's importance to a popular play when even inconclusive evidence indicates play doctors have worked on the script. It is definitely impossible to determine all revisions made by play doctors. And when even an acknowledged author's reputation does not insure the popularity of a play, any attempt to find reasons why plays have run five hundred or more performances must be made on some impartial basis other than the work of authors, adaptors, directors, producers, or play doctors.

Stars

IF an author's reputation is discounted as a basis for establishing a long run, the next drawing power to be considered is the actor who gets top billing above the title of the play. The theory that stars draw long lines to the box office gained in popularity in the early 1900s, when productions often centered around the stars. Charles Frohman selected scripts specifically for Maude Adams or Billie Burke. David Belasco built plays around Lenore Ulric, Blanche Bates, Mrs. Fiske, and Mrs. Leslie Carter. Moreover, several plays have substantiated the theory that a star determines the success or failure of a production.

Henry Fonda's excellent performance plus his box office value as a motion picture star helped prolong the run of *Mister Roberts* in New York. When Fonda left the cast, box office receipts dropped over ten thousand dollars per week. After Fonda joined the road company, receipts for that company often exceeded the grosses in the same cities where *Mister Roberts* had previously played with another cast.

If a star's box office magnetism makes a drama successful, the star's name becomes inseparably linked with the play, frequently overshadowing the importance of the play or of the author. Such close associations include Frank Bacon and *Lightnin'*, with Bacon, the star, more important than Bacon the collaborating dramatist; Helen Hayes and both *Victoria Regina* and *Happy Birthday;* and Katharine Cornell and *The Barretts of Wimpole Street*. Even Tallulah Bankhead in the revival of *Rain* could not make critics forget Jeanne Eagels in the original production, for most of them mentioned Miss Eagels in their reviews of the Bankhead revival. Although in one particular season there were eight road companies of *Peg o' My Heart* touring the United States and Canada simultaneously, critics still associated the role of Peg with Laurette Taylor.

A cursory sampling of plays with five hundred or more performances would seem to indicate that stars are responsible for establishing long runs. Ralph Bellamy, for example, has appeared in four long-running plays: *Tomorrow the World, State of the Union, Detective Story,* and *Sunrise at Campobello*. Perhaps Mr. Bellamy's drawing power in the 1940s in *Tomorrow the World* could have been associated with his reputation as a motion picture star. In *State of the Union* he appeared with an excellent costarring and supporting cast, but his appearance in these two plays earned him the starring roles in *Detective Story* and *Sunrise at Campobello*. As further proof of Bellamy's importance to *Detective Story,* the road company, with another star in the leading role, closed before completing its scheduled tour. When Bellamy's television commitments prevented his going on the road at the end of the New York run, the management closed the show rather than risk a second unprofitable road tour. *Sunrise at Campobello* without Bellamy also failed to duplicate its New York success on the road.

Elisabeth Bergner is responsible for the 585 performances of *The Two Mrs. Carrolls*. Maurice Evans kept *Dial M for Murder* running for more than five hundred performances. Gertrude Berg and Sir Cedric Hardwicke were the principal reasons for the long run of *A Majority of One*. *Lightnin'* closed on the road when Frank Bacon died.

A closer examination of the plays, however, raises doubts about the drawing power of the stars. Many of the long runs succeeded without box office names; others continued their runs in spite of numerous cast changes; and still others created new stars out of featured players or virtually unknown performers. There were exceptions, of course. No critic would challenge the statement that without Helen Hayes *Happy Birthday* would never have run 541 performances. Yet Miss Hayes's box office magnetism could not convert *The Wisteria Trees* into a long-running success. Maurice Evans did not duplicate his success in *Dial M for Murder* when he appeared in *The Aspern Papers,* a financial failure. In addition to *Mister Roberts,* Henry Fonda originated the lead in another long-running play, *Two for the Seesaw,* but three of Fonda's more recent plays, *A Gift of Time, Critic's Choice,* and *Silent Night, Lonely Night,* were either failures or, at best, moderate successes.

Many of the top names in the theater are not associated with plays which have run five hundred or more performances in New York. There is not one play in the list which featured or starred Katharine Cornell, Alfred Lunt, Lynn Fontanne, any of the three Barrymores, George Arliss, Tallulah Bankhead, Judith Anderson, or Leslie Howard. Although Gertrude Lawrence had a long run in the musical *The King and I,* she never appeared in a drama which ran five hundred performances. Some of these stars, however, have appeared more than five hundred times in one play if the road performances are counted. The Lunts, particularly, have had long road tours. Katharine Cornell's tours with *The Barretts of Wimpole Street* were very extensive. But none of these stars has appeared for five hundred or more consecutive performances in any one play on Broadway.

Life with Father is a classic example of the drawing power of a play regardless of the cast. The leading roles were originated by Howard Lindsay and Dorothy Stickney, whose performances pleased the critics. Other actors, however, received the same warm appraisal from the press. Some of the critics, for example, were almost ecstatic about the performances given by Percy Waram and Lillian Gish when *Life with Father* opened in Chicago. Nor were Mr. Lindsay and Miss Stickney the principal box office draws on Broadway. As the play continued its long run in New York, the cast changed with comparatively little effect on the gross receipts. By the time *Life with Father* closed, eleven actors had played Father Day. In addition to Howard Lindsay and Percy Waram, they were Arthur Margetson, Wallis Clark, Donald Randolph, Louis Calhern, A. H. Burns, Harry Bannister, Edwin Cooper, Stanley Ridges, and Brandon Peters. Lillian Gish did not appear on Broadway in the role of Vinnie, but her sister, Dorothy Gish, was one of the eight actresses to play Mother Day in New York. The others were Nydia Westman, Lily Cahill, Mary Loane, Margalo Gillmore, Elaine Ivans, and Muriel Kirkland. *Variety* did report that toward the end of the long run, *Life with Father* played to unprofitable business for a number of weeks. The drop in receipts, however, should be attributed to the length of the run rather than to the lack of star names, for the producers kept the play running to establish a new long-run record. Box office receipts improved when Mr. Lindsay and Miss Stickney rejoined the cast in the 397th week of the run, but again, there were other factors for the improved grosses such as additional publicity and reduced admissions. The new publicity blurbs would have interested most theatergoers, for the news stories reported, quite accurately, that the original stars re-entered the company to celebrate the 3,183rd performance, the one which surpassed the record held by *Tobacco Road*.

Henry Hull gave a remarkable performance as Jeeter Lester in *Tobacco Road*. Mr. Hull also deserves part of the credit for converting the play from a failure into a success because he accepted the minimum Equity salary in the early weeks of the run to cut expenses and to keep the play open. On the other hand, it would be ridiculous to attribute the seven-year run to his excellent performance as Jeeter, since box office receipts did not drop when his successor, James Barton, proved to be equally effective in the role. James Bell, Eddie Garr, and Will Geer, who followed Barton in the New York cast, gave additional proof that the role was not associated with any one performer. John Barton, uncle of James, and Taylor Holmes were also successful in the profitable touring companies.

In many respects, the case history of *Harvey* almost parallels that of *Tobacco Road*. In both plays the original star received rave press notices. The major difference, however, was that Henry Hull's performance drew better notices than the play. On the other hand, although critics were almost unanimous in praising Frank Fay's performance as Elwood P. Dowd, the alcoholic hero of *Harvey,* they devoted as much if not more space to a discussion of the humor and merits of the comedy, which later received the Pulitzer Prize. In fact, the box office receipts increased when James Stewart, the first substitute for Frank Fay, played the role for six weeks, an increase easily explained because, in the 1940s, New York audi-

Tobacco Road, three of the Jeeters—Charles Timblin, Will Geer and James Barton

ences were intrigued with the personal appearance of the top-rank-
ing motion picture star. During the lengthy run of *Harvey,* Joe E.
Brown, who had starred in the road company, also appeared in the
New York cast, as did Jack Buchanan, James Dunn, Bert Wheeler,
and the producer himself, Brock Pemberton, who played Elwood
for one Actor's Equity benefit performance.

Sally Middleton, the heroine and perhaps the most important of
the three characters in John Van Druten's *The Voice of the Turtle,*
was first played by Margaret Sullavan, but the play continued to
draw capacity houses when Betty Field replaced her. Not only Miss
Field but also Florence Rice, K. T. Stevens, Martha Scott, Louise
Horton, Beatrice Pearson, and Phyllis Ryder appeared as Sally
Middleton in the New York production and in road companies during the long run.

Arthur Miller's Willy Loman in *Death of a Salesman* is apparently
another actor-proof role. Gene Lockhart, who replaced Lee J. Cobb,
the first Willy Loman, was in turn succeeded by Albert Dekker.
When Dekker left the cast to exchange roles with Thomas Mitchell,
star of the road company, Robert Simon, the understudy, played
Willy Loman until Mitchell joined the New York cast.

Born Yesterday opened out of town with Jean Arthur, but Judy
Holliday stepped into the role of Billie Dawn before the play reached
Broadway. Although Judy Holliday and the play are usually linked
together, Billie was played by Jan Sterling, Cara Williams, and
Eleanor Lynn before the New York run ended, and later by Mary
Martin in the television production.

Rosalind Russell and *Auntie Mame* are almost synonymous since
Miss Russell starred in both the stage play and the motion picture.
Miss Russell left the cast before the end of the run in New York
and was replaced by Greer Garson, who, in turn, was followed by
Beatrice Lillie. Constance Bennett, Sylvia Sidney, and Shirl Con-
way also played Auntie Mame in the road companies.

Rather than credit the stars with the long-running successes, it
seems more logical to credit the plays with enhancing the reputations of the actors. *Born Yesterday* placed Judy Holliday and Paul
Douglas in the top ranks of Broadway performers. *Claudia* made
Dorothy McGuire a star. It was not until Jessica Tandy played
Blanche DuBois in *A Streetcar Named Desire* that critics called her
a second Jeanne Eagels. The same play catapulted Marlon Brando,

whose previous experience had been in secondary roles in *I Remember Mama, Truckline Cafe,* and *Candida,* to eventual stardom in Hollywood. Helen Menken's great success came with *Seventh Heaven.* Monty Woolley, a featured player, earned star billing as Sheridan Whiteside in *The Man Who Came to Dinner.* Neither the late Mady Christians nor Oscar Homolka had ever approached the popular approval they received during their long run in *I Remember Mama.* It might be added that they never again equaled it.

Quite a few actors should be singled out for memorable performances in other long-running plays. Henry Travers and Josephine Hull aided *You Can't Take It with You* with their expert interpretations respectively of Grandpa Vanderhof and Penny. Lee Tracy drew excellent notices for his performance as the hoofer in *Broadway,* produced in the 1920s, and, more than thirty years later, for his performance in *The Best Man.* Shirley Booth, who had shown her flair for comedy in *Three Men on a Horse* and *My Sister Eileen,* demonstrated her dramatic ability in *Tomorrow the World.* To assert blandly that the performances of these actors were not responsible for long runs would be nonsensical, for excellent performances are almost always essential to commercial success. But to maintain that the performers overshadowed the play in importance would be equally nonsensical, for even expert acting does not guarantee a long run. Josephine Hull could not salvage *Minnie and Mr. Williams.* Although critics have always praised her performances, Shirley Booth has appeared in several unsuccessful plays in recent years, and her greatest dramatic success, *Come Back, Little Sheba,* ran less than one season.

It is not derogatory to an excellent cast, therefore, to say the play itself is frequently of the greatest importance in establishing a long run. There were no stars in such comedies as *Janie, Junior Miss, Dear Ruth, The Doughgirls,* or *Sailor, Beware!* Expert acting immeasurably helped *Three Men on a Horse, What a Life, Kiss and Tell,* and *Brother Rat,* but the plays themselves and George Abbott's swift-paced direction were even greater assets. *Dead End, The Children's Hour,* and *Street Scene* enhanced the reputations of the authors, Sidney Kingsley, Lillian Hellman, and Elmer Rice, respectively, rather than the actors. With the exception of Canada Lee, none of the cast members of *Anna Lucasta* were known to Broadway theatergoers. The original Anna, the very photogenic

Hilda Simms, drew remarkable publicity spreads in such magazines as *Life,* but Anna proved to be another actor-proof role when succeeding actresses continued in the long run. Sidney Poitier's motion picture reputation brought him the starring role in *A Raisin in the Sun,* but Claudia MacNeil was quickly elevated to stardom when Poitier left the cast. There were no starring roles in *The Tenth Man, Strictly Dishonorable, Personal Appearance,* or *Bird in Hand.* It would probably be difficult for even a seasoned playgoer to recall the cast of Leon Gordon's *White Cargo* or the Mary Roberts Rinehart–Avery Hopwood mystery, *The Bat.* Most theatergoers know Anne Nichols wrote *Abie's Irish Rose,* but it is doubtful if these same theatergoers could recall as easily the names Mathilde Cottrelly, Bernard Gorcey, Howard Land, Alfred Wiseman, Robert B. Williams, Marie Carroll, John Cope, Harry Bradley, and Dorothy Grau, who comprised the original cast.

The importance of the star cannot be minimized, for the star may, and often does, have enough popular appeal to keep a production running five hundred performances. But when the production runs one thousand performances or more, with only the few exceptions mentioned, the cast has changed, often almost completely, and it is the play itself which draws patrons to the box office for a prolonged run. To find out what makes Broadway's biggest hits, therefore, the most logical method left is to analyze the plays and their Broadway productions.

1900
to
1950

Popular
Fare

IN discussing what makes drama run five hundred performances, one long-running production should be excluded. Although *The Ladder,* produced in 1926, ran 789 performances, it certainly does not belong in any list of popular plays. It does have the distinction of establishing two records, neither of which has any connection with popularity. First, from a commercial point of view, it is the greatest failure in the New York theater, with losses estimated from $750,000 to $1,500,000; and second, it is the only commercially produced drama presented without admission charges. The producer, who felt the play had a message, tried selling tickets at reduced rates to draw larger audiences. Then he offered refunds to dissatisfied patrons, but attendance did not pick up until he decided to admit the public free of charge. After eight months, the management again sold tickets and attendance dropped. At the end of the second year, the producer closed the show. According to reports, there were only a handful of people in the audience at the last performance. There are no available texts of the play and the few references in theatrical histories to *The Ladder,* which presumably dealt with reincarnation, are anything but complimentary.

Whether *Separate Rooms* could be called a popular play or

whether it should be called a product of ingenious management, which offered such inducements as reduced rates or two tickets for the price of one, is debatable. In the last ten years, more than one successful play, including *Mary, Mary,* has resorted to the two-for-one ticket policy to prolong the run. The basic difference between *Separate Rooms* and more recent production, however, is that *Separate Rooms* flourished almost exclusively as a bargain price attraction while the more current popular shows have resorted to reduced rates only after running at least a season. Cut rates did not go into effect for *Never Too Late,* for example, until the last year of the run.

Separate Rooms, produced in 1940, is primarily a framework for obvious gags, with little or no attempt to make the characters believable. The plot concerns a newspaper columnist, his younger brother, who is a playwright, and an actress who marries the playwright for convenience rather than for love. Through a series of contrived situations, the newspaper columnist forces the actress to become a model wife.

The printed text includes a page with excerpts from New York reviews to help amateur producers with their publicity. The excerpts, taken out of context, are highly complimentary, but the original criticisms are another matter. For example, one excerpt reads, ". . . authors have stuffed it nearly to the choking point with theatrical gags," but Herrick Brown had written, ". . . its numerous authors have stuffed it nearly to the choking point with theatrical gags. Not all of them are fresh and quite a few of them are decidedly not for the squeamish. . . ." A second excerpt reads, "frequent funny lines," but John Chapman had said, "There are fairly frequent funny lines, but most of them sound as though one of the collaborators had said, 'This is a good gag. Let's put it in here.' "

Several long-running plays, not quite so contrived as *Separate Rooms,* might also be dismissed as undistinguished drama that entertained audiences. The popular appeal depended more on the interpretations of the stars than on the cleverness of the plot. Three of these plays, *East Is West, Kiki,* and *The Gold Diggers,* all produced before 1923, had long runs because they provided tours de force for Fay Bainter, Lenore Ulric, and Ina Claire, respectively.

East Is West, produced in 1918, deals with Ming Toy, who is to be sold on the Chinese Love Boat, a woman market, to the ruthless Chang Lee. Billy Benson, son of the American ambassador to China, persuades his friend, Lo Sang Kee, to buy Ming Toy and take her to San Francisco where she will be the ward of Lo Sang Kee. The second act takes place one year later in America. Billy has fallen in love with Ming Toy. Racial barriers, however, prevent his marrying her. At the beginning of Act IV, the situation seems hopeless, but the audience and Billy are both startled to learn that Ming Toy is not Chinese, that she had been kidnapped when she was a child, and that her father had been one of the most distinguished American scholars.

The story is almost a rehashed version of *Madame Butterfly,* except for its obviously imposed, happy ending which, according to reports, the authors tacked on when the producer balked at presenting the play in its original draft. The dialogue undoubtedly would have to be more effective on the stage than it is in the text. Ming Toy speaks a combination Chinese-American dialect which strains for humor in such lines as, "Oh, will be so glad to go to America. So glad to see Statue of Liberty hold big punk stick." It might be added that the talking picture version with Lupe Velez speaking the Chinese-American dialect in a Mexican accent did not offer any improvement.

In his essay, "Stage Illusions," Charles Lamb wrote, "We confess we love in comedy to see an audience naturalized behind the scenes, taken into the interest of the drama, welcomed as bystanders, however." Many playwrights have used this process of naturalizing to give audiences the advantage of knowing more than the actors on stage. For example, if a character hides behind a screen or door, or if one actor confides secret information to another, the audience then knows more about the plot development than some of those involved in the action, and therefore anticipates what will probably happen. The suspense increases because the audience is not sure the plot will turn out as it hopes it will.

If *East Is West* had used this trick device by informing the audience that Ming Toy was American but Billy Benson believed she was Chinese, the play would have illustrated Lamb's theory of naturalizing. Such a revision would have meant rewriting more than one scene instead of the last few pages of the script, but the added naturalization would have created a sympathetic Ming Toy instead of a Chinese-American hoyden, and the audience could have anticipated a happy ending.

East Is West was a personal triumph for Fay Bainter, whose portrayal of Ming Toy entertained audiences for 680 performances, but the theatergoer who has never seen Miss Bainter in the play cannot visualize the charm of the character from the printed page.

Kiki, the David Belasco adaptation of André Picard's play, produced in 1921, established a six-hundred-performance record for an American production of a French play. *Kiki* is the slight story of a Parisian coquette who acts like a trollop. The final revelation that she is a "good girl" is almost as contrived as the ending in *East Is West.* What's more, it is false to the characterization of the gamin who bites and scratches the men who try to put her out of an office into which she has forced her way, and who feigns catalepsy to prevent being thrown out of a man's apartment. There is one hint that Kiki is not as bad as she appears when the hero, on whom she has forced her attention, tries to kiss her; in this scene she fights and kicks to keep him away. If audiences had known why Kiki repulsed the man after she had tried so hard to attract him, the situation would have become plausible.

The silent motion picture version followed the play closely. When Mary Pickford made *Kiki* as an "all talking–all singing" musical picture in the 1930s, however, her reputation as "America's Sweetheart" assured audiences that Kiki would be a good girl, that she would marry the hero, and that the ending would not be illogical. It is fascinating to speculate what motion picture producers would do to the story today if they presented an updated version.

In 1921, the chief entertainment features of *Kiki* were Lenore Ulric's acting and David Belasco's production. The cleverness with which Miss Ulric played Kiki—particularly in her cataleptic-fit scene—or the ingenious direction, staging, and lighting Belasco contributed to all his productions, cannot be visualized from reading the typewritten manuscript, the only available text of the play. The reader is overcome with detailed stage directions and hard-to-read dialogue and fails to discover what made the comedy run six hundred performances.

It is much easier to see from the manuscript the reason that the Avery Hopwood farce *The Gold Diggers,* which Belasco produced in 1919, charmed audiences. The ending is not contrived, as in *Kiki* and in *East Is West.* Moreover, the author used Lamb's theory of naturalizing by letting the audience know that the heroine, Jerry

Lamar, is deliberately sacrificing her own reputation to prove that a little chorus girl, whose marriage is opposed by a stern guardian of the prospective groom, is not as bad as the other chorus girls. The audience, well aware of Jerry's scheme to make the guardian believe she is a "gold digger," is not surprised when the guardian learns the truth and marries her. In fact, what concerns the audience most is how long it will take the stuffed-shirt guardian to realize that he is wrong.

The character types which audiences enjoyed included the brash chorus girl, the chorus girl who is good to her old-fashioned mother, the innocent chorus girl, the bewildered juvenile, and the stern guardian who falls in love with the glamorous star. The plot, in 1919, was funny but slight. Today, after at least one silent motion picture version and several talking pictures made and released with varying titles in a whole series of gold-digger musicals, the story is hackneyed.

The Gold Diggers depended largely upon Ina Claire's perform- ance as Jerry for its effectiveness, which unfortunately cannot be visualized in reading the typewritten text, the only available version on paper. *The Gold Diggers,* like *Kiki,* also benefited from Belasco's staging and direction. Although critics referred to the play as "empty comedy" and "claptrap," the humorous treatment of sex, a naturalized audience which was aware of Jerry's deception, and Ina Claire's sparkling performance must have offered enjoyable enter- tainment to keep the play running for 720 performances.

Another Belasco production, *The Boomerang,* by Winchell Smith and Victor Mapes, produced in 1915, was not a tour de force for a star nor did it present an unusual story. The frothy plot deals with Dr. Gerald Sumner who tries to cure his first patient, Budd Wood- bridge, of his moody jealousy of Grace Tyler. Dr. Sumner suggests that Budd pretend to be in love with Virginia Xelva, Dr. Sumner's office nurse; but the plan boomerangs when Dr. Sumner thinks Virginia is in love with Preston De Witt. In the last act, Budd and Grace are reconciled, and the final curtain falls as Dr. Sumner takes Virginia in his arms.

Belasco's production helped account for the run of 522 perform- ances. In the first and last acts, Belasco used a fully equipped doc- tor's office on stage, even to running water. In an era when Belasco dominated the theater world with his use of stage innovations, new methods of lighting, and authenticity of details, the physical production undoubtedly interested theatergoers. The story itself, though trite, was another magnet, for it presented a new type of medical treatment. Although the words *psychiatry* and *psychology* were never mentioned, Dr. Sumner's treatment of Budd, even to the point of injecting distilled water and pretending that it was an important serum, added a novel twist. And since Dr. Sumner was trying to cure jealousy rather than a physical ailment, audiences undoubtedly were interested to see how the plan worked.

If one love story interested an audience, then two love stories made the play doubly interesting. The audience, naturalized in the second act about Dr. Sumner's plans, kept wondering whether the scheme would be successful. In the third act, the audience suspected that the plan would boomerang; and when Dr. Sumner began to show that he was jealous, the audience settled back with an "I knew it" attitude, and waited patiently for the play to end logically. Because it did, not for just one love affair but for two, the theatergoer went home contented.

Just as Belasco's production helped the popularity of *The Boomerang,* the combination of Belasco as producer and Charles Klein as author contributed to the popular success of *The Music Master,* produced in 1904. The play should really be called a tour de force for David Warfield, one of Belasco's top stars, since it gave him a role that capitalized on strong emotion and sentiment. Most theater historians praise Warfield's performance but dismiss the play as "popular fare."

The Music Master tells the story of Herr Anton Von Barwig, who has come to America to find the man who had run off with his wife and small daughter. Von Barwig has hunted for sixteen years for his lost child; and then, by coincidence, the girl, now called Helen Stanton, comes to his studio to ask him to teach a young child in whom she is interested. Von Barwig recognizes his daughter and persuades her to take piano lessons so that he can be with her. Helen feels an attachment for Von Barwig which she cannot explain. Several months later, Henry Stanton, the villain, discovers that Von Barwig has been teaching Helen. He tells the servants to refuse to admit him, but Helen discovers the order and countermands it. When Von Barwig and Stanton finally meet, Von Barwig threatens to reveal Helen's identity. Stanton tells him that if he does, the

Crugers will refuse to accept her as a daughter-in-law. At this point, Von Barwig says, "Then if they don't take her—I take her! If they don't want her, I want her! I'm selfish; I'm selfish," a speech that became one of the most quoted of the early 1900s. In Act III, on her wedding day, Helen learns who her father really is and returns to his studio to take him back to Leipzig with her on her honeymoon. The curtain falls on a tearful but happy reunion.

David Warfield's performance as Von Barwig impressed audiences enough to keep the play running for 540 performances. The play itself, however, also had popular appeal. In the first place, the dramatist naturalized his audience by revealing in the first act that Von Barwig knew he had discovered his daughter. The audience wanted father and daughter reunited and the happy ending was again the outcome of its wish. If the drama had ended any other way, it is doubtful if even Warfield's performance could have given it such a long run. In the second place, Helen, the heroine, triumphed over the villain, a dramatic situation which always pleases audiences. In the third place, the entire drama is crammed with sentimental touches including a love affair between Poons, a young German musician whose attempts to speak English are funny, and Jenny, the maid, whose fractured German is even funnier; a scene in which the freaks in the museum where Von Barwig had been playing send him a farewell gift; and finally, the big reunion scene in the last act when Helen tries to get Von Barwig to admit that he is her father by repeating, "Who giveth this woman to be married?" until Von Barwig finally says, "I do."

Critics were more kindly disposed to the second long-running play by Charles Klein, *The Lion and the Mouse,* produced in 1905. They liked not only the acting but also the theme. The play was presented at the time Theodore Roosevelt was fighting the big trusts, and the villain of the drama was rumored to be John D. Rockefeller. Act I takes place in the home of Judge Rossmore where Shirley Rossmore, who has just returned from Europe, learns that her father was the latest victim of John Ryder, the most powerful financier in the United States. Judge Rossmore, who has handed down a decision unfavorable to Ryder's interests, is accused of taking a bribe in the form of shares of stock. Although the Judge had written two letters to Ryder asking him about investing money—letters which would have cleared the Judge—Ryder refuses to acknowledge the letters or to produce them for court evidence. Act I also reveals that Shirley and Ryder's son, Jeff, are in love.

Act II takes place in John Ryder's private office in his New York residence. Ryder has decided that Jeff should marry Kate Roberts, a senator's daughter, so that he can be sure that Roberts, an influential member of the senate, will be favorably disposed to his business deals. In the time lapse between Act I and Act II, however, Shirley had written a novel, under the pen name of Sarah Green, about a man who strongly resembles Ryder. Ryder, therefore, had invited Sarah Green to his home to learn where she had obtained so much information that paralleled his own life, and also to ask her to work on his biography. After some persuasion, Shirley agrees to stay at the Ryder home and tells Jeff she wants to get possession of the letters which her father had written.

When Act III opens, Shirley had ingratiated herself with both Mr. and Mrs. Ryder. Ryder tells her the fable of the lion and the mouse and asks her to gnaw the ropes that tie Jeff to the Rossmore girl. By the end of the act, Ryder learns that the Rossmore letters are missing. At the climax, Shirley reveals her identity and announces she has the letters, which she intends to take to Washington. In Act IV, Ryder admits Shirley has defeated him, but he is so anxious to have her as a daughter-in-law that he will help clear her father's name.

Implausible as the story may sound in synopsis, it has strong melodramatic moments. The talking picture version made in the late 1920s reveals more definitely the power of the climax. In the early days of sound films, producers experimenting with talking pictures tried the novelty of making several reels of silent film and then, to heighten the effect, putting the last reel in sound. *The Lion and the Mouse* provided an admirable vehicle for this combination. The cast, headed by Lionel Barrymore and Mae McAvoy, mimed through most of the picture, but, in the final sequence, spoke the dialogue and proved in the late 1920s that the climax was still as exciting as it had been a quarter of a century earlier.

In addition to the strong climax, the timely theme, and the excellent portrayals of Edmund Breese as Ryder, Grace Elliston as Shirley, and Richard Bennett as Jeff, *The Lion and the Mouse* had other qualities which insured its long run. It epitomized the popular situation of the triumphant heroine, which pleased audiences particularly with this play because the woman triumphed over so ruthless a man as John Ryder. Next, it contained scene after scene in which the audience knew more than some of the characters—that is, in which the audience was naturalized. The spectators enjoyed watching Shirley fool the great John Ryder and also imagined where Shirley had learned the intimate secrets about Ryder's personal life —his love affair with a girl in Vermont, his morbid fear of death. The naturalized audience also hoped that Shirley would obtain the letters, clear her father's name, and marry Jeff. Since Ryder not only withdrew his objections to Shirley as a daughter-in-law but actually pleaded with her to marry his son, the audience, prepared for the happy ending, received an extra bonus. Such lines as Ryder's, "I want your respect—I want to earn it—I can't buy it," may seem ludicrous today, but the dramatic vigor of the play kept *The Lion and the Mouse* running for 686 performances, a record that was not equaled for thirteen years.

The Two Mrs. Carrolls, Martin Vale's murder melodrama produced in 1943, has nearly as strong a climax as *The Lion and the Mouse* but bogs down with a hackneyed plot. Martin Vale (pseudonym for Mrs. Marguerite Veiller) constructed a play that suffers by comparison with other long-running psychological murder melodramas such as *Angel Street* and *Dial M for Murder* which have better continuity and greater suspense.

The Two Mrs. Carrolls tells the story of an artist who tries to poison his second wife. The first wife, whom he has also tried to poison, learns of his plan and arrives in time to warn the heroine, the second Mrs. Carroll. The cast includes such familiar characters as the devoted wife who does not suspect her husband's murderous intentions, the noble ex-suitor of the wife who arrives at the opportune moment, the obvious siren who would like to be the third Mrs. Carroll, and the artist who becomes enraptured with the siren's beauty and insists upon painting her portrait. Although the ending is not as contrived as the ending of *East Is West* or *Kiki,* it is still unconvincing. Earlier in the play, the audience learns that the poison which Carroll is giving his wife works slowly. Yet, in the final episode, Carroll, to avoid capture, drinks the poison and dies almost instantly.

There are two possible explanations for the play's phenomenal success. *The Two Mrs. Carrolls* was produced in 1943 during the booming World War II years when a greater number of Broadway shows than usual had long runs. Even the Margaret Webster production of *Othello* ran 296 performances, the only Shakespearean production to run over 250 consecutive performances in the history of the New York theater.

A second and more definite explanation is Elisabeth Bergner's interpretation of the second Mrs. Carroll, which impressed both critics and audiences. Critics who ripped into the play still wrote favorably of her performance. Anyone who reads the play, however, without the benefit of seeing or hearing Miss Bergner, remains unimpressed. The first act does little to arouse suspense; the plot develops far too slowly; and the dialogue, when read, seems downright dull. *The Two Mrs. Carrolls* is, at best, a conventional melodrama which provided Elisabeth Bergner with a tour de force that interested audiences for 585 performances.

Unlike plays with heroines who entertain audiences but not readers, *Happy Birthday,* the Anita Loos comedy produced in 1945, has a heroine whose charm even the reader can grasp. The slight plot concerns Addie Bemis, a meek librarian who secretly admires a bank clerk. She follows him into a bar where he is having a rendezvous with an obvious hussy. Addie drinks pink ladies, and, as the evening progresses, gets into a series of misadventures, and finally charms the bank clerk away from her rival.

Reviews of the comedy ranged from approval to disapproval, but whether *Happy Birthday* was a modern version of *Cinderella,* as some critics thought, or whether it was an original comedy, did not disturb audiences who came primarily to see the star, Helen Hayes. The cast included an assortment of typical denizens of a cocktail bar, but all interest centered around Helen Hayes, whose performance as Addie dominated the show. Miss Hayes delighted audiences when she sang, danced, became riotously drunk, and captivated the hero. The effective production, embellished with music and trick effects, added to the enjoyment. For example, as Addie became more intoxicated, the stage became darker, and the bottles lighted up one by one, glowing in brilliant colors. The audience was not completely naturalized in Lamb's conception of the word, but it did anticipate that Addie would triumph over the other woman, and the obviously happy ending came as no surprise. *Happy Birthday* was not a distinguished play, but it was an amusing, if conventional, comedy which definitely owed its popular run of 563 performances to Helen Hayes's tour de force as Addie.

Janie, the Josephine Bentham–Herschel Williams comedy produced in 1942, has no role so colorful as Addie to recommend it nor does it have a particularly original plot. At least four of the New York drama critics compared *Janie* to the Jerome Chodorov–Joseph Fields comedy, *Junior Miss,* and most of these critics were not complimentary to *Janie* in their comparisons. *Janie* does have to its advantage a timely story for 1942, that of a sixteen-year-old girl who gives a party for soldiers stationed in a camp near her home town. Janie's parents are upset when the party gets out of hand and the boys overrun the house. All turns out well, however, because the party gives Janie's father the chance to meet an influential man from Washington whom he had been trying to contact for business priorities.

Today, *Janie* is dated comedy. In the 1940s, many of the situations were funny; in the 1960s, they seem labored and forced, and some of them appear to be little more than variations of the overused situations found in plays about adolescents, such as the scene in which the father discusses sex with his adolescent child. The familiar characterizations include harassed parents, adolescents, and a precocious child, Janie's younger sister.

Janie, like *The Two Mrs. Carrolls,* was produced in the lush World War II years. The economic prosperity of the theater, the timeliness of the story, and the chance to laugh and forget the serious side of the war that *Janie* gave audiences helped account for its run of 642 performances.

Although critics ignored or lightly dismissed the eleven plays mentioned thus far as popular fare, they were, for the most part, somewhat more kindly disposed toward *White Cargo, Is Zat So?, Sailor, Beware!, Personal Appearance, Brother Rat, Room Service, Seventh Heaven, Within the Law,* and *Bird in Hand.*

Most historians of the drama dismiss Leon Gordon's *White Cargo,* produced in 1923, with brief comments that express little approval or disapproval. The plot concerns Longford, an idealistic young Englishman, who struggles against the effects of African jungle heat and dry rot. He avoids whiskey and native women until he meets Tondeleyo, a half-caste, voluptuous, native girl who undermines his resistance. Longford insists upon marrying Tondeleyo to preserve his respectability, but when he is finally disillusioned by the realization that she is thoroughly wanton, he is ready to be shipped back to England as white cargo.

The first act is long and talky and builds much too slowly to avoid dullness until Tondeleyo finally enters and says, "Me—Tondeleyo," and the curtain falls. But once Tondeleyo has appeared, the second and third acts become more forceful. The plot develops logically, and Tondeleyo and Longford are both convincing characters. The play impressed Burns Mantle sufficiently to say he regretted not being able to include *White Cargo* as one of the ten best plays of the 1923–1924 season. It had enough dramatic and sensational appeal to flourish for 864 performances on Broadway and also proved to be a popular success in the strawhat theaters, particularly with Ann Corio, ex-burlesque queen, playing Tondeleyo. At the New York première, one or two critics called *White Cargo* a "torrid" drama. Perhaps the theme and action may have been torrid for 1923, but in comparison with *Rain,* a more torrid play of the same era, *White Cargo* is merely tepid.

Is Zat So?, the James Gleason–Richard Taber comedy produced in 1924, is not as realistic as *White Cargo* in theme but is far more realistic in dialogue. A liberal use of slang is combined with fragmentary speeches which require the actor's interpretation, gestures, and vocal inflections to be effective. Such expressions as "Is Zat So?" "T'row it away," "t'ink," "know'd" illustrate why many critics called the play unliterary. This dialogue as spoken on stage by James Gleason and Robert Armstrong, however, became colorful, realistic, and extremely effective.

Is Zat So? tells an amusing story about Chick, a lightweight boxer, and Hap, his manager, who are penniless. They accept temporary positions as footman and butler in the Fifth Avenue home of a socially prominent New Yorker, C. Clinton Blackburn, who is a weakling. Hap and Chick give Blackburn intensive exercises, build him up physically, and finally expose his brother-in-law, Robert Parker, as a thief. The high spot of the play is the second scene in Act II, which includes a prize fight between the chauffeur, Duffy, and Chick, who loses the fight. Even the brief stage directions in the printed text indicate the effective byplay of the scene, the action in the ring during the three-minute rounds, the screaming when Chick falls, and the ad-libbing of the spectators during the fight. Since the prize fight is staged in the Blackburn home, the play contrasts the action of the sports arena with the elegance of a Fifth Avenue mansion and gives the audience the vicarious pleasure of watching a boxing match in an unusual setting. This sequence, along with the logical plot development, the excellent performances of James Gleason as Hap and Robert Armstrong as Chick, and the ultimate victory of the rehabilitated socialite whom the audience wanted to triumph over his scheming brother-in-law, kept *Is Zat So?* running for 618 performances.

George Jean Nathan called *Sailor, Beware!*, produced in 1933, and *Personal Appearance*, produced in 1934, "theatrical naughty postcards." Of the two, the Kenyon Nicholson–Charles Robinson comedy, *Sailor, Beware!*, is by far the rowdier. Some critics have called it bawdy or boisterous. Other critics have insinuated that the script underwent heavy revisions and deletions to make the comedy palatable for audiences. In fact, writing a synopsis of the play without using a blue pencil is difficult.

The two principal characters are Chester Jones of the U.S.S. *Dakota,* nicknamed "Dynamite" by his shipmates because his lovemaking breaks down all feminine resistance, and Billie Jackson, a café hostess in Panama City, nicknamed "Stonewall" because she always defends her virtue against all masculine sieges. When Dynamite meets Stonewall, Dynamite's shipmates and Stonewall's co-hostesses begin betting on the winner. As the play progresses, Dynamite makes stronger attacks, Stonewall puts up stronger resistance, and the bets keep getting bigger and bigger. Finally, Lieutenant Loomis of the United States Navy saves the whole situation by stopping all bets. Meanwhile, Dynamite and Stonewall have fallen in love and all ends well.

Sailor, Beware! was frank and adult in its treatment of sex. The authors stressed the humor and used no serious moments to temper the fun. Because *Sailor, Beware!* satisfied the need for comedy in the depression year of 1933, it found ready audiences and became one of the first plays produced during the barren theater years of the early 1930s to run five hundred performances. After *Sailor, Beware!* is called funny, boisterous, or rowdy, however, there is little more to say about its popular success other than it was an enjoyable evening's entertainment, even if the audience could forget the play as soon as it was over.

Lawrence Riley's *Personal Appearance* basically is as raucous as *Sailor, Beware!* but appears to be more subtle because it uses contrasting and more fully developed characterizations. The story concerns a motion picture actress, Carole Arden, who is making a personal appearance tour through Pennsylvania. Her car breaks down and she is forced to spend the night in a small town between Scranton and Wilkes-Barre. There she meets a handsome but naïve gas station attendant whom she tries to seduce. Gene Tuttle, her public relations manager, helps break up the romance. The laughs started the very first moment Carole met the gas station attendant because of her futile attempts to seduce the unsuspecting boy— another example of an author's use of Lamb's theory of naturalizing the audience. The audience's awareness of Carole's amorous pursuits and the boy's innocence resulted in one of the biggest laughs in the final scene when the young man told his fiancée he wasn't sure just what Miss Arden was trying to do.

Carole Arden burlesques the motion picture sirens of the 1930s, including Mae West, to whom several references are made in the play. Gladys George gave an excellent performance as Carole in the stage version, but Mae West starred in the motion picture and, in a sense, burlesqued herself.

The comedy comes not only from the situations but also from the dialogue. Carole, for example, uses malapropisms just often enough to provide effective humor. She says to the woman in whose home she is staying, "Our car broke down and I couldn't resist running in to see if the interior was as picturesque as the ulterior." To make Carole's garbled vocabulary even more ridiculous, Tuttle often acts as a foil. When Carole says to the young gas station attendant, "Your naviette appals me," and Tuttle says, "His what?", Carole snarls, "You heard me," and Tuttle says, "I was afraid I did."

Although the characterization is broadly written, Carole is not entirely ludicrous or unsympathetic. Several short episodes explain her actions and make her a real person rather than a caricature. The best sequence is a serious moment when Tuttle defends Carole, explaining how she started as a waitress in a cheap restaurant and worked her way up to her present status as a glamorous star. If she now appears affected and rather silly, Tuttle says, the fault is not entirely hers, for Hollywood has helped her become that way.

Personal Appearance differs as a Hollywood satire from other plays about theatrical stars and the entertainment world. It is the story of a Hollywood actress but not of Hollywood. The contrast between Carole and the small-town folk gives the play a novel approach by taking an actress out of her natural setting and putting her in surroundings more familiar to the audience. The play is not without defects. The plot is conventional; many of the gags are too dependent on the period of the early 1930s and date the dialogue; at least one character, the movie-struck home-town girl, is an exaggerated caricature; and the pace of Act I is uneven. The prologue, Carole's personal appearance in a motion picture theater, sets a fast tempo which the first act fails to sustain until Carole reappears and again livens up the action.

Audiences enjoyed *Personal Appearance,* nonetheless, for many reasons: the humorous situations and dialogue; the lampoon of a movie actress; Gladys George's expert performance as Carole; the incongruity of a Hollywood star in a rural community; and the popular situation of the triumphant woman, in this case the small-town girl whose fiancé prefers her to the glamorous Hollywood star. All these combined to keep *Personal Appearance* on Broadway for 501 performances.

Brother Rat, produced in 1936, and *Room Service,* produced in 1937, are almost identical to each other in construction. *Brother Rat* is a series of ludicrous situations involving a group of students at Virginia Military Institute; *Room Service* is a series of farcical situations involving a theatrical producer without funds who tries to hold a hotel room until his play is produced. Both plays have fast action, fast pace, and humorous characters who become more and more involved in impossible situations.

Most critics liked *Brother Rat* by John Monks, Jr., and Fred F. Finklehoffe. In the 1936–1937 theatrical season it was the third-produced but best-rated play about life in a military school. The first two, *So Proudly We Hail* and *Bright Honor,* were serious dramas about the harmful influences of such military institutions. *Brother Rat* approached the problem as farce and exposed the antics of the cadets at lightning speed through a maze of complications until the final curtain.

The plot concerns Bing Edwards, V.M.I.'s best baseball pitcher, who is in danger of failing in several courses. Moreover, Bing, who is secretly married, is about to become a father. Since the marriage is a violation of school regulations, Bing is afraid he will be exposed and expelled. His roommates, Billy and Dan, who try to help solve his problems, only add to his troubles. Although Bing loses the big game, he does graduate. He also wins a three-hundred-dollar prize for being the first father in his class.

The play is full of gags, with several of the best ones used as curtain lines. At the end of Act II, for instance, Bing's roommates have succeeded in getting Bing arrested, through no fault of his own, for hazing a new cadet, for neglecting his duty as a room orderly, for writing a check without funds, and for pawning a saber which belongs to the Institute. Billy and Dan start arguing about who is responsible for the trouble and keep raising their voices until they are shouting. Bing looks up and says, "Quiet! You want to get us into trouble?" Illogical as the line may be, its humor typifies the gags and curtain lines throughout the play.

The characters are types rather than individuals. According to the script, Joyce is a "blonde, Southern prom-trotter"; Mrs. Brooks, "an elderly Southern gentlewoman"; Bing, a "healthy-looking Southern college athlete"; and Claire, "the glass-wearing Phi Beta Kappa type—not very attractive but very likeable." The characters, however, were of secondary importance in popular appeal. What the audience enjoyed most were the fast action, the rapid succession of funny gags, and the exaggerated situations. *Brother Rat* had one other mark of popular distinction. When it ran 577 performances, it upset a belief prevalent among Broadway showmen that plays about baseball were seldom successful.

Room Service by John Murray and Allen Boretz represents a better blending of humor, dialogue, and action. The raffish characters in *Brother Rat* are undisciplined cadets whose antics and impoliteness are too farfetched to be convincing to most audiences as typical of student behavior in a staid military institute. In *Room Service,* the assortment of Broadway-type, raffish characters resembling Damon Runyon creations include a "shoestring" play producer, his cronies and associates, an irate hotel manager, a threatening hotel investigator, and a bewildered young playwright. The strategic maneuvering of these characters to hold a hotel room, the gag lines and involved complications, and the characters themselves are enough in keeping with the Broadway locale to make the play convincing as well as amusing.

Room Service thrived on its humor. Critics called it one of the funniest shows of the season and even sedate theatergoers enjoyed the hilarious story of the "shoestring" producer who has the play, the actors, the theater, but no capital. To raise funds, the producer sells 10 per cent of the show to a hotel manager and then moves his entire staff and cast into a room in the hotel. When the manager threatens to throw everybody out, the producer persuades the playwright to pretend he is sick. That scheme doesn't work; so the playwright is forced to pretend he has committed suicide. The producer and his associates then hold a funeral service to keep stalling for time because the first performance of the play is in progress. Finally, the producer gets word that the performance is over, the play is a great success, and everyone, including the hotel manager, is happy.

The situations and dialogue appealed to Broadway theatergoers who knew the character types excellently played by Sam Levene, Eddie Albert, Philip Loeb, Betty Field, and others. George Abbott's name as director also helped at the box office because *Room Service* was his fourth long-running success in a row following *Three Men on a Horse, Boy Meets Girl,* and *Brother Rat.* The play itself may have been too localized, however, to appeal to theatergoers unfamiliar with the New York theater area, which probably accounts, in part, for *Room Service*'s five hundred performances, a low figure in comparison with other Abbott-directed farces.

The 704-performance record for Austin Strong's *Seventh Heaven,* produced in 1922, on the other hand, does not indicate the tremendous popularity of the play, for *Seventh Heaven* might have had a much longer run if John Golden had not joined with other producers who closed their successful attractions during a dispute with Actors Equity Association. Audiences enjoyed the emotional appeal of *Seventh Heaven* although many of the critics who disapproved of the melodramatic plot did not. Even before the play went into production it met with heavy opposition. Directors and producers rejected it, and several leading actors, including William Gillette, Douglas Fairbanks, and Lionel Barrymore, turned down the script. When John Golden agreed to stage the production, he and Strong revised the story and characterizations to combine a romantic love interest with a story of Parisian slum life into a play with dramatic and emotional appeal. Despite the presence in the cast of a dope fiend, a sewer rat, a pickpocket, and other denizens of the slums, the treatment of these characters is idealistic rather than realistic in a plot that is superficial and naïve. In the first act, for example, police have arrested a group of women and try to arrest Diane. In an effort to befriend her, Chico, the hero, insists that she is an honest woman. When the police ask him to prove it, he hesitates and then says she is his wife. The action indicates that the police have rounded up the prostitutes of the area, but the dialogue never states the purpose of the raid. John Golden, in discussing his revisions, admitted he had changed Diane from a prostitute to a pickpocket.

The development of the entire plot is as naïve as this sequence. Chico takes Diane to Seventh Heaven, his small attic on the seventh floor. Three days later, when Chico must go to war, he decides that since there is not enough time to arrange for a proper marriage ceremony, he and Diane will perform the ceremony themselves by addressing *le bon Dieu* and taking their vows as man and wife. The sophisticated audiences assume that Chico and Diane have been lovers, but there is no indication of an affair in the dialogue.

With all its superimposed innocence and resulting weaknesses in characterization and plot development, there still remains enough good dramatic impetus to explain the popularity of *Seventh Heaven*. The highly emotional quality of the play is most evident in the climaxes at the end of each act. The second act ends as Diane is about to go down to the street to see Chico march by. Nana, Diane's absinthe-drinking sister who has always beaten and bullied Diane, enters and prevents Diane from leaving. When Nana pulls out a whip, Diane stands motionless, but as Nana raises the whip to strike, Diane suddenly springs at her, struggles, takes the whip away, and lashes Nana until she stumbles off stage. Diane then throws the whip at the door, runs to the window, and shouts to Chico, "I am brave!"

The third-act climax is equally melodramatic. Diane is disillusioned, for Chico has been reported dead. Just when everything appears hopeless, Chico bursts into the room and insists Diane should have been told he had been wounded but not killed. Chico is blind, but he maintains, as he has done all through the play, that he is a "very remarkable fellow." The tearful lovers are reunited, and the audience believes, as Diane does, that the remarkable Chico will regain his eyesight.

The tremendous popular appeal of *Seventh Heaven* as an emotional melodrama is also evident in its phenomenal success in motion pictures. In 1928, the first film version won Oscars for Janet Gaynor, who played Diane, and Frank Borzage, the director. The theme song, "Diane," composed for the picture, became an instant favorite and retained its popularity beyond two subsequent remakes in talking pictures.

In many respects, the pre-production history of Bayard Veiller's melodrama *Within the Law,* produced in 1912, resembles that of *Seventh Heaven.* Several producers rejected the script before William A. Brady decided to produce it with Emily Stevens in the role of Mary Turner. When the play opened in Chicago but met with little approval, Veiller sold all rights to his agents for three thousand dollars, and Brady sold his interest to Arch Selwyn, who put Jane Cowl in the leading role, restaged the play, and brought it to New York where it ran almost two years. It should be added that after the play had become an established success, Selwyn paid Bayard Veiller one hundred dollars a week for each company, although he was not legally required to do so. Figures vary on the number of companies, but six to eight is a safe estimate. Veiller's share of the profits, if he had kept his rights to the author's royalties, would have been far more lucrative.

Within the Law tells the story of Mary Turner, who is accused of shoplifting, pleads innocent, but is convicted and sentenced to a year in prison. After her release, Mary, determined to get revenge, organizes a group which operates in shady deals that are always, however, within the law. To further her plans, she marries Robert Gilder, son of the man who sent her to prison, but when she learns that her associates are planning to operate outside the law and rob the Gilder home, Mary tries to stop the burglary. In the third act, set in the Gilder home, the lights suddenly go off, and when they come on again, a man is lying on the floor evidently killed by a bullet although there has been no sound of gunfire. Mary immediately announces her husband shot the man and that he is justified in the act since he shot to protect his home. The police take Mary and her husband to headquarters for further questioning, but the fourth act brings a confession from Joe Garson, the killer. The same act also brings a letter from the real shoplifter completely exonerating Mary, who then admits she has fallen in love with her husband, a fact which the audience has known for two acts, and the couple is reunited for a happy ending.

Lamb's theory of naturalizing an audience easily explains what transformed *Within the Law* from a failure in Chicago to a sensation in New York. The climax occurred in the third act when the criminal used a gun with a silencer, but, according to stories heard along Broadway, the scene failed to impress audiences because they were unfamiliar with such a device. In his revisions, the producer added a new scene in the second act in which Joe Garson pointed a gun at a vase on the opposite side of the stage. Almost instantly the vase shattered, although there was no sound. Garson explained that he had used a new gadget called a silencer. In the third act, therefore, when the lights were turned up and a man lay dead, the naturalized audience immediately jumped to the conclusion that Garson had used the silencer, and the scene as well as the whole play gained greater impact.

Jane Cowl's performance as Mary Turner delighted audiences, as did the popular situation of the victorious heroine, for Mary triumphed not only over the employer who had imprisoned her unjustly but also over the law. The 541-performance record in New York is only a partial indication of the play's success, for *Within the Law* toured the country for several years followed by at least three versions in motion pictures.

John Drinkwater's *Bird in Hand,* produced in 1929, differs almost completely from most of the preceding popular plays. It has intellectual appeal but lacks dramatic and emotional appeal. Any attempt to analyze its run of five hundred performances leads only to confusion. In fact, the popularity of *Bird in Hand* puzzled critics, who admitted quite frankly that they could not explain why it had been successful in New York. Reviews ranged from such favorable comments as "ideal entertainment" to "an interminable bore," depending upon the critic's reaction to the extreme talkiness of the play, which included long discussions of class distinctions in England.

The slight story which holds these discussions together concerns Thomas Greenleaf, an innkeeper, who objects to his daughter's marrying Gerald Arnwood, son of Sir Robert Arnwood, squire of the county. Three guests at the inn are drawn into the argument to determine whether Thomas or his daughter has the right viewpoint concerning class distinctions. Finally Sir Robert himself is consulted and he decides the young couple should marry.

Bird in Hand is a well-written, literate drama; it does have intellectual appeal in its arguments for and against class distinctions; and it does have adequate character motivation. On the other hand, it has but little action or plot to make it sufficiently diverting to be entertaining theater. English critics have referred to *Bird in Hand* as a typical English farce, but the humor is not characteristic of American farce because it is quaint and at times obvious rather than boisterous. For example, Mr. Blanquet is dancing with Mrs. Greenleaf, but Mr. Godolphin, the barrister, also wants to dance with her. When he tries to cut in, Mr. Blanquet reminds him that possession is nine points of the law, and Mr. Godolphin replies, "I am the law." American critics have called it a character comedy, but it is doubtful whether New York audiences would be well enough acquainted with such characters as the English innkeeper, the English barrister, the English squire, the wealthy merchant's sophisticated son, and the rebellious daughter to keep the play running five hundred performances.

The success of *Bird in Hand* on Broadway, however, might be attributed to the triumph of the young lovers over the objections of their parents as well as to the daughter's triumph over her father. Furthermore, *Bird in Hand* kept the audience completely informed by explaining every step of the romance in detail, and by presenting its arguments so logically that the audience anticipated the final curtain and was gratified to see the play end happily.

Four
Record Breakers

Four of the greatest successes in the New York theater, *Abie's Irish Rose, Lightnin', The Bat,* and *Peg o' My Heart,* should also be included among the popular plays which appealed more to audiences than to critics. Even the more favorable reviews called the plays pleasant or entertaining but never distinguished or impressive.

Almost without exception, every historian of American drama has referred to *Abie's Irish Rose*'s phenomenal success as an exam- usually made that all New York critics disliked the comedy is not ple of a play which prospered in spite of the critics. The statement correct, for several, including William B. Chase of *The New York Times,* wrote rather favorable reviews. Of those criticisms which condemned the play, Robert Benchley's jibes are perhaps the best known. In the old *Life* magazine devoted to humor in the 1920s, Benchley not only wrote a derogatory review but also included a new barb each week in his column about current shows. For example, in 1922 he wrote, "People laugh at this every night, which explains why democracy can never be a success"; in 1923, "Where do the people come from who keep this thing going? You don't see them out in the daytime"; in 1924, "The play which made Edwin Booth famous"; in 1925, "We understand that a performance of this play in modern dress is under way"; and in 1926, "Closing soon (only fooling)." Turning out such quips must have developed into a nightmare, for Benchley's struggles each week to say something clever but different made him hate the play so much, it is said, that he refused to walk on the same side of the street as the theater where it was playing.

The popularity of *Abie's Irish Rose* cannot be dismissed as casually as it is in the Benchley bulletins, for the comedy was not an immediate success. Box-office receipts during the first few weeks of the run were very low, and, if Broadway stories are accurate, Arnold Rothstein, the gambler, financed the temporary deficits until *Abie's Irish Rose* built into a sound commercial success.

The story deals with a Jewish boy, Abie, and a Catholic girl, Rosemary, who are married by a justice of the peace. To overcome the objections of Abie's family, Rosemary poses as a Jewess and the young couple are married by a rabbi. Before the play is over, they have been married again by a priest. The two quarreling families finally give their blessings to the marriage when Rosemary and Abie have twins and name one for each grandfather.

If the action or the characterizations had been developed with greater skill, *Abie's Irish Rose* might have been a more important drama, for there is a decided similarity between the basic plots of *Abie's Irish Rose* and *Romeo and Juliet*. It is even a matter of court record that Anne Nichols sued Universal Pictures for using her play as the basis for the film series, *The Cohens and the Kellys,* and lost the case because George Jean Nathan testified that *Abie's Irish Rose* went all the way back to Shakespeare's tragedy.

With the theme of religious tolerance and the Romeo and Juliet love story, *Abie's Irish Rose* could have been a serious play, but Miss Nichols has developed it as pure farce. The problems involving the young lovers, the three marriage ceremonies, and the arguments between the grandfathers, Solomon Levy and Patrick Murphy, are meant to be hilarious and exaggerated, and, as a result, they are sometimes humorous but always unconvincing farce situations. Moreover, Miss Nichols has made her characters types rather than individuals. Solomon Levy and the Cohens are stock Jewish comedians, faintly reminiscent of Weber and Fields; Patrick Murphy is the typical stock Irish comedian. Even in the 1920s, they were familiar to audiences which had seen similar characters in vaudeville, in revues, and in burlesque.

The wide variance in criticisms of *Abie's Irish Rose* is understandable. Some critics who liked the play thought it pointed up a lesson in prejudice and religious tolerance. Others who disliked it, often quite violently, thought the play was basically tragic and deserved a more serious treatment than a combination of a Romeo and Juliet love story with old jokes and stock characterizations assembled without distinction. To most critics, *Abie's Irish Rose* was a decidedly unliterary play, a fourth- or fifth-rate farce with a first-rate theme of social significance. Audiences, nevertheless, enjoyed the jokes, the dialogue, the situations, and the characters because they were familiar and typical, which helped *Abie's Irish Rose* become the longest-running play in the New York theater from the time it surpassed *Lightnin'* in 1925 until *Tobacco Road* surpassed it in 1939.

The phenomenal success of *Abie's Irish Rose* extended far beyond the Broadway scene. All over the country it ran for months in cities which normally kept shows only one week; it ran for weeks in towns that were formerly one-night stands. As great a money-maker as it was in the 1920s, it has now become almost a theatrical nonentity. Revivals in the 1930s and 1940s met with little public support but with strong opposition from religious leaders and a younger generation with a growing resentment toward racial caricatures. A second motion picture version similarly turned out to be a dismal failure. Today, *Abie's Irish Rose*'s only distinction is that it held the record as Broadway's longest-running play for fourteen years.

Unlike *Abie's Irish Rose,* which became popular because it had farcical humor, *Lightnin'*, the Winchell Smith–Frank Bacon comedy produced in 1918, became popular because Frank Bacon was the star. Theatergoers often forgot the names of cast members in *Abie's Irish Rose,* but they never forgot Frank Bacon in *Lightnin'* for two very definite reasons. First, all the action revolved around Lightnin' Bill Jones, and second, the play resembled Joseph Jefferson's production of *Rip Van Winkle* in story, in characterization, and in Bacon's acting which, according to critics, he patterned very closely on Jefferson's performance as Rip. Lightnin' Bill Jones bore a marked resemblance not only to Rip but also to characters in earlier plays such as *A Temperance Town* and *Tennessee's Pardner;* it was, therefore, in spite of the individuality which Bacon gave the role, a character familiar to American audiences. The play itself was a forerunner of the Will Rogers cycle of motion pictures and had the same warm, audience appeal, the same blend of melodrama and humor. Will Rogers, in fact, later starred in the motion picture version of the play.

The story of *Lightnin'* more than casually resembles the Joseph Jefferson version of Rip Van Winkle, for both plays concern a lovable drunkard whose wife is long suffering and almost loses her property to the villain but is saved by the lovable drunkard. *Lightnin'* more specifically tells the story of Bill Jones and his wife, who own the Calivada Hotel, almost lose the hotel when scheming lawyers persuade Mrs. Jones to sell it, and wind up in the divorce court when Lightnin' refuses to sign the deed to the hotel. Millie Jones and her suitor, John Marvin, quarrel when Millie sides with her mother against John, who is acting as attorney for Lightnin'. At the end of the play, Lightnin' outsmarts the lawyers and wins back his wife, making it possible for Millie and John to reconcile.

Probably the dramatists' most original contribution was the colorful setting of the Calivada Hotel, situated on the state line between Nevada and California, one half of the hotel in each state. A woman who wanted a divorce, therefore, could live in the Nevada half of the hotel to establish residence and, at the same time, use the California address to trick her friends into believing she had gone to a California resort. The dividing boundary line down the center of the stage made some of the situations hilarious, particularly when police from one state could not cross the line to serve a summons in another state.

Lightnin' included still one other popular ingredient in its homespun, folksy humor, particularly in Lightnin' Bill's exaggerated tall yarns. At the beginning of the play he announced that he had been a spy once with Buffalo Bill. In the second act, he elaborated on his experiences with Buffalo Bill and added that he had been an Indian fighter and had "shot Sitting Bull when he was standing." Later, he said he had driven a swarm of bees across the plains in the dead of winter and never lost a bee. This type of gag may have been conventional rather than distinctive, but it enabled Bacon to give a memorable performance.

In addition to the humor, Bacon's performance, and the sure-fire plot, such popular situations as a misunderstanding between young lovers, a hero who outsmarts a villain, and a final scene with multiple reconciliations all helped *Lightnin'* become the first play to run more than one thousand performances in New York, with a final total of 1,291 performances.

The Mary Roberts Rinehart–Avery Hopwood melodrama *The Bat,* produced in 1920, has no character as enchanting as Lightnin' Bill but it does have greater suspense, for it is a complex, tightly written melodrama. Based on Mary Roberts Rinehart's successful novel *The Circular Staircase, The Bat* has an excellent plot and is one of the better mystery plays of the 1920s. The story concerns a large sum of money hidden in the home of Miss Cornelia Van Gorder, which brings several visitors to the home to search for the treasure, including a cashier who is accused of taking funds from the bank; a detective whom Miss Van Gorder has hired to solve the mysterious activities in her home; and The Bat, a notorious thief. Not until a murder has been committed, the cashier has been cleared of guilt, and the supposed detective has been exposed as the criminal, is the mystery finally solved. In addition to the device of having the criminal masquerade as the detective, the authors incorporate several other situations which heighten the suspense, such as the sudden and mysterious appearance of the shadow of a bat on the walls of the house; a secret chamber in the garret; and a mysterious character called "The Unknown," in reality the detective hired by Miss Van Gorder and whose true identity is not revealed until the last few minutes of the play. The information concerning the real detective and the false clues given the audience add to the complexity of the mystery and, of course, heighten the suspense, but do not result in an illogical or contrived ending. As a result of precise writing and careful construction, every clue or situation is in keeping with the ultimate solution.

The characters in a melodrama are often conventional types, but Lizzie, a frightened maid, is an exceptionally well-written characterization, one easy to visualize even in reading the text. She not only accentuates the mystery with her terror but also provides comic relief with her hysterical dialogue. Many critics have said that May Vokes, who played Lizzie in New York, helped immeasurably to make the play a popular success. Even more important, the excellent dramatic structure, the heightened suspense, and the logical development of a complex plot all combined to give *The Bat* a run of 867 performances, making it the only long-running mystery in the 1920s and 1930s in spite of the number of melodramas patterned on it.

If a literary critic were to classify the fourth record breaker, *Peg o' My Heart*, the J. Hartley Manners comedy produced in 1912, he would probably call it a tour de force and credit the long run to Laurette Taylor's superb acting. There is certainly no denying Miss Taylor's importance to the play nor the critics' praise for her interpretation of Peg. Even the famous Sarah Bernhardt, while she was appearing at the Palace Theater in 1913, asked to see the fabulous Taylor performance and attended a special morning presentation of *Peg o' My Heart* arranged for her benefit, at which she was the only person in the audience. Yet the play outside of New York did record-breaking business without Laurette Taylor, for when she decided not to go on the road, other actresses were only too willing to have the role. In fact, as many as seven and eight companies toured the United States and Canada during one season, all doing profitable business.

Some critics have called *Peg o' My Heart* mere "popular fare," and again there is no argument, for the play is a sentimental comedy that entertained audiences but offers no great dramatic originality. The story is about Peg, whose mother, a British noblewoman, had married an Irish commoner, had been disowned by her family, and had gone to America with her husband. In the first act, the audience learns that Peg's mother has died and that Peg is returning to England to live with Mrs. Chichester, her mother's sister. Under the terms of a will made by Peg's uncle, Mrs. Chichester, who is temporarily penniless, is to receive a thousand pounds to teach Peg to act like an English lady. Since Peg's father has not told her the specifications of the will, she cannot understand why he has sent her to England. In Act I, called "The Coming of Peg," she meets Sir Gerald Adair, whom everyone in the play calls Jerry. In Act II, "The Rebellion of Peg," she falls in love with Jerry but still does not know he is a member of the nobility. Peg disobeys her aunt by going to a dance with Jerry and finds when she returns that her cousin Ethel is planning to run away with a married man. Peg upsets the plan, pretends she is the culprit, and the curtain falls as

Ethel faints before she can tell her mother the truth. "Peg o' My Heart," the last act, opens with Peg determined to go back to America to be with her father. She learns the truth about Jerry and has a marriage proposal from her cousin Alaric and another from the solicitor, Mr. Hawkes, both of whom know that Peg will receive five thousand pounds a year if she fulfills the terms of the will. When Peg finally hears the stipulations made in the will, she still plans to go back to America but then, at the last moment, decides to stay and marry Jerry.

A terse synopsis does not explain the popularity of the play, but a closer examination shows that *Peg o' My Heart* includes a great many situations which audiences always enjoy. In the first place it epitomizes Lamb's theory of naturalizing an audience, for the spectators know more than the characters in every situation. The audience knows the terms of the will from the outset and wonders how Peg will learn the truth. The audience sees Christian Brent, the married man who is attempting to seduce Ethel, make advances to Peg. Even when Peg tells her about Brent, Ethel refuses to believe what the audience has seen. After Peg stops Ethel from running off with Brent, the audience is again naturalized, for Ethel's mother and brother rush onstage but are unaware of what has actually happened previously. When Jerry comes to take Peg to the dance, Peg warns him that her aunt will refuse to let her go but that she will sneak out of the house and meet him after all the others have gone to bed. Mrs. Chichester, of course, refuses to give her permission. Peg signals to Jerry behind Mrs. Chichester's back that she will meet him outside, and again the naturalized audience is delighted in sharing the secret.

Peg o' My Heart also includes more than one variation of a second popular dramatic situation, the triumphant heroine, for Peg outsmarts Mr. Brent and his plan to seduce Ethel, proves her superiority over her shallow British cousins, definitely outwits her aunt, and marries the British nobleman. A great deal of the play revolves around a third situation popular in the American theater, young lovers who overcome all obstacles. Even Peg admits that she and Jerry should not marry because she lacks the education a nobleman's wife should have, and she believes that Jerry would soon be ashamed of her. But the audience wants a happy ending and gets it, because all obstacles are pushed aside in the last minute of the play.

Not to be overlooked is the conventional but humorous dialogue, particularly in many of Peg's speeches. Peg, who has arrived with a huge dog named Michael, sees Ethel holding a small lap dog and says, "Where's the rest of that?" Later, again referring to the dog, she says, "I thought it was her knitting until it moved." In the last act when she asks Alaric if he had been willing to sacrifice himself by marrying her for her money and he admits he had, Peg says, "There's a great hero lost in you, Alaric."

With all these popular situations blended into a play that enabled Laurette Taylor to captivate theatergoers, *Peg o' My Heart* ran 603 performances on Broadway and could have run longer if Miss Taylor had not grown tired of playing the role. Not that Miss Taylor or the author, Mr. Manners, ever regarded the role of Peg lightly. Oliver Morosco, who originally produced the play on the West Coast, sold the film rights, which he thought he owned, to Paramount Pictures. Manners and Taylor fought the sale in court, won the case, prevented the completed picture with Wanda Hawley as Peg from ever being released, and then sold the film rights to Metro. The silent motion picture was subsequently made starring Laurette Taylor.

It would simplify any discussion of what makes a long run on Broadway if it were possible to say that *Peg o' My Heart* symbolized the popular play, and that any drama which combined the same strong central characterization, the naturalized audience, the woman's triumph, the obstacles to young love, and the humorous dialogue would automatically be a success. The history of *Peg o' My Heart*, however, indicates that public tastes keep changing, for, in the 1920s, when Laurette Taylor revived the comedy on Broadway, it closed after eighty-eight performances.

Nine
Best Plays

A Broadway producer once said that a play had to run six weeks to outlive bad reviews, which does not mean that a good review will always establish a popular success. Favorable criticisms, however, often do help dramas achieve long runs. Most of the plays of 1900–1950 discussed in this chapter have, in addition to their long runs, the critics' approval. Burns Mantle, for example, included all the plays among the ten top plays of the season in his *Best Plays* series. Five of these productions are comedies, of which Joseph Fields's *The Doughgirls,* produced in 1942, is the rowdiest, resembling *Sailor, Beware!* in bawdy humor and in lack of subtlety.

The play broadly satirizes the hotel shortage in wartime Washington, the philandering Army officials, the women in their lives, the Russian female guerrillas, and the civilian war workers. The prime purpose of the comedy is to present humorous situations, dialogue, and characterizations which would appeal to a wartime audience. The obvious dialogue is crowded with lusty gags. Typical is the argument between Harry Halstead and Vivian, whom he plans to marry. Harry is jealous because General Slade has hired Vivian and is monopolizing her time. Harry insists he will not spend his evenings alone nor sleep alone; and when Vivian says, "But,

Harry, the General does his best work at night," Harry says, "So do I." The doughgirls are reminiscent of the chorus girls in *The Gold Diggers,* but they are much franker and more outspoken. Perhaps the most humorous doughgirl is the Russian guerrilla, Natalia, who takes a brisk walk to Baltimore and back just for the exercise but who is disgusted with Vivian's dog, which she took along with her, because "he couldn't took it—he goes tired on me—So I have to carry him halfway home." Some critics objected to the characterization of Natalia because they felt she was a thinly disguised caricature of a famous Russian guerrilla fighter whose heroism had made headlines. Nonetheless, Natalia, superbly played by Arlene Francis, accounted for much of the laughter. When Natalia offers to pawn Vivian's diamond and ruby clips to get enough money to pay the hotel bill and asks Vivian how much she would like to get, Vivian tells her, "I got five hundred last time, but I had to cry a little." Natalia pats her gun and says, "I get six hundred—he cries a little."

The Army officials and their doughgirl friends—perhaps better called their unmarried wives—along with the Washington Administration officials who control priorities, the lady judge who is thought to be a real judge who can perform the marriage ceremony for Harry and Vivian but who is finally exposed as the judge of a pie-eating contest, and the other characters who drift in and out of the plot are caricatures, but they are realistic enough to make *The Doughgirls* entertaining. The obvious situations, the raucous gags, and the broad satire of a timely theme all appealed to a theatergoing public in search of laughter during the first year of World War II and enabled *The Doughgirls* to run 671 performances.

F. Hugh Herbert's *Kiss and Tell,* produced in 1943, also flourished in the lush theatrical war years when patrons swarmed into the New York theaters and, like *The Doughgirls,* satirized a wartime situation. *Kiss and Tell* concerned the problem that parents of teen-age girls faced when their daughters met amorous young soldiers. Like *Janie,* it dealt with adolescents in wartime, but it was a more convincing comedy.

The story is about fifteen-year-old Corliss Archer, whose older brother Lenny marries Mildred Pringle shortly before he goes overseas. Since the Archers and the Pringles are not on friendly terms, Corliss is the only other member of both families who knows that Lenny and Mildred are married. When Mildred discovers that she

Kiss and Tell, Joan Caulfield, Robert White, Tommy Lewis, Judith Parrish
and Richard Widmark

is pregnant, Corliss, who has gone with Mildred on her visits to the doctor, tells her parents she has gone to the doctor because she is having a baby and names Dexter Franklin, a seventeen-year-old neighbor of the Archers, as the father. This provokes bitter arguments not only within the Archer family but also among the Archers, the Pringles, and the Franklins. Finally, Mildred receives a telegram telling her Lenny is to be decorated for shooting down three Nazi bombers, Mildred confesses she is married, the Archers and the Pringles give their blessings to the couple, and all three families forget about their quarrels.

The audiences' familiarity with the story and the situations accounts in part for the long run of 957 performances. The marriage of Lenny and Mildred is a variation of *Abie's Irish Rose* without the religious angle; the Archer-Pringle feud is a variation of the Montague-Capulet feud in *Romeo and Juliet;* and Corliss' pretense of approaching motherhood to shield Mildred is a variation of the popular dramatic situation—mistaken identity, which, if poorly written, could be offensive and in bad taste. *Kiss and Tell* amuses rather than offends.

The humor is not restricted to obvious gag lines but often arises out of the characterizations. Corliss, for example, as an adolescent trying to act mature, uses malapropisms and usually has a foil to correct her and to heighten the humor. When Corliss says, "Knowing a girl's right age affects a man's entire physiology," Mrs. Archer says, "I think you mean psychology, don't you?" and Corliss answers, "All right, but it makes all the difference in the world the way a man treats you."

Unlike the bawdy dialogue and double entendre in *The Doughgirls,* frankness in *Kiss and Tell* is kept to a comparative minimum. In fact, F. Hugh Herbert has often resorted to understatement for greater effect. In the scene between the Franklins and the Archers just before Corliss disrupts both households with her pretense, Mr. Franklin says, "Know what we just heard? It's true about the little Hoffman girl," and Mrs. Archer says, "Oh *no!*" Mrs. Franklin says, "Oh *yes!*" and Mr. Archer groans, "Oh *God.*"

The characters in *Kiss and Tell* are also familiar to audiences and include a twelve-year-old precocious youngster; a family servant who gives as well as receives orders; an irate father; a wise, understanding mother; and an awkward seventeen-year-old boy whose favorite expression is "Holy cow!" These are types rather than individuals, but the situations involving them and the humorous dialogue make them convincing small-town folk in a typically American comedy of family life that entertained audiences with its timely story during the early World War II years.

Norman Krasna's *Dear Ruth,* produced in 1944, also flourished during World War II. In situation and theme *Dear Ruth* resembles *Kiss and Tell,* for both plays deal with soldiers and adolescents, and both are based on the theme of mistaken identity. *Dear Ruth* tells the familiar rather than original story of an adolescent, Miriam, who writes love letters to Lieutenant Bill Seawright but signs them with her older sister's name, Ruth. When Bill returns from overseas on leave, the plot settles into the conventional situation of mistaken identity in which everyone except Bill knows who really wrote the letters. After a whirlwind courtship, Bill marries Ruth.

Here again the playwright uses the device of tipping off—naturalizing—the audience to information unknown to one character, by revealing in Act I that Ruth did not write the letters. The audience wonders how long it will take Bill to discover the truth. Although he goes away after he finds out, and although Ruth plans to marry Albert, her fiancé, the audience still expects Ruth and Bill to marry. In the last few minutes of the play when Bill returns and Ruth's father, a judge, performs a hasty ceremony, the audience gets a photo finish and leaves the theater contented. The naturalized audience also enjoys the episode in which everyone but Albert sees the humor of Ruth's predicament; the scene in which Bill discovers, to his chagrin, that Miriam has written the letters; and Ruth's dilemma when Bill tries to make love to her with Ruth and the audience fully aware that Albert is hovering upstairs. The audience also enjoys Albert's anger when Bill announces that he and Ruth are engaged, and no one tells Bill that Ruth is already engaged to Albert.

The humor ranges from the obvious gag to the quieter family joke. Albert is displeased because Ruth has not told Bill about the letters, and Ruth says she would like to have a son like Bill. When she adds that Bill is twenty-four, Albert says, "You're twenty-two. Won't that be a little difficult?" Ruth's parents discuss the suitability of Albert as a prospective husband, and Mrs. Wilkins calls him the Kummer boy, to which Judge Wilkins replies, "Thirty-four's no boy." At times the humor has serious undertones. Miriam insists she is not sorry for what she has done. "I've given a soldier to the war," she says, and Mrs. Wilkins adds, "His mother'll be happy to hear that." Most of the humorous episodes involving Bill have sufficient sentiment and human interest to make him appealing, particularly to women in the audience.

A closer analysis of the play, however, discloses several weaknesses in the plot. For example, audiences might wonder why Ruth, who is wholesome and attractive, would become engaged to Albert, who is stodgy and domineering; or why Bill, after spending an evening with Ruth, would not realize that she could never have written the letters Miriam sent exposing capitalism, discussing sex life in the Soviet, or telling how much she liked Cracker Jack. There are, however, enough laugh-provoking episodes to make audiences overlook the implausibilities.

The characters, as in *Kiss and Tell,* are familiar types, but Krasna made them convincing enough to win audience sympathy and blended them with a timely war story and with humor, to make *Dear Ruth* one of the popular comedies of the 1940s with a run of 683 performances.

My Sister Eileen, produced in 1940, differs from all three war comedies in plot, for it is not a timely story but is based on Ruth McKenney's experiences when she and her sister first came to New York. Miss McKenney herself had collaborated with Leslie Reade on a dramatization of her stories, but the play was never produced. When Jerome Chodorov and Joseph Fields adapted the adventures of the McKenney sisters, they exaggerated actual experiences and blended individual sketches into a unified play which has since served as the basis for a long-running musical comedy, *Wonderful Town,* a television series, and at least two motion pictures.

The plot concerns Ruth Sherwood, an aspiring author, and her sister Eileen, an aspiring actress, who lease a basement apartment in Greenwich Village and run into a series of difficulties, mostly with men, including a newspaper reporter with dishonorable designs on Eileen, a soda fountain manager with similar designs, a landlord whom Eileen is forced to slap, a man who thinks Ruth and Eileen are friends of the prostitute who formerly rented the apartment, and a group of young officers from a Brazilian training ship who follow Ruth home from Brooklyn and change their objective to Eileen when they reach Greenwich Village. Ruth falls in love with Mr. Baker, a magazine editor, but thinks he is in love with Eileen. To add to the confusion, intermittent blasting for a subway tunnel directly below the girls' apartment violently shakes the walls at periodic intervals. One month after the girls have arrived, they are disillusioned because Eileen has spent a night in jail and Ruth's stories have all been rejected. In the last few minutes of the play when Ruth gets a staff appointment on a newspaper, having impresed the editor with her story about the Brazilian Navy, the girls decide to stay in Greenwich Village and sign a new lease on the apartment.

In spite of a variety of disconnected episodes and an assortment of eccentric characters who drift in and out of the rambling plot, Fields and Chodorov have given the comedy an exaggerated continuity as well as popular appeal by emphasizing the characterizations and setting. *My Sister Eileen* capitalizes on the attraction Greenwich Village has always had for sight-seers by presenting the character types and living conditions audiences have associated with the area. Ruth and Eileen, as bewildered, small-town girls, provide contrast not only for the metropolitan setting but also for the mounting confusion of the action. Their difficulties in adjusting to the Bohemian life, therefore, make the play appealing to anyone who has wanted to live in the Village or who has thought of coming to New York in search of a career. *My Sister Eileen* ran 865 performances or almost one year longer than *Room Service,* which also dealt with a limited locale in New York, because *Room Service* appealed mainly to native New Yorkers, but *My Sister Eileen* not only entertained New Yorkers who knew the area but also provided a curious, if somewhat bowdlerized, presentation of Bohemian life for theatergoers unfamiliar with Greenwich Village.

The play is filled with broad gags, most of them delegated to Ruth. When Mr. Appopolous, the landlord, who fancies himself to be a painter, tells the girls he is taking a picture out of their apartment for exhibit, Eileen says she will hang the Sunday funnies in its place. Ruth adds, "You must excuse Eileen, Mr. Appopolous. I keep telling her not to confuse the artist with his personality, but she still thinks you're a louse." Later, when Ruth introduces Mr. Appopolous to the magazine editor, she says, "Bob, this is our landlord— Rasputin." Frank, the soda fountain manager, says he has always wanted to live in a Greenwich Village studio apartment, but with his position in the drugstore, he must keep up appearances. "I see," Ruth says, "where the Liggetts speak only to the Walgreens and the Walgreens speak only to God."

The gags are obvious but appeal to the audience because they characterize the girls. Ruth's wit makes her flippancy convincing. Eileen, who does not sparkle as a conversationalist, learns to capitalize on her charm by smiling at the soda fountain manager to get a free lunch, or smiling at a man on a bus so that he will say he saw her pay her fare when she did not. In spite of her appeal, Eileen lacks Ruth's self-reliance, but her dependence upon Ruth wins sympathy for both girls, who are more realistic than the sophisticated women who capitalize on charm in *The Doughgirls* or *The Gold Diggers*.

The romantic ending usually found in popular comedies is minimized with just a faint suggestion that Ruth may marry Mr. Baker. The love story is sacrificed for a gag finish in which the girls are again duped by Mr. Appopolous who assures them they will no longer be bothered by drilling under the apartment. As soon as they agree to stay, an explosion fairly rocks the apartment and Mr. Appopolous announces, "Now they are blasting." The musical comedy version, *Wonderful Town,* ends on a more positive note with Ruth in Mr. Baker's arms, but in *My Sister Eileen,* even the hint of a love story is enough to keep the audience contented because the play entertains with clever lines, amusing characters, and funny situations. More than a little credit for the play's popular appeal belongs to Shirley Booth's sparkling performance as Ruth in the original cast. Her infectious voice and her ability to give punch lines emphasis without exaggeration delighted audiences in *My Sister Eileen* as much as they have in the 1960s on the television series "Hazel."

Clifford Goldsmith's *What a Life,* produced in 1938, and directed by George Abbott, has the accelerated tempo and exaggerated situations of other Abbott productions such as *Room Service* or *Brother Rat,* but the play itself has a more serious undertone than these farces and is more universal in both story and characterization. Perhaps *What a Life* really tells two stories. The first, dealing humorously with student-faculty problems in high school, is a delightful satire on teachers, teen-age students, and high school

My Sister Eileen, Shirley Booth and Jo Ann Sayre

activities. The second deals with family problems that arise when parents dominate the lives of their children unreasonably. Mr. and Mrs. Aldrich, for example, expect Henry to be brilliant and to attend Princeton because Mr. Aldrich is a brilliant Princeton graduate. When the high school principal tells Mrs. Aldrich that Henry spends most of his time in classes drawing pictures, Mrs. Aldrich says, "If we'd let him, he'd waste his time in exactly the same way at home. Mr. Aldrich simply won't permit such nonsense." The audience, knowing Henry's one talent is his ability to draw, sympathizes with Henry rather than with his parents. The situations involving Henry's efforts to obey his parents and keep out of trouble are convincing rather than mere exaggerated farce situations. After Henry pleads with Mr. Bradley, the principal, not to send a letter home, and Mr. Bradley asks Henry what he would do if he were principal, Henry says, "I think I'd give myself another chance, Mr. Bradley. You don't understand my parents. Sometimes even I don't understand them."

Henry also appeals to audiences because he is not a static character. When the play begins, he is a failure. He has no confidence in himself and he evades the truth so often that when he tries to be honest no one believes him. Because his mother insists that he make the highest grade in an examination before she will allow him to take Barbara to a dance, Henry resorts to cheating. In the third act, Henry gains enough confidence in himself to persuade his mother that he should attend art classes. Even more important, Henry learns he does not have to apologize for himself or be afraid to tell the truth. Earlier in the play, Henry told Barbara he could not take her to the dance because his uncle was seriously ill. In the last minutes of the play, when Barbara asks if his uncle is much worse, Henry says firmly, "He died . . . seven years ago." Then he admits he cheated so he could take her to the dance, that he would still like to take her, and that all he needs is thirty cents for carfare. As the curtain starts to fall, he asks, "Can you lend me thirty cents?"

The gag ending is not so contrived as the final line in *My Sister Eileen* and ends the play happily to the satisfaction of the audience. Clifford Goldsmith traveled around the country talking to high school assemblies and is said to have written about his humorous experiences in *What a Life*. As a result, the play appeals equally to students, to teachers, and to parents because the atmosphere, the dialogue, and most of the action are realistic.

The popularity of *What a Life,* which ran 513 performances, was not limited to the 1930s. The character of Henry Aldrich became the basis of a radio serial as well as a series of motion pictures in the 1940s. The same characters and situations might be equally popular in the 1960s, for the television serial, "Dobie Gillis," did not seem too far removed from the adventures of Henry Aldrich in *What a Life.*

The First Year and *Claudia* are leisurely paced, realistic, and, at times, sentimental stories dealing with young married couples. Both plays pleased the critics more than the five previous comedies, for both were nominated for drama awards, *Claudia* for the Critics' Circle Award in 1941 and *The First Year* for the Pulitzer Prize in 1921.

Critics approved of Frank Craven's *The First Year,* produced in 1920, as a new type of comedy dealing with the low-salaried little man and his struggle to get rich. The play tells the story of Grace, Tommy, and Dick. Grace marries Tommy, but one year later, Dick comes to dinner and spoils Tommy's plan to sell land to the railroad. Grace and Tommy quarrel, Grace goes home to her mother, and then she reconciles with Tommy after he maneuvers the sale.

The realistic characterizations and dialogue distinguished *The First Year* from other comedies of the same period. When Grace tells her uncle, a physician, that she can't make up her mind whether to marry Tommy or Dick and asks for his opinion, he says, "I set Dick's leg once when he had broken it at football, and I could have wished he was my own son, the way he took it. . . . I brought Tommy into the world . . . well, I wish he had been my son, too." The homespun, folksy tone of the dialogue made Grace, Tommy, and Dick believable characters who appealed to audiences.

By present standards, *The First Year* would probably never have a long run, for at least one episode, the business transaction, is not even remotely convincing. Tommy, who is in the real-estate business, buys several lots because he thinks the railroad plans to use the land for a new road. Even if audiences accept the premise that railroad executives would disclose their plans before buying the land, they would question the business tactics of the purchasing agent, Mr. Barstow, who comes to Tommy's house to make a deal with instructions to make a down payment of five thousand dollars.

Mr. Barstow cancels the entire transaction because Dick, who knows nothing about the purchasing division, blandly says the railroad has no intention of using the land. When Mr. Barstow comes back and tells Tommy he has called the president of the company and has found out that Dick was wrong, Tommy refuses to sell at the original price of $100,000 and forces Barstow to pay an additional $25,000. The entire transaction is as exaggerated and as unconvincing as a situation in farce. In 1920, audiences enjoyed rags-to-riches stories about men who rose rapidly to success, and accepted the business transaction as realistic comedy. In the 1960s, however, audiences enjoy the same story of rapid success when it is absurdly exaggerated, as in the musical comedy *How to Succeed in Business without Really Trying,* aptly summarized in its title.

Audiences today might also object to serious undertones which detract from the wholesomeness of the characters. Grace leaves Tommy, a devoted husband, because he fails in a business deal but returns after he acquires sudden wealth. Moreover, the play offers audiences no assurance that Grace and Tommy, who have quarreled bitterly in their first year of marriage, will not have the same bitter quarrels in the second year. In the 1920s, nevertheless, in comparison with such plays as *Kiki* and *East Is West, The First Year* entertained audiences as a realistic comedy about small-town characters and small-town life.

Rose Franken's *Claudia* is almost the antithesis of *The First Year* in timeliness. Today, *The First Year* is an outmoded comedy, but *Claudia* gains merit in retrospect as a play which deals with emotions not changed or influenced by economic conditions. When *Claudia* was produced in 1941, critics wrote favorable rather than enthusiastic reviews, but the public endorsed the production with a long run of 722 performances. Critics now generally acknowledge *Claudia* to be an original and significant American character comedy.

Claudia is not merely a tour de force, even though it made a star of Dorothy McGuire; the play itself has popular appeal. Miss Franken has counterbalanced a slight plot with strength in characterization, more emphasis on dialogue than on dramatic action, and more character development than plot development. In the first and second acts, light banter blends with serious overtones; in the deeply emotional third act, humor counterbalances the sentiment.

The story deals with Claudia, a young, immature wife whose emotions are confused because her attachment to her mother is as deep as her affection for her husband. This conflict interferes with her complete happiness in marriage, but she begins to mature when she learns her mother is dying and that she can no longer be dependent upon her. *Claudia* presents the relationship between husband and wife, not in homespun dialogue and unconvincing situations as in *The First Year,* but in adult, frank discussions, including several references to sexual relationships, which never startle or shock the audience.

The play deals with sentiment and emotional problems but is singularly free from the bathos and overemphasis characteristic of women's radio or television serials. Rose Franken has avoided sensationalism by underwriting the pathos, particularly in the scenes between mother and daughter. The strong attachment is always evident but is never discussed in exaggerated dialogue. This underwriting, coupled with the technique of naturalizing the audience, results in effective drama. For example, early in the play, David scolds Claudia for listening in on the neighbor's telephone conversations, and Claudia admits she loves to eavesdrop. In the second act, after David finishes a telephone conversation with Mrs. Brown who has told him the doctor's diagnosis, Claudia enters looking stunned. The naturalized audience knows immediately that she has been listening in on the extension phone and is therefore prepared for Claudia's reactions in the emotional scene which follows. The audience also suspects that Mrs. Brown is dying of cancer, although the illness is never mentioned specifically, for neither Claudia nor her mother discuss the malady with each other. Mrs. Brown, unaware that Claudia has overheard the telephone conversation, admits she is a coward and is afraid to tell Claudia. When David suggests that Claudia tell her mother she knows and Claudia says she wishes she could, but that she and her mother have never said such things to each other, David says, "I don't think you'll have to say them . . . in words. It's not your system." The system does work, for, at the end, Mrs. Brown realizes that Claudia knows.

In addition to underwriting to avoid sentimentality, Rose Franken adds touches of bittersweet humor which lessen the pathos of the last act. David, for example, tells Mrs. Brown she must stay with them, now that she is ill, and Mrs. Brown says, "I'd rather die!" Both Mrs. Brown and David are startled by what she has said, but then Mrs. Brown begins to laugh.

All through the play the humor develops naturally out of situations without resorting to forced gags. Claudia is examining her bank statement and insists the bank has made a mistake. Her mother and David tell her that banks do not make mistakes, which begins a series of arguments with David on the losing end, for even when he says that banks use adding machines, Claudia says, "What does that prove? We use a washing machine and look at your shirt last week." This type of repartee adds little to the plot, but it develops idiosyncrasies of the characters and makes them individuals rather than a typical wife, a typical husband, and a typical mother-in-law.

Perhaps the audience's familiarity with the characters helped account for the play's wide popularity. A great many theatergoers had read Rose Franken's stories and novels based on the adventures of Claudia and David and enjoyed seeing the characters come to life on stage. The fact that *Claudia,* although nominated for a prize, did not receive the award indicates that the critics in 1941 probably gave more consideration to plays dealing with dictators, possible invasions, and preparations for war. To the public, however, Rose Franken's well-written *Claudia* had more popular appeal and ran longer than any of the war plays presented the same season.

Both *Anna Lucasta* and *Detective Story* illustrate the difficulty of predicting which plays will have long runs, for neither seemed to be the type of drama that would run five hundred performances in the 1940s. The popular appeal of Philip Yordan's *Anna Lucasta,* produced in 1944, surprised a great many critics. Listing *Anna Lucasta* as a "Best Play" surprised many others, for the drama is uneven and disappointing. It is a curious combination of pathos and humor, realism and escapism, strong characters and weak motivation. The discordant mixture of comedy and tragedy as well as the inconsistencies in the plot possibly resulted from heavy doctoring and numerous revisions before the play reached Broadway. In the original version, presented in Harlem by the American Negro Theater, *Anna Lucasta* ended tragically; in the revised version, the play ended happily but unconvincingly.

The plot seems to be a combination of several timeworn situations, for *Anna Lucasta* tells the familiar story of the prostitute who falls in love and is regenerated, as well as the familiar story of the city slickers who try to swindle the innocent country boy, but these situations are not blended to sustain a unified plot. The revisions and doctoring are not entirely responsible for the unevenness which is evident even in the story of Anna, whose father, Joe Lucasta, has turned her out of his home because of her promiscuity, although the play implies that Joe has an unnatural attraction toward his daughter. When Joe's friend, Otis Slocum, asks him to find a wife for his son Rudolf, all the Lucastas except Joe decide that if Anna were to marry Rudolf, the Lucastas could get his money. Joe objects, of course, but the rest of the family goes ahead with the plan. Immediately after the wedding, Anna learns that Joe has told the Slocums the truth about her and that he will also spoil any chance Rudolf might have of getting a teaching position. Anna runs off with a former lover but comes back to Rudolf when her father dies. This contrived plot could have dramatic force, but the motivation for the action is almost always unconvincing. Audiences may accept the fact that Anna realizes her father's insane jealousy will wreck Rudolf's career, but her decision to leave with her former lover, Danny, shortly after the wedding ceremony, comes too quickly to be realistic. The engagement scene is equally unconvincing. Rudolf meets Anna for the first time, talks to her a few minutes, kisses her just as Mrs. Lucasta walks into the room, and within a short time persuades her to marry him. Perhaps the most unrealistic part of the play is the contrived, happy ending. Anna has returned to her former haunts and has tried to commit suicide. When the bartender gives her a note from Rudolf saying, "Darling—isn't it enough that I love you?" she goes back to Rudolf, who is waiting outside.

Much of the humor seems incongruous with the serious plot, but, at times, particularly in the barroom scenes, it does provide comic relief. Blanche, a streetwalker, has stolen a pair of binoculars; and when she offers them to the bartender, he says, "You ain't any different from those hoodlums in Europe who's stealing countries." Blanche says, "I get a pair of binoculars and right away I'm Hitler."

The long run of 957 performances obviously indicates *Anna Lucasta* had popular appeal, perhaps in the characterizations, which were not meant to represent a typical Negro family. Although played on Broadway by an all-Negro cast, the original script, *Anna Lukaska,* concerned a Polish family. The title became *Anna Lucasta* when the American Negro Theater produced the play in Harlem. Interestingly enough, the first motion picture version, starring Paulette Goddard, dealt with a white family; the second version, starring Eartha Kitt and Sammy Davis, Jr., reverted to the stage play. The long run on Broadway may have resulted from the audience's familiarity with such characters as the bullying brother-in-law, the flippant streetwalker, the understanding bartender, and the patient mother who welcomes her erring daughter. Audiences definitely liked Rudolf because he was not a simple country boy but a shrewd young man, far more clever than the Lucastas who tried to swindle him. Villains in American melodrama from Simon Legree down to the present-day portrayal of ruthless public figures have always fascinated audiences, and Joe Lucasta is no exception. In fact, his villainy is a combination of the stern father in old-fashioned melodrama and the repressed Reverend Davidson in *Rain*. The most individualized character, however, is Anna, who, in spite of her past, gains audience sympathy as Joe becomes more and more vindictive.

The critics' objections to the contrived ending are understandable, but if the theory is true that most popular plays give audiences the endings they want, then *Anna Lucasta* could not end unhappily. Furthermore, allowing Anna to live made possible a second popular situation, Anna's triumph over her father and over Danny, the lover who deserted her. One final contributing factor to the long run could have been the economic prosperity of the New York theater, for *Anna Lucasta* flourished on Broadway during the entertainment boom of World War II.

Sidney Kingsley's *Detective Story,* produced in 1949, is a much better written melodrama than *Anna Lucasta* and might have been a prize-winning play if it had not been produced the same season as Arthur Miller's *Death of a Salesman.* The story concerns Detective McLeod, whose rigid ethical ideals prove to be his downfall when he discovers a moral lapse in his wife's past. The plot is developed through a series of incidents that reveal McLeod's insistence that all criminals must be prosecuted regardless of extenuating circumstances, that leniency in police systems encourages crime, and that McLeod believes he is justified in using his own methods to enforce the law if he thinks it necessary. McLeod, who shows no leniency to a hardened criminal who will get a life sentence if convicted, is equally relentless with a bewildered young war veteran whose employer is willing to drop charges if the young man will return misappropriated funds. When the police lack sufficient evidence to prosecute Dr. Schneider, an abortionist who is responsible for the death of a young woman, McLeod disobeys orders and manhandles Schneider. This encounter becomes the major incident in the drama, for McLeod learns that his wife has also been a patient of Schneider's. At first McLeod is embittered and cross-examines his wife as though she were a criminal. Then he tries to reconcile with her, but she accuses him of being as sadistic as his father, whom he hated, and says that this hatred has made him merciless to anyone whom he thinks is an evildoer.

Detective Story effectively dramatizes the necessity for placing the power of the courts in more than one man by showing that no individual, even an idealistic McLeod, should have the legal authority to determine who is right and who is wrong. To emphasize his ideas concerning democracy, Kingsley uses a newspaper reporter, Joe Feinson, to make philosophical comments. When one of the officers gets a ticket for parking in front of the criminal court building, Feinson arranges to have the charges dropped by threatening to print a story about the judge who is responsible for giving parking tickets to policemen on duty. Callahan, the policeman, is bewildered at the idea of a reporter's fixing a ticket for a policeman, and Joe says, "The law keeps you in line, we keep the law in line, the people keep us in line, and you keep the people in line. . . . That's democracy."

Kingsley's extensive research before writing the play, his associations with detectives, and the months he spent visiting police headquarters are evident in the realistic characterizations and authentic dialogue that give *Detective Story* the same audience appeal as a suspenseful documentary recording of police court activities. The convincing characterizations include a cross section of types seen in precinct police stations such as a shoplifter who one of the policemen says is "just a slob," an eccentric woman who demands police protection from her neighbors because she knows they are blowing atomic vapors right through the walls, a smooth-talking lawyer, and two hardened criminals. The police officers, too, are realistic characters rather than the caricatures of policemen often found in melodramas. McLeod may seem a bit theatrical, but his actions emphasize his rebellion against the practice of what he calls "coddling criminals."

The documentary method of projecting the story retards the plot development in the first act, which is little more than a panorama of activities in the police station. The third act, however, moves rapidly to a melodramatic conclusion when McLeod, shaken by his wife's accusation that he is as sadistic as his father, as well as by the realization that he cannot give up his ideals, deliberately steps in front of an armed prisoner who kills him. This ending is in keeping with the characterization, for, by placing himself in the position where he will be shot, McLeod enables the other officers to disarm the prisoner. At the final curtain, there is no compromise with escapism for popular appeal such as the ending in *Anna Lucasta,* but the audience accepts the reality because it knows there could never be a logical reconciliation between McLeod and his wife.

With its documentary appeal and vivid characterizations as well as the critics' approval and Ralph Bellamy's expert performance as McLeod, *Detective Story* had sufficient power to draw audiences for 581 performances. The popular appeal, however, seems to have been limited to the New York area, for the play fared poorly on its road tour, possibly because it lacked Bellamy's forceful portrayal of McLeod, and possibly because the plot was not the type usually found in popular drama.

Comedies
the Critics
Liked

THIRTEEN long-running comedies produced between 1920 and 1950 have had not only approval of the critics but also unusual popular appeal for the public. Three of the comedies ran more than one thousand performances, and a fourth, *Life with Father,* established a longevity record in the New York theater.

Of the thirteen, *Three Men on a Horse,* written by John Cecil Holm in collaboration with George Abbott and produced in 1935, was the only comedy not selected as one of the ten best plays of its season. To some critics, *Three Men on a Horse* resembled other typically contrived farces produced in the 1920s and 1930s. To audiences, however, the play had greater appeal and ran longer than most of the farces using the same feverish pace, staccato dialogue, and assortment of raffish characters.

The story deals with Erwin Trowbridge, a meek suburbanite, who writes greeting-card verses and whose hobby is picking winners in horse races, although he never trusts his uncanny luck enough to place a bet. Erwin, tired of being bullied by Clarence, his brother-in-law, and by Mr. Carver, his employer, offers little resistance when a group of gamblers shanghai him and inveigle him into making their selections. His consistency in picking winners delights the gamblers until they discover that Erwin is not betting. They find a list of horses with names crossed out, suspect Erwin is double-crossing them, and force him to place a bet. The wrong horse wins, the gamblers grow menacing, and then, at the crucial moment, the radio announcer flashes the news that the winning horse has been scratched and that the new winner, Mr. Khayyam, the horse Erwin picked, is paying off twelve to one. With new confidence, Erwin bellows orders to everyone on stage, including Mr. Carver. To add to Erwin's triumph, Clarence has lost all his money betting on the list Erwin had discarded; and Mr. Carver persuades Erwin to come back to work at a substantial increase in salary.

The role of Erwin, as well as his importance to the plot, gives *Three Men on a Horse* greater audience appeal than *Room Service,* in which the one small-town character is subordinated to the Broadway "shoestring" producers who dominate the plot and action. In *Three Men on a Horse,* all situations revolve around Erwin, whose bewildered participation in the frenzied activity surrounding him emphasizes the humor. Just as the Sherwood girls are a decided contrast to the Greenwich Villagers in *My Sister Eileen,* Erwin, the suburbanite, is a decided contrast to the gamblers, the ex-follies girl, and the hotel employees feverishly placing bets. The satire inherent in other characters also appeals to audiences: Mr. Carver, who burlesques the gruff business executive; Mabel, the one-time follies girl who gets out of breath trying to demonstrate her former chorus routines; and Patsy, the arrogant, blustering horse-race better.

Three Men on a Horse also satirizes the greeting-card industry. Erwin's poems, amusing in themselves, develop into ludicrous combinations of sentiment and gags when the gamblers, who have torn up the verses, try to piece them together again. Erwin has written a sentimental poem about going to church on Sundays, and Charlie, who can't find the last line Erwin had written, adds, "So now I don't ever get drunk no more on Tuesdays and Mondays." Even funnier is the scene in which Erwin dazzles Patsy with his Mother's Day verses, or the moment when Erwin's uncanny prediction brings sudden wealth to elevator operators and scrubwomen as well as to the professional gamblers.

The humor, the excellent construction of the comedy, and the triumph of Erwin, which earned him an almost worshipful awe from his wife, all had popular appeal, as did the effective performances of Sam Levene as Patsy, Shirley Booth as Mabel, William Lynn as Erwin, and Millard Mitchell as Charlie. The long run of 835 performances given to *Three Men on a Horse* by New York audiences influenced the production of two musical comedies based on it. The first, *Banjo Eyes,* starring Eddie Cantor, closed after 126 performances bcause illness forced Cantor to leave the show; and the producers, who had revised the script to fit Cantor, realized they could not find a suitable replacement. The second musical version, *Let It Ride,* even with George Gobel and Sam Levene in the cast, failed. Perhaps audiences had seen too many versions of *Three Men on a Horse,* including television productions, motion pictures, and stage revivals. Perhaps, too, the play, characteristic of comedies of the 1930s, had become outdated.

Boy Meets Girl, the Bella and Samuel Spewack farce produced in 1935, consists of a series of unconvincing, exaggerated situations as rowdy as *Room Service* and as full of gags as *The Doughgirls,* but *Boy Meets Girl* appears to be even more exaggerated and accelerated than other formula farces. From the opening curtain to the final episode, there is no slacking of pace or tempo, or few, if any, quiet interludes to relieve the humor.

The story, a deliberate lampoon on the activities of Hollywood writers, producers, and actors, concerns Benson and Law, two script writers whose antics stir up a mounting maze of confusion. They bedevil their producer with whirlwind escapades; act as godfathers to Happy, infant son of Suzie, a studio waitress, who has discovered that her husband is a bigamist; write scenarios which make Happy one of the biggest baby stars in Hollywood; and plague Larry Toms, star of the studio's Western pictures, for whom they also write scenarios. Benson and Law believe all stories are based on variations of the formula "Boy meets girl—boy loses girl—boy gets girl," and Suzie's romance in the play verifies their formula, for Rodney, an English nobleman, meets Suzie, loses Suzie, and then marries Suzie.

One or two critics have raised minor objections to the lack of morality in *Boy Meets Girl;* audiences, evidently, have not. The play does have censorable lines and situations, but the moral tone is not so pernicious as the bawdiness of *Sailor, Beware!* or the extreme earthiness in *Tobacco Road,* because the sex angle is not the major theme. The authors have made Suzie, the expectant mother, a victim of circumstances, who has married in good faith, not knowing her husband was already married.

The characters are cleverly conceived but they remain caricatures. Rodney is a satire of a well-bred Englishman with no sense of humor who is determined to be an actor; Larry Toms, a stereotyped cowboy star whose dialogue is limited to such expressions as "mighty fond"; and C. F. Friday, a bewildered, overworked producer subservient to the chief executive of the studio. Benson and Law are rumored to be fictionalized portraits of two Broadway playwrights whose antics in Hollywood were the despair of producers and actors, but audiences unfamiliar with the real-life counterparts can still enjoy the humor. Benson and Law deliberately scheme to torment their victims, neither giving them any consideration nor receiving any consideration from them. They are as ruthless and self-centered at the final curtain as they were in the opening scene. Their actions and dialogue develop the plot, but they remain static characterizations.

Boy Meets Girl is a clever satire on the motion picture industry with an undertone of criticism, a humorous indictment of the follies of Hollywood. The farce, for example, reveals the blunders of research advisors in costumes. Rodney, who is wearing the uniform of the Coldstream Guard, justifiably informs C. F., the producer, that the uniform is not authentic. C. F. promptly fires Rodney and then orders the hat, the one authentic item in the costume, to be changed. The use of background music is ridiculed, particularly when the studio song writers audition a ballad, "Pain in My Heart and My Heart's on my Sleeve," with lyrics that are a compilation of stock phrases and a melody stolen from an old tune in the studio's files. Benson and Law's staccato dialogue as they weave hackneyed situations into a scenario becomes a laughable commentary on motion picture plots. Episodes involving Happy's roles in the scenarios and the reluctance of actors to appear with Happy because babies steal the best scenes burlesques the trite pictures made with child stars. These situations are hectic and exaggerated, but the underlying basis of truth often makes the most incredible scene appear authentic to audiences who enjoy the dramatized absurdities of behind-the-scenes activities in Hollywood.

At times the humor is obvious and contrived but, nonetheless, hilarious, such as the scene in which Benson and Law make an overseas telephone call in Larry's hospital room while Larry is out. When he returns and objects to Law's using the telephone, Benson says, "If that's the way you feel about it—here's your nickel." Equally ridiculous is Suzie's radio broadcast when she announces that Happy couldn't possibly eat all the products he endorses in advertisements, or the episode in which Larry proposes to Suzie and acts the bashful hero, just as he does in the films, while Suzie gives a synopsis of the first picture in which she remembers seeing Larry, and Larry interrupts periodically to utter his stock phrase, "Mighty fond."

Primarily, however, the clever satire, perhaps the best satire on Hollywood produced on the New York stage, distinguishes *Boy Meets Girl* from a great many other long-running farces. The run of 669 performances also results from the play's popular appeal, aptly summarized in the title which has become a stock phrase to illustrate one of the most popular situations on Broadway.

Blithe Spirit and *Arsenic and Old Lace,* both produced in 1941, deal humorously with murder. In *Blithe Spirit,* the plot to kill is planned by a ghost; in *Arsenic and Old Lace,* by a homicidal maniac and two gentle but addlepated ladies.

Noel Coward's *Blithe Spirit,* subtitled "An Improbable Farce," is a fantasy concerning a husband haunted by the ghosts of his wives. With the possible exception of the final scene, the tempo never reaches the frenzied pace of a farce because the plot stretches one humorous situation over three acts. The story deals with Charles Condomine and his second wife, Ruth, who invite a medium, Madame Arcati, to give a demonstration in their home. During the séance, Madame Arcati goes into a trance and Charles alone hears the voice of Elvira, his first wife. When Madame Arcati leaves, Charles sees the ghost of Elvira, but Ruth neither sees nor hears Elvira and cannot understand Charles's strangely fantastic conversations with his first wife until Charles convinces Ruth that Elvira's ghost is in the room. Several days later, while Elvira is still haunting the house, Ruth insists Elvira wants to involve Charles in a fatal accident so that he will join her in the spirit world. While driving into town to ask Madame Arcati to help rid them of Elvira, Ruth is killed, for Elvira has tampered with the mechanism of the car which she thought Charles would use. When Madame Arcati tries to exorcise Elvira, she causes the ghost of Ruth to appear instead. Finally, after several futile demonstrations, Madame Arcati makes both ghosts disappear, and Charles readily admits he is glad to be rid of both wives.

Although many critics have called this ludicrous plot "shallow," audiences have found it extremely amusing, even though the first two acts merely involve the problem of Charles's difficulty of living with his very much alive second wife and the ghost of his first wife. The humor is most hilarious when the audience shares Charles's ability to see and hear Elvira and is able to enjoy the perplexity of the situation and the maddening bewilderment of Ruth who imagines that everything Charles says is addressed to her. For example, Ruth says, "I am not going to stay here arguing any longer," and Elvira says, "Hurray!" Charles turns to Elvira and snaps, "Shut up!" but Ruth, thinking he is still talking to her, says, "How dare you speak to me like that." The situation grows worse as Charles tries to explain and Elvira keeps interrupting, until Charles says, "Be quiet. You're behaving like a guttersnipe," and Ruth stalks off the stage. The humor of the situation becomes even more effective in the next act when Ruth realizes that Elvira is present, but since she cannot hear Elvira and must rely on Charles to tell her what Elvira is saying, Ruth insists he is not telling her the truth. The more desperate Ruth becomes, the more humorous the scene becomes because the audience hears all three sides of the conversation.

In the third act, when the ghost of Ruth appears and Charles must cope with the spirits of two wives, the situation, conversely, is not nearly as funny, for the audience has lost its position of advantage. Even when Madame Arcati returns and restores some degree of interest because she cannot see or hear the ghosts, the humor never regains the effectiveness of the first two acts, Madame Arcati provokes some laughter with her ridiculous gestures, but she is unable to arouse the same degree of hilarity that Ruth does in her frustrated attempts to communicate with Elvira's ghost or as the maid does when she enters the room, takes off a phonograph record, and then, seconds later, when Elvira starts the record again, goes screaming out of the room.

Charles, Elvira, and Ruth, with their charming but often superficial manners, their unconvincing, morally loose banter, and their almost arrogant unconcern for people beneath their own social level, are amusing but brittle characters. Madame Arcati is the most whimsical character, created solely to evoke laughter, delightfully amusing but unconvincing. She is a theatrical personality rather than a human characterization, dependent almost wholly upon the interpretation of the actress to make the humor effective, for she must speak ridiculous chatter without lapsing into annoying silliness which would pall rather than amuse audiences.

Perhaps the play is fluffy and shallow, but it is, nevertheless, entertaining shallowness, particularly in those scenes which naturalize the audience. Much of Coward's humor has literary allusions, such as Elvira's comment that she was playing backgammon with Genghis Khan when she received the call to revisit the earth, or Elvira's expressed contempt for Madame Arcati's demonstrations: "Merlin does all this sort of thing at parties and bores us all stiff with it."

One additional factor which contributed to the popular run of 657 performances should not be overlooked. *Blithe Spirit* played on Broadway during the first year of World War II, a time when audiences sought relief from tragedy and horror; and Coward's play gave them the opportunity to laugh, even at death.

In 1964, a musical comedy based on *Blithe Spirit* called *High Spirits* gave Beatrice Lillie the chance to delight New York audiences with her portrayal of Madame Arcati, a role that fitted her talents admirably. The ending was also changed by having Madame Arcati and Charles drink wine which Elvira has poisoned. The Madame and Charles then go into a ghoulish but fast-paced and humorous death scene. The musical, which was rumored to have had trouble on the road, went through a series of revisions with Gower Champion being called in to stage several dance sequences that highlighted the production. *High Spirits,* however, in spite of Miss Lillie's delightful clowning, did not duplicate the long run of Coward's *Blithe Spirit.*

The ghoulish ending in *High Spirits* is reminiscent of the tone throughout Joseph Kesselring's *Arsenic and Old Lace,* which combines the humor of farce with the mystery and suspense of melodrama. The plot is almost purely melodramatic. Mortimer Brewster discovers to his horror that his sweet old aunts, Abby and Martha, have murdered twelve men. His brother, Jonathan, who looks like

Boris Karloff, and was played in New York by Karloff himself, has also killed twelve men. Jonathan returns to the Brewster home where he almost gets one more murder to his credit, but the police arrive in time and take Jonathan to prison. Mortimer learns he is illegitimate and not an insane Brewster, as he had feared; and at the final curtain, the audience has good reason to believe that Abby and Martha may get their thirteenth victim and triumph over Jonathan.

Ghoulish as this plot may sound in synopsis, the play itself is almost pure farce, for the dialogue is peppered with gags which ridicule the plot and dispel any preceding moments of horror. For example, just after Martha and Abby have shocked Mortimer by revealing that they are responsible for the murder of Mr. Hoskins, whose body is stuffed into the box under the window, Martha insists the next time she takes the little Schultz boy to the movies, she will not allow him to drag her to "another of those scary pictures." And when Martha tells Mortimer her formula for adding arsenic, strychnine, and cyanide to elderberry wine, she and Abby take as much pride in revealing the secret as though they were giving him their prize-winning recipe from the county fair. Teddy Brewster, who resembles Teddy Roosevelt and imagines that he actually is Teddy Roosevelt, is anything but a serious characterization. To Teddy, the stairs leading to the second floor are San Juan Hill, and he never dashes up without shouting, "Charge!" The holes he digs in the cellar are locks for the Panama Canal, and the victims of Martha and Abby which he buries in these holes have died of yellow fever.

Although Howard Lindsay and Russel Crouse, who produced *Arsenic and Old Lace,* have consistently denied doctoring the script, they have not convinced critics who insist the producers transformed the show from melodrama to farce by adding humorous embellishments. Regardless of who is responsible for the final draft, *Arsenic and Old Lace* cleverly ridicules the hackneyed improbabilities of the old-fashioned murder plays. When these early melodramas were revived in the 1920s and 1930s and were played as comedies, audiences hissed the villains and applauded the heroes. *Arsenic and Old Lace* capitalizes on this vogue by incorporating the jeers and boos into the script. By inserting the laughs in opportune situations, the play satirizes the very form of melodrama, and the audience, instead of booing the villain, laughs at the satire as well as the villain. All this accounts, in large measure, for the phenomenal popularity of the play.

Contrast, if well drawn, is always a popular dramatic technique, and *Arsenic and Old Lace* abounds in contrast moving swiftly from laughter to fear, and from terror to hilarity. The melodramatic scenes have humorous overtones, and the farcical episodes have macabre undertones. The episodes involving Jonathan's attempt to murder Mortimer are bloodthirsty and harrowing, for the audience never doubts that Jonathan would torture Mortimer by giving him a long, lingering death; on the other hand, the episode in which Martha and Abby offer a glass of their lethal elderberry wine to lonely Mr. Gibbs is highly amusing because the audience has a morbid fascination in Mr. Gibbs's plight and would probably be entertained if he smacked his lips and expressed delight with the drink, as Abby said one of their other gentlemen had done.

Abby and Martha are studies in contrast, for they speak and act like two devout, gentle souls who epitomize benevolence; yet they are elated with their swift and painless mode of poisoning. Mortimer, the only member of the Brewster clan not tainted with madness, adds further contrast. In the midst of the frenzied excitement, he fears for his own sanity and acts as though he were the demented Brewster while Abby and Martha proceed with their household duties as though they were the sane Brewsters who must humor him, just as they humor Teddy. The more perplexed and agitated Mortimer becomes, the more reserved his aunts become, since they believe their little murders are no concern of his. The audience, therefore, is not too surprised to learn, in the very last few minutes of the play, that Mortimer is not a Brewster after all.

Contrast also emphasizes the satire of character types familiar to audiences. Jonathan, who lacks a sense of humor, is amusing not only because he resents his resemblance to Boris Karloff but also because his actions satirize the murderous villains Karloff has played in horror pictures. In the road company, Erich Von Stroheim, who had been billed in Hollywood as "the man you love to hate," played Jonathan, and the references in the play, of course, were changed to Von Stroheim. The character of Mortimer holds up to ridicule the prejudiced theater critic who has made up his mind to write a bad review even before he attends the performance. The police officers, O'Hara and Rooney, are blundering officials who can't recognize criminals from their descriptions. Rooney, for example, talks to headquarters on the telephone and repeats a detailed description of Jonathan's assistant, Dr. Einstein, while he stares blankly at Einstein. Then, after completing his call, Rooney thanks Einstein for signing papers which will commit the Brewster sisters to an asylum and lets him walk out. Unlike Abby and Martha, who are satirical portraits of the kindly Lady Bountifuls of earlier dramas, Teddy, the least complex of the Brewsters, is merely a caricature. He is a harmless lunatic who does not indulge in homicide but is content to pursue his career as a Roughrider, to dig locks, blow bugles, call cabinet meetings, and bury corpses.

The technique of naturalizing the audience, which is used rather consistently throughout the play, adds further impact to the climaxes. At the end of Act II, Dr. Einstein insists the number of murder victims for both the aunts and Jonathan is equal—twelve each. Just as Jonathan says that all he needs is one more victim, Mortimer enters and says, "Well, here I am." The effectiveness of this curtain speech is emphasized by the audience's complete awareness and Mortimer's unawareness of the impending danger. The audience is again more informed than Mr. Witherspoon at the end of the play when the sisters offer him the elderberry wine and Witherspoon says, "I thought I'd had my last glass of it." This naturalization, combined with the emphasis on absurdity, the effective satire, and the excellent performances of Boris Karloff, Josephine Hull, Jean Adair, and Allyn Joslyn, entertained audiences for 1,444 performances, making *Arsenic and Old Lace* one of the longest-running productions in the history of the New York theater.

Junior Miss, produced in 1941 and adapted by Jerome Chodorov and Joseph Fields from Sally Benson's stories in *The New Yorker,* ran only half as long as *Arsenic and Old Lace*. The comedy did not get unanimous approval from the critics, but it did entertain audiences with its well-drawn characterizations.

The plot deals with Judy, a thirteen-year-old adolescent who stumbles through a series of contrived situations and finally, in the last act, develops into a junior miss, very much like her older sister, Lois. Judy's insatiable appetite, her desire to wear clothes like her sister's, and her fear of meeting her first date who is coming to look her over before asking her to a dance, are amusing and make audiences sympathetic with her problems. There is a slight resemblance between Judy and Booth Tarkington's Penrod in that both adolescents compare incidents in their lives to stories they have seen in the movies. Penrod uses a melodramatic movie plot to weave a fictional account of his sordid home life so that his teacher will not punish him for neglecting to do his homework. Judy, on the other hand, uses movie plots to draw parallels with situations she imagines are happening in her own life. For example, she thinks that her uncle, who has been away for years, has served a prison term. The romance she deliberately plans for her uncle is also inspired by the movies, but the romance is neither farfetched nor unconvincing when it does materialize.

Judy is more immature and more wholesome than her inseparable friend, Fuffy, who is obviously funny when she applies a different shade of nail polish on each finger so that Judy can help her pick the right color. Fuffy's exaggerated bad manners and brashness, however, emphasize Judy's milder actions and escapades. Without Fuffy to serve as contrast, Judy would be an irritating youngster rather than a likable and amusing child.

Lois and her entourage of young boy friends satirize pseudo-sophisticated teen-agers who patronize their elders and tolerate parental authority. By comparison with junior misses in such plays as *Janie* or *Kiss and Tell,* Lois is more restrained and more realistic in her disgust with Judy, her distress at her father's treatment of the variety of escorts who trail her, and her deliberate casualness with these escorts. The adults are also amusing but lack the individuality of Judy and Lois. Mr. and Mrs. Graves are typical understanding parents; J. B. Curtis is a domineering senior member of a successful law firm; Ellen, his daughter, typifies the young woman dominated by her father; and Hilda, the maid, closely resembles Hazel, the humorous maid in the *Saturday Evening Post* cartoons and, more recently, the principal character in the popular television series. As a farcical character, Hilda is more successful at insolent repartee than at being a maid. In fact, many of the good gag lines are delegated to Hilda. She picks up her Christmas packages and sneers, "Gloves—handkerchiefs—bedroom slippers—and that same tired toilet water I wouldn't use on a dog," and follows that comment three lines later with, "I'll open them down at the department store when I exchange them." Immediately after Hilda sneers at her gifts, Fuffy and Judy exchange identically wrapped packages containing identical imitation leather purses, except for the color. The girls are not so obviously funny as Hilda, but they are more convincing.

Fields and Chodorov have succeeded in adapting Miss Benson's characters to the stage more than they have in dramatizing the disconnected short stories into a unified play. They have taken Judy's escapades, Lois' disgust with Judy, an imaginary triangle, a situation which threatens the Graves family with financial disaster, and a secondary romance between Uncle Willis and Ellen Curtis and interwoven them by maneuvering and assembling incidents so that the humor inherent in the original stories often lacks spontaneity in the adaptation.

In spite of the obviously contrived result, *Junior Miss* had popular appeal. Audiences, particularly those familiar with *The New Yorker* stories, enjoyed seeing Miss Benson's characters come to life. The humor in the obviously inserted gag lines and in the quieter, more convincing scenes, plus the amusing portrait of adolescents and teen-agers, pleased audiences enough to keep the play running for 710 performances.

Although Clare Boothe's *The Women,* produced in 1936, is not an adaptation of short sketches, it shows better dramatic skill than *Junior Miss* in maneuvering episodic scenes into a unified and logical plot sequence. The play is almost a series of variations on the Spewack formula, "Boy meets girl—boy loses girl—boy gets girl," for the principal story concerns Mary, who is married to Stephen, divorces Stephen, and finally remarries Stephen. Among the secondary plots, Peggy is happily married, then goes to Reno for a divorce, changes her mind, and returns to her husband. More than half the other women in the cast are either meeting men, losing men, or getting men.

The Women is a clever piece of craftsmanship unfolding a variety of complicated marital relationships and affairs of wives and mistresses without introducing a single male character on stage. Miss Boothe's use of an all-feminine cast is not unprecedented in the theater, but she is the only dramatist who accomplished this feat in a popular play. Artificial sequences and devices such as telephone conversations and gossip sessions in a kitchen, a fitting room, a beauty salon, and a drawing room are written with deliberate cleverness rather than subtlety, for the audience is always conscious of Miss Boothe's ingenuity in keeping men off stage. *The Women* has the same clever theatricality in its humor, particularly in curtain speeches. For example, after Janie, the maid, and Maggie, the cook, have discussed Mary's impending divorce, Maggie says as the last line of the scene, "The first man who can think up a good explanation of how he can be in love with his wife *and* another woman, is going to win that prize they're always giving out in Sweden."

Miss Boothe never misses an opportunity to ridicule feminine fads. She includes jokes about psychoanalysis, diets, divorce, and fashion. Some of these quips, such as Edith's comment on watercress sandwiches, "I'd just as soon eat my way across a front lawn," are witty enough for audiences to remember after leaving the theater. Other quips are often little more than good cartoon gag lines. There is a constant interlacing of dialogue with humorous commentaries on pregnancy, "kept" women, and sex. None of these lines is subtle, many are vulgar, but often they are more amusing than the vicious jibes throughout the play which illustrate woman's inhumanity to woman. Probably the most typical example of vitriolic humor occurs in the Arden Beauty Salon episode. Edith admits she has been gossiping with a newspaperwoman and has repeated some gossip Sylvia told her which could wreck Mary's marriage if it were printed. When Edith tells Sylvia she forgot she was talking to a journalist, Sylvia says she can fix everything by calling the columnist and saying that Edith had been lying, but Edith objects. Sylvia tells her not to worry, for the story will be old news in a day or so. Moreover, Sylvia adds, "You know the awful things they printed about—what's her name—before she jumped out the window? Why I can't even remember her name, so who cares?" After Sylvia leaves, Peggy insists upon calling Mary, but Edith warns her to avoid getting involved. "I've never had a fight with a girl friend in all my life," says Edith. "I hear no evil, I see no evil, I speak no evil." The utter absurdity of Edith's speech should be funny, but the audience's awareness of Sylvia's maliciousness, Edith's stupidity, and Mary's helplessness makes the scene effective but not amusing.

The humor which grows out of the action stimulates better audience response. When Sylvia, the most vicious woman in the play, becomes hysterical, gets into a fight with Miriam, and bites her, Lucy, the maid, grabs Sylvia, drags her across stage, forces a bottle of spirits of ammonia under her nose and says, "Listen, Mrs. Fowler! You've got the hy-strikes." The situation is doubly effective because the audience laughs at Lucy and gets great satisfaction in watching someone manhandle Sylvia.

The play projects a series of satirical portraits of idle, wealthy, and often vulgar women more vicious and unsympathetic than any group of women ever presented in a long-running drama. The principal characters include Mary, the faithful wife; Crystal, the ruthless "kept" woman; Sylvia, the unfaithful wife, gossip, and troublemaker; Edith, the anually pregnant woman; Flora, the silly, aging countess, much married and much divorced; and Peggy, the simplehearted wife bewildered by the viciousness which surrounds her. Paradoxically, Mary, the only noble woman in the group, is the least interesting. When Crystal tells Mary, "Saint or no saint, Mrs. Haines, you are a hell of a *dull* woman," she is voicing the opinion of the audience. In the final scene, however, even noble Mary learns to claw as the other women have. The minor characters represent a greater variety of types and include gossiping beauticians, maids, a secretary in love with her employer, an outraged hospital nurse who has no sympathy for her wealthy patients, a debutante and her dowager mother, and a placid maid in a ladies' powder room. Some of these characters are amusing, others are raucous, but all are familiar types frequently used only for gag lines.

Audiences enjoyed the theatrical skill demonstrated in the maneuvering to keep men off stage as well as the technique of giving them information not known by all the characters—naturalization —in almost every scene. In the opening episode, Sylvia tells Edith that Mary's husband is unfaithful, and the audience waits in suspense to meet Crystal and to see which woman will triumph. In the second scene, when a manicurist tells Mary how Crystal met Mr. Haines, not realizing that she is telling the story to Mrs. Haines, the naturalized audience watches closely to get Mary's reaction. In the final scenes, the audience knows Crystal has been unfaithful to Stephen and wonders how Mary will learn the facts and then wheedle the truth out of Crystal. Moreover, Mary's reconciliation with Stephen gives the audience the ending it wants and once again uses the popular situation in which the right woman triumphs. The appeal of the naturalized situations is offset, in part, by the audacious frankness which often descends into vulgarity, and by the lack of subtlety, but Miss Boothe's cleverness in creating a unified play from diversified episodes makes even the unsavory characters palatable.

Several production factors also accounted for the popularity of *The Women,* particularly with feminine audiences who crowded the matinee performances. Multiple scene changes, for example, added to the entertainment. The producers used a revolving stage divided into several sections, and entranced audiences as curtains closed and reopened almost instantly on a complete new stage set. The actresses changed outfits for each new scene to provide a continuous fashion show of the latest styles from negligees to street dresses, from sports outfits to formal gowns. Intimate peeks into a beauty salon, a night-club powder room, a fitting room in an exclusive dress shop, an apartment in Reno for divorcées, and even a bathroom gave audiences the vicarious pleasure of observing the actions of unconventional and malicious Park Avenue socialites in a multiplicity of complicated love affairs. Expert performances by Margalo Gillmore in the thankless role of Mary, Ilka Chase as Sylvia, Phyllis Povah as Edith, and Betty Lawford as Crystal also helped *The Women* run for 657 performances.

The first motion picture production of *The Women* featured an all-star, all-feminine cast including Norma Shearer as Mary, Rosalind Russell as Sylvia, Joan Crawford as Crystal, Paulette Goddard as Miriam, Joan Fontaine as Peggy, Mary Boland as The Countess, and Hedda Hopper as a newspaper columnist. According to stories heard in Hollywood, many important actresses were anxious to become part of such a star-studded cast. The producers had planned to have Hedy Lamarr play Crystal, but Joan Crawford was so eager to play the role, so the story goes, that she offered to do it without salary. Later, Metro-Goldwyn-Mayer refilmed the play but introduced male characters and distorted the effective, conniving touches Miss Boothe had been able to create with only women in the cast.

The puritan would probably consider *Strictly Dishonorable,* produced in 1929, and *The Voice of the Turtle,* produced in 1943, as immoral as *The Women* although both are more subtle in their discussions of sex. Both plays concern men of affairs who begin their amorous pursuits with dishonorable intentions and then become completely captivated by young, appealing heroines. Both plays blend overtones of disarming dialogue with undertones of immorality. The heroines in the two plays differ, however. In *Strictly Dishonorable,* Isabelle is virtuous. At the climax, Count di Ruvo warns Isabelle to lock the door, walks out of his apartment, and does not return until the following morning. In *The Voice of the Turtle,* Sally has been disillusioned in love by two previous affairs. Sergeant Bill Page, who has spent the first night of his leave sleeping on the couch in Sally's living room, decides after making love to Sally and being repulsed that he would rather go to his hotel room than spend a second night alone on the couch. Just as he is about to leave, Sally calls him back into the bedroom. The contrast between the two heroines indicates the extent to which the audience's views on morality changed from 1929 when heroines in popular comedies were expected to be innocent in spite of temptation, to the public's acceptance, in 1943, of a slightly promiscuous heroine. Isabelle and Sally, however, are both more winsome than any of the characters in *The Women.*

Preston Sturges' *Strictly Dishonorable* is a leisurely paced comedy of a romance between a naïve Southern girl and an Italian nobleman who meet in an intimate speak-easy. There are none of the hoodlums, bootleggers, racketeers, or vindictive policemen which other dramatists have included in plays about typical speak-easies of the 1920s. *Strictly Dishonorable,* which could easily have been a heavy-handed satire ridiculing speak-easies, bibulous officers of the law, and virtuous heroines, presents an amusing portrait of the friendly atmosphere of the speak-easy, the casual relationships between police and bar owners, and almost justifies Isabelle's willingness to accept the Count's attentions by making Henry a nagging, uncivil fiancé.

All of the characters, with the exception of Henry, are likable. Count di Ruvo is converted from a charming villain who would seduce the heroine into a charming hero. Tomaso Antiovi, the friendly, paternal speak-easy owner, operates his establishment as though it were within the law. A judge, in fact, lives directly above the speak-easy. The audience is not surprised when Henry mistakes the identity of the judge, who is sitting at the bar and talking across the room to Isabelle, and calls him a jailbird. Mulligan, the policeman, comes into the speak-easy, not to get a drink or to stage a raid, but merely to retrieve Isabelle who has refused to leave with Henry. Mulligan tells the judge Henry has gone to headquarters demanding a search for Isabelle's kidnappers and has described the judge as "an old, broken down barfly, a regular bum."

Mulligan and the judge have some of the wittiest lines in the play. When Isabelle suggests that Mulligan might like an Italian chocolate and is told that he would rather have a drink, Isabelle says, "But policemen never drink on duty," and Mulligan says, "It just seems like never." This remark typifies the humor which flows through the play and seldom appears to be inserted like an obtrusive gag.

Isabelle is a combination of Southern charm and innocence. Her helplessness appeals to all the men from the judge who wants to protect her, to the Count who marries her. Both the Count and Isabelle are convincing characters, for, if they were not, the climax of the second act, which takes place in the Count's apartment, would be ludicrous rather than humorous. As the Count helps Isabelle undress, he realizes more and more that she is not an experienced, worldly woman, and when he places Isabelle on the bed, he picks up a large Teddy bear, puts it beside her, says, "There! So you won't be frightened," and walks out of the room while Isabelle shouts the curtain line, "I'm not a baby! I'm not a baby!"

The light treatment throughout the whole bedroom scene made it amusing rather than offensive. Women in the audience were aware that they were seeing a play about seduction, but they overlooked the immorality because of the humor of Isabelle's inexperience in love-making and the Count's gradual change from a seducer to a protecting bridegroom. Because *Strictly Dishonorable* gave audiences what they believed was an authentic picture of the prohibition era with no attempt to condemn or condone the speak-easy and because it entertained audiences with a racy story, clever characterizations, and witty dialogue, it established a run of 557 performances, making it one of the very few plays produced between 1929 and 1933 to exceed the five-hundred-performance mark.

John Van Druten's *The Voice of the Turtle,* basically a variation of *Strictly Dishonorable,* spreads a thin plot over six scenes. By ingenious dramatic structure and by fully developed characterizations, however, the comedy becomes a playwright's tour de force. With a small cast of only three characters, one of whom appears in two brief scenes, Van Druten creates a delightful full-length play which never lags and seldom resorts to obvious devices such as telephone conversations to break up long passages of dialogue.

The first scene introduces all three characters. Sergeant Bill Page has come to New York on leave to spend the weekend with Olive, who turns him over to Sally, a young actress, because she has a rendezvous with a lieutenant commander. The next three scenes concentrate on the development of the love story between Sally and Bill, created so cleverly that the audience never gets bored watching just two characters. In the last act, Olive comes back to reclaim Bill who, by this time, prefers to stay with Sally. The people who influence the lives of the three characters are discussed sufficiently to enable the audience to identify the lieutenant commander with whom Olive spends the weekend; Bill's first sweetheart, a girl he met in Paris and whom he meets again in New York; the leading man in Sally's new play; and the theatrical producer, the second man with whom Sally has had an affair. The play, however, deals almost exclusively with Sally and Bill.

The most important and convincing character is Sally, an individualized combination of artlessness and sophistication. Unlike Isabelle in *Strictly Dishonorable,* who is innocent and helpless, Sally is more mature and realistic. Olive, the other woman, is as immoral but not so crass as the characters in *The Women,* for although she personifies many of the traits Clare Boothe's women discuss, she seldom descends to the same level of frank or vulgar dialogue. Olive not only arranges the meeting between Sally and Bill but also acts as a foil for Sally. In contrast to Olive, Sally, who is not a conventional heroine, becomes almost winsome and wholesome. Olive is calculating; Sally is impulsive. Olive is brash and earthy; Sally is naïvely curious. The scene in which Olive discusses morality with Sally definitely contrasts Olive's acceptance of easy virtue with Sally's concern over her own unconventionality. The less favorably Olive is presented throughout the play, the more sympathetic Sally becomes to audiences, who understand why Bill would fall in love with her. Bill, the third character, combines the maturity and perception of David in *Claudia* and the youthful appeal of Lieutenant Seawright in *Dear Ruth* with his own individualized charm.

The physical production of the play fascinated audiences. The stage setting, representing the interior of a three-room apartment with full view of kitchen, living room, and bedroom, helped develop the plot and prevented the two character scenes from lapsing into

The Voice of the Turtle, Margaret Sullavan and Elliott Nugent

static dialogue. Van Druten kept the action flowing without interruption of curtain waits or scene changes by having the actors move freely and naturally from one room to another as though they were in an actual apartment rather than on a stage set. Audiences enjoyed this fluidity of action, particularly when the complicated stage set gave them the advantage of watching simultaneous action in two rooms. For example, when Olive came back and Bill hid in the bedroom, the audience relished the idea of watching Bill get out of the apartment without Olive's discovering that he had been there.

The long run of almost four years cannot be credited to the original cast. The excellent performances of Margaret Sullavan, Elliott Nugent, and Audrey Christie helped the initial momentum at the box office, but the popular draw continued through a whole series of replacements in all three roles, for it was the play itself that audiences came to see in the second, third, and fourth seasons.

The love affair did arouse adverse comments from those critics who objected to the underlying immorality. Audiences, however, accepted the frankness of the realistic plot because it was timely for the 1940s. The story of a soldier on leave who hoped he would return home after the war aroused the same hope in audiences that other young men like Bill would return. Furthermore, the sympathetic characterizations of Sally and Bill in a wartime romance written with candor and without resorting to either extreme of vulgarity or euphemism helped establish *The Voice of the Turtle* as the seventh longest running play in New York, with a total of 1,557 performances.

Van Druten's Sally is an innocent ingénue in comparison with Billie Dawn, Garson Kanin's heroine in *Born Yesterday,* produced in 1946. Kanin presents Billie boldly and without reservation as a trollop, an ex-chorus girl who has become the mistress of a wealthy junk dealer, never letting the audience forget that Billie has been promiscuous. Yet, at the final curtain, Billie is converted into a rather sympathetic heroine who will marry Paul Verrall, the hero. *Born Yesterday* indicates even further the change in public attitude toward unconventionality in the acceptance of Billie as a heroine. Immoral women presented as boldly as Billie in other popular plays have not been sympathetic characterizations. Crystal, the mistress, and Sylvia, the gossip, in *The Women,* are satirized and are not triumphant in the last scene. The four women in *The Doughgirls* are farcical characters, created for laughs rather than sympathy. Billie, however, is never an exaggerated or unconvincing heroine. She not only dominates the play but also wins audience approval in her triumph over Harry Brock, the junk dealer, again illustrating the popular appeal of a play in which the woman wins.

More than one critic has commented on the similarity between *Born Yesterday* and the legend of Pygmalion, for Kanin's play is a modern version of the story of the sculptor who falls in love with the statue he has created. *Born Yesterday* concerns Harry Brock, who brings Billie, his beautiful but stupid mistress, to Washington where he hopes to organize a cartel. Brock, oblivious to his own crudeness, realizes Billie cannot stay with him in Washington unless she acquires decorum and poise, and hires Paul Verrall, a newspaper reporter, to teach her the social graces. Under Verrall's guidance, Billie is transformed into a beautiful and humanized woman. When she realizes the full extent of Brock's ruthless plans, she gives Verrall sufficient evidence to incriminate Brock, who becomes violent. Billie, no longer afraid of him, threatens to expose him if he steps out of line, and then promises to return the documents at the rate of one a year if he makes no further attempts to become involved in crooked deals. Just like Pygmalion, Paul has fallen in love with the new woman he has created, and Billie has fallen in love with Paul, a situation which the audience anticipated even in the first act. At the final curtain, the audience is content to know Brock's industrial plans are ruined and Billie and Paul are to be married.

Born Yesterday combines the humor of farce and the suspense of melodrama. The raucous lines in the first act, Billie's two mink coats, Billie's first encounter with Paul when she is the one who makes the improper advances, and Brock's apologies for vulgarities which Senator Hedges and his wife do not understand, are touches of farce. The exposure of a junk dealer with fascist inclinations, the bribing of a senator to pass a bill which would help organize a cartel, the brutality of Brock when he discovers Billie has stolen documents which will incriminate him, and the suspense in the last act when Brock threatens Billie and Paul with physical violence are melodramatic. In 1946, the tone of the play and the final triumph of Billie seemed exaggerated and amusing. In more recent years, with reports of the Kefauver investigation and the exposure of high-ranking officials accused of taking bribes, the situations are more realistic.

Born Yesterday is profuse in its use of vulgarity to illustrate Billie's stupidity and Brock's coarseness. Kanin, however, has tempered the vulgarity as well as any embarrassment the audience might experience by placing a foil on stage who is shocked or stunned by the dialogue and action. For example, Billie's dialogue shocks Senator and Mrs. Hedges, and their discomfort convinces Brock that Billie needs to learn the art of polite conversation. Both Ed Devery, Brock's lawyer, and Paul are embarrassed each time Brock shouts at Billie. Paul, in fact, who proves to be the most convincing foil, is disgusted, then embarrassed, and finally infuriated with Brock's treatment of Billie. In the second act, when Paul makes an obvious reference to Billie's relationship with Brock, Billie is almost as embarrassed as Paul had been in the first act. This use of contrast, primarily through the presence of someone on stage who reacts squeamishly, makes the dialogue palatable without reservations.

The humor is most raucous in episodes which concern the commonness of Billie or Brock, but not all the humor is embedded in vulgarity. There are good gags to relieve the tension in the melodramatic scenes. When Billie refuses to sign any more documents for Brock until she has read them, he loses his temper. In the midst of the argument, Billie says, "You're just not couth!" to which Brock shouts, "I'm just as couth as you are!" In the last act, Brock is convinced he must marry Billie to protect his industrial empire because she has signed enough documents to own a controlling interest in his enterprises, but when Brock tells Billie they are getting married, Billie says, "No," and then adds the seemingly incongruent but ludicrous afterthought, "In fact, I've never been so insulted."

The quieter type of humor satirizes political corruption, pseudo-literary journalists, and educational systems. Billie explains she has learned never to say *ain't* because her teacher "would slug you if you did it." Billie tells Verrall she has read his column and adds, "Well, I think it's the best thing I ever read. I didn't understand one word." After Paul has given her a simplified explanation, Billie points to the article and says, "Well, why didn't you say so?"

Much of the entertainment comes from Kanin's characterizations, which he has not kept static. Billie changes from a vulgar, self-centered mistress into a softer, more humane heroine. Paul, through his association with Billie, loses some of his pomposity. Brock changes from the confident, domineering bully to an angry, baffled bully unable to accept defeat. Kanin is equally successful with the minor characterizations. Senator Hedges is a mild, ineffectual congressman who accepts bribes even though he cannot possibly persuade other congressmen to change their votes. Devery, Brock's attorney, is a convincing portrait of a man who sacrifices his career and ideals to become associated with men he knows are his inferiors.

Whether *Born Yesterday* would have been such a phenomenal popular success without Judy Holliday and Paul Douglas is questionable. Miss Holliday, incidentally, did not originate the role of Billie Dawn. Jean Arthur, who played the role in the road tryout, took ill and Miss Holliday was brought in as her replacement. If the story is true that the producers hoped to find another movie star to play the role and hired Miss Holliday as a temporary substitute, her sparkling performance must have made them change their minds very quickly, for she was superb. Paul Douglas, better known at that time as a sports announcer, also proved to be ideally cast as Brock. Miss Holliday's hippy undulations and nasal falsetto entranced audiences as did Paul Douglas' malevolent physical prowess and vigorous finger snapping. Although reports from audiences that saw replacements in the roles during the last year or so of the run indicate that Billie and Brock still emerged as realistic characterizations, credit for the initial success and tremendous box office power of the play belongs to Miss Holliday and Mr. Douglas. Their performances, along with the excellent plot and humor, helped *Born Yesterday* become not only one of the ten best plays of 1945–1946 but also one of the most popular postwar comedies, with a total run of 1,642 performances, making it the fifth longest running play on Broadway.

Harry Brock, the boorish egotist, resembles Aubrey Piper in George Kelly's *The Show-Off*, produced in 1923. Both Harry and Aubrey are loud show-offs. Harry is as egotistical about exploiting his crude but effective business tactics as Aubrey is about his ability to create impressions of grandeur. In 1946, the egotist, as personified in Brock, was a malevolent social menace. In 1923, the egotist, as personified in Aubrey Piper, was a harmless, irritating Babbitt.

The Show-Off was originally a one-act sketch called *Poor Aubrey* and played in most of the better vaudeville houses around the country. The cast included only four characters: Aubrey, an egomaniac whose folly was readily apparent to everyone; Mrs. Fisher, his mother-in-law, a garrulous, lonely widow who disapproved of Aubrey; Amy, his wife, who acted primarily as a buffer to prevent her mother and husband from arguing; and Mrs. Cole, a visitor, who brought out the worst in both Aubrey and Mrs. Fisher. In elaborating the short sketch into a full-length play, Kelly did not stretch the plot thin to span three acts or supplement it with obvious padding. He avoided these pitfalls by improving the character development and by adding other members of the Fisher family including Mr. Fisher, and two children, Clara and Joe. As the central figure in the one-act play, Aubrey was almost a caricature rather than a characterization. In the three-act play, however, Aubrey became more realistic. He was still foppish, wore a carnation and a toupee, still laughed raucously and exaggerated his social position, but he was more assured, more boastful, and was, apparently, insensitive to the barbs of the other characters.

Although the plot is of minor importance, the play never lags. The first act establishes the characterization of Aubrey as well as Amy's infatuation for him and her blindness to his faults. The expository opening scene builds to an excellent entrance for Aubrey. First, he is discussed by the family; then he is heard off stage but does not make an entrance. He and Amy laugh intermittently in the off-stage parlor while Mrs. Fisher, who listens at the wall, repeats their conversation to Joe and Mrs. Fisher. Finally, when Aubrey does appear, the audience is well prepared for his exaggerated dialogue and gestures.

In the second and third acts, Aubrey is the same audacious braggart, but he gains sympathy, not through his own actions but through the other characters who realize that he is devoted to Amy. For example, Clara reveals that her husband, Frank Hyland, had been in love with someone else before he married her and that her marriage is not a happy one. For that reason, Clara is willing to tolerate Aubrey because she knows that Aubrey, in spite of his faults, loves Amy. Joe, who has sold an invention for a fabulous sum, wants to give Aubrey a share of the money because it was Aubrey's distorted account of the process which helped Joe perfect his idea, and it was Aubrey's bluffing with the business executives which forced them to pay twice the amount Joe would have taken for his chemical discovery. Aubrey's dealings with big business, however, are just as incredible today as the railroad transactions in *The First Year.* Modern audiences would have difficulty believing that Aubrey could outsmart business executives when his lies, his pompousness, and his braggadocio would be evident to anyone who talked to him more than five minutes. At the final curtain, nevertheless, Aubrey settles down to read the financial page, triumphant not only over big business but also over his mother-in-law, for it is Mrs. Fisher who speaks the final and very significant curtain line, "God help *me,* from now on."

The well-written characterizations account largely for the popularity of *The Show-Off.* Critics have compared Aubrey with characters created by Molière and Dickens, but Aubrey is an individualized satirical creation. If the other people in the play laughed at him, he would be thoroughly ridiculous, but Amy's unfaltering admiration encourages him in his expansive exaggerations. The wrong actor playing the role could easily have alienated audience sympathy, but Louis John Bartels gave a remarkable performance that audiences enjoyed. Like Judy Holliday in *Born Yesterday,* Bartels was not the producer's first choice for the dominant role. He had been signed for a minor part in the show, but when plans to get a well-known comic under contract to another producer fell through, Bartels got the chance and pleased both audiences and critics. Curiously enough, the characterization was altered in motion pictures. The first version in the silent films made Aubrey a ludicrous character, but the first remake in talking pictures starring Spencer Tracy softened the role, eliminated the fopperies and the toupee, although Aubrey still retained his brashness and bragging. The second remake in talking pictures starring Red Skelton played down Skelton's ability to clown, made Aubrey less boisterous, and permitted Skelton to play a more sympathetic role than any of his predecessors.

Other characters also appealed to audiences. Mrs. Fisher represented not only a distressed mother but also a curiously sympathetic characterization of an unsympathetic woman. Clara was a convincing portrait of an unhappy wife whose dialogue had underlying tones of bitterness. When Mrs. Fisher said that if Amy "makes her bed, let her lie in it," Clara replied, "Well, that's the trouble, Mom; it isn't always the same person that makes the bed that lies *in* it— very often somebody else has to lie in it."

The dialogue for the most part was realistic with no obviously inserted gags or deliberately clever lines, even in Aubrey's profusive triteness. The humor was in the situations depicting the helplessness of the Fishers to cope with an undesirable Aubrey as well as the inevitable frustration of coping with a triumphant Aubrey. Kelly, who subtitled the play, "A Transcript of Life," offset the irritable qualities of his hero by making both the audience and the characters in the play realize that Aubrey, in spite of his faults, was disposed to benevolence.

Critics recognized the merits of *The Show-Off,* even stirring up a controversy concerning the Pulitzer Prize which several members of the committee felt *The Show-Off* deserved in preference to the prize winner, *Hell Bent for Heaven.* Undoubtedly the committee's dissatisfaction brought *The Show-Off* new publicity which intrigued theatergoers into seeing the play. The performance record indicates that audiences also preferred *The Show-Off,* for the realistic presentation of middle-class family life and Louis John Bartels' effective performance had enough popular appeal to give the play a run of 570 performances.

The Show-Off might easily be a subtitle for the George S. Kaufman, Moss Hart comedy, *The Man Who Came to Dinner,* produced in 1939, which also deals with an egotistical hero. Both plays emphasize character more than plot but differ in character types and in humor. *The Show-Off* deals with lower middle-class people who are neither witty nor clever; *The Man Who Came to Dinner,* with members of café society who make no effort to restrain their barbed witticisms, as well as members of the theatrical world, who are forced upon a wealthy middle-class family.

The plot deals with Sheridan Whiteside, who has come to Mesalia, Ohio, on a lecture tour. He accepts an invitation to dinner at the Stanley's but slips on the front stairs, breaks his leg, and is forced to remain in the Stanley home. When the play opens and Whiteside makes his first appearance in a wheelchair, he proceeds to upset the entire household. He bullies the host; encourages the son, Richard Stanley, to leave home; encourages the daughter, June

Stanley, to marry a labor organizer; entertains an assortment of guests from convicts to theatrical celebrities; insults the local towns-people without provocation; and almost breaks up a romance between Maggie, his secretary, and Bert Jefferson, the local news-paperman. Whiteside faces defeat at the hands of Mr. Stanley, grows remorseful, helps Maggie reconcile with Bert, but just as he is leaving the house, he slips again, and the play ends in utter con-fusion for the Stanleys.

The entertainment in *The Man Who Came to Dinner* is largely the humor and characterization. Critics enjoyed the play enough to nominate it for the Critics' Circle Award, and called it "brilliant," and "American comedy at its best." Kaufman and Hart, it is said, were inspired to write the comedy after Alexander Woollcott had spent a weekend with them. Hart is reputed to have said, "Wouldn't it be terrible if he broke a leg and had to stay," and almost instantly the collaborators knew they had a basic plot. Many dramatists have tried to emulate this type of farce-comedy dealing with well-known figures, but few have equaled the characterization of Sheridan Whiteside because the popular appeal of the role is not the delib-erate satire on a famous celebrity. Whiteside is amusing to audiences who are not acquainted with Woollcott's venomous wit, his florid radio broadcasts, his interests in criminology, and his wide circle of friends, all of which are written into the play. Sheridan Whiteside is an ill-tempered, ill-mannered egotist who might easily have annoyed audiences if he were permitted to triumph as Aubrey Piper did in *The Show-Off*. Instead, in the last act Whiteside must attempt to rectify his error in thwarting Maggie's love affair. That he is willing to admit his faults makes him more sympathetic and more entertaining.

In addition to Whiteside, other characters are recognizable as thinly disguised portraits of celebrities. Beverly Carlton, the English playwright, is a take-off on Noel Coward and is a younger facsimile of Whiteside; Banjo, the Hollywood actor, romps through the play just as audiences imagine Harpo Marx would romp off screen; and Lorraine Sheldon is an almost libelous satire on several actresses, none of whom the critics have dared to identify too specifically. Lorraine's promiscuity may be exaggerated in the accounts White-side and Carlton give of her many romantic affairs, but her actions on stage are realistic enough to depict a temperamental, egotistical, and lustful actress. The humor and appeal to audiences does not exist only in proportion to the spectators' familiarity with Woollcott's eccentricties, Coward's cleverness, or Harpo Marx's wild antics, for the dramatists have made the characters entertaining in themselves. Kaufman and Hart have also included enough townspeople to heighten the humor by providing a specific contrast to the celebrities. These characters include the Stanleys, whose home Whiteside completely disrupts; Miss Preen, the nurse, a perfect foil for Whiteside's most vicious barbs; Dr. Bradley, the small-town physician with literary ambitions; and Mrs. McCutcheon and Mrs. Dexter, Mesalia clubwomen too awed by the presence of Sheridan Whiteside to realize how completely he is ridiculing them.

Maggie Cutler, Whiteside's secretary, combines the contrast in characterization, for she has the sharp cleverness of Whiteside and his friends as well as the honesty of the townspeople. Of all the characters, Maggie alone has the integrity to tell Whiteside how completely selfish he is. In the first act when Maggie informs Whiteside that she has fallen in love with the local newspaperman and Whiteside threatens to break up the romance, Maggie reminds him that she knows what a devil he can be, that he needn't try to tell her he's thinking of her happiness when all he really is worried about is breaking in a new secretary, and she concludes, "Don't you dare to try any of your tricks. I'm on to every one of them." In the third act, it is Maggie again who makes the effective speech which piques Whiteside into realizing that Maggie's romance is not so superficial as he had imagined. Maggie says, "You are a selfish, petty egomaniac who would see his mother burned . . . at the stake . . . if that was the only way he could light his cigarette."

Sometimes the humor in the play arises from the fast-paced action, such as the episode in which Banjo carries the struggling Miss Preen on stage and then proceeds to make love to the bewildered nurse as though she were a motion picture glamour girl. At other times, the humor is a succession of clever barbs and cynical gags reflecting Whiteside's keen wit, such as his epithet to Miss Preen, whom he calls "Miss Bed Pan." The humor becomes slapstick in such episodes as the contrived manner in which Whiteside and Banjo lock Lorraine in a mummy case to get rid of her. Whiteside's triumph over the Stanleys is another exaggerated but funny situation. The Stanleys have threatened to evict Whiteside but are cowed into submission

The Man Who Came to Dinner, Monty Woolley

when Whiteside suddenly remembers that Harriet, the eccentric sister who lives with the Stanleys, is another Lizzie Borden, that her real name is Harriet Sedley, and that she murdered her parents with an ax.

Monty Woolley, ideally cast as Sheridan Whiteside, immeasurably aided the popular run of 739 performances. He looked the part, had the right touch of acidity in his voice, and made the audience love him in spite of his nastiness. Clifton Webb played Whiteside in the road company, and even Alexander Woollcott must have been pleased with the Kaufman-Hart lampoon, for he played the burlesque of himself in an out-of-town production. But the success of the characterization on Broadway belongs to Monty Woolley, whose brilliant performance entertained audiences in both the stage play and the motion picture.

The satiric, humorous appeal of *The Man Who Came to Dinner* is far different from the emotional appeal of *I Remember Mama* or the family appeal of *Life with Father*. Both *I Remember Mama* and *Life with Father* are adaptations from series of short sketches, reveal superior craftsmanship in correlating disconnected episodes into a unified play, combine sentiment and humor, and present sympathetic strong characterizations.

John Van Druten's *I Remember Mama*, produced in 1944, veered sharply from the conventional form of popular drama and presented a series of disconnected episodes linked through the medium of a narrator. Van Druten based the play on Kathryn Forbes's *Mama's Bank Account* and used six of her sketches and minor incidents from three others to create a group of kaleidoscopic portraits which formed a unified play through the dominance of Mama and the sentimental picture of family life. Just as he had done in *The Voice of the Turtle*, Van Druten again manipulated a stage setting to permit freedom of movement. By dividing the stage into three sections, each with a revolving platform, he constructed the play to simulate the effect of a continuous motion picture and blended the action from one scene to the next without curtain waits. When isolated episodes did not develop logically, Katrin, the oldest daughter, acted as narrator to correlate the action.

The story deals with a Norwegian family living in San Francisco. The principal characters are Mama, Papa, their son Nels, and their daughters Katrin, Christine, and Dagmar; Mama's sisters, Jenny,

Sigrid, and Trina; and Mama's brother, Chris. In the first scene, Mama, Papa, and the children gather around the kitchen table on Saturday night. Papa opens his pay envelope and Mama apportions the money for the week. When Nels explains that he will need more money if he is to attend high school, Mama and Papa examine the little bank in which they keep money for emergencies, and decide they do not have enough money for Nels unless they go to the big bank, which they must not do. The family plans its strategy and, after much maneuvering, Mama announces, "Is enough! We do not have to go to the bank!" This scene sets the pace for ensuing episodes in which Mama plans and schemes to pay bills which include an operation for Dagmar and a graduation gift for Katrin. In the final scene, when Katrin, who has always wanted to be a writer, gets a check for five hundred dollars for her first story, Mama asks what she will do with the money. Katrin says she must first get Mama a warm coat and then let Mama put what is left in the bank. Mama hesitates, then confesses she does not have a bank account, in fact has never had one, and has never told them before because she did not want the children to be afraid. But now, Mama says, "With five hundred dollar, I think I can tell."

The basis for Katrin's story, called "Mama and the Hospital," is the climax of Act I. Dagmar is rushed to the hospital for an ear operation, but the doctor has sent Dagmar to the clinic to cut down on expenses. When Mama wants to see Dagmar after the operation, the nurse tells her visiting hours are over and that no one will be able to visit the clinic until the next day. Reluctantly, Mama goes home and decides to scrub the floor. The children remind her that she had just scrubbed it yesterday, but Mama says, "Comes a time when you've got to get down on your knees." In the midst of her scrubbing, she sits up, says, "I think of something!" and the curtains close. Two scenes later, when Mama reappears at the hospital, she gives Katrin her hat and coat, takes a pail and mop out of a closet, and gets down on her knees. The audience, knowing what Mama is planning, almost purrs in satisfaction as Mama scrubs and crawls toward the corridor leading to the clinic. When she returns and announces to Katrin that now she can tell Papa Dagmar is fine, Katrin asks if Mama will try to see Dagmar again before tomorrow afternoon, and Mama says, "No! That would be against the rules."

Van Druten's craftsmanship is evident in his reshaping of the original material, elaborating the emotional appeal, and emphasizing Mama until she dominates almost every scene of the play. For example, Van Druten has added an episode between Mama and Mrs. Moorehead which illustrates Mama's persuasiveness. Katrin has written quite a few stories but has been unable to sell any. When Mama learns that Mrs. Moorehead, a famous author, is in town, and that Mrs. Moorehead's main interest is cooking, Mama goes to the hotel and meets Mrs. Moorehead, who informs her bluntly that she never reads unpublished material. Mama immediately changes the conversation to cooking, particularly Norwegian cooking, captures Mrs. Moorehead's interest when she says she has never given her recipes to anyone, not even her own sisters, and soon maneuvers Mrs. Moorehead into agreeing to read one of Katrin's stories while she writes out a recipe. Mrs. Moorehead advises Katrin to write about things she knows rather than about incidents she imagines might happen. Mama thinks this is good advice and suggests that Katrin write a story about Papa, to which Katrin agrees until she gets the sudden inspiration to write about Mama and the hospital.

Van Druten has also vitalized other characters in the original stories without detracting from Mama. For example, he has taken lame Uncle Chris, who appears in only one of Miss Forbes's sketches, and built him into a major character who bullies his sisters Sigrid, Jenny, and Trina, shouts at the children, and terrorizes everyone except Mama. The aunts are shocked that Uncle Chris is living with a woman who is not his wife. All through the play, the aunts wonder what Uncle Chris does with his money. When they learn he is dying, they go to his home; but Uncle Chris refuses to allow anyone except Mama and Katrin, and the woman whom he introduces as "Yessie," to stay in the room with him. Uncle Chris asks Mama to sell his heavily mortgaged home and give the few hundred dollars to Yessie. After Mama rejoins the aunts outside, she takes out a notebook Chris has given her that reveals he spent most of his money taking care of lame people and paying for operations which would permit children to walk and not go through life limping as he had done. Aunt Sigrid is shamed by the final notation about her own son, Arne, for Uncle Chris had insisted that Arne's fractured kneecap be operated upon and had paid for the operation so that Arne might walk again.

Audiences enjoyed the emotional appeal in these episodes, but their enjoyment was enhanced by Van Druten's ability to give the dialogue dramatic power. He changed lines, simplified the action, and, on occasion, added an almost lyrical cadence. Miss Forbes, for example, wrote, "But the first awareness was of Mama," which Van Druten revised to "But first and foremost I remember Mama." When Mama protests that she must tell Dagmar she did not cure the cat because it would not be good for Dagmar to believe that Mama could fix everything, Papa said, in the original story, "Leave her alone . . . she will learn the sad things soon enough." In the play, however, Papa says, "Is best thing in the world for her to believe."

The humor which appealed to audiences did not depend upon witty lines or clever speeches. The courtship of shy Aunt Trina and Mrs. Thorkelson, an undertaker, if written by a less skillful playwright, might easily have become a slapstick romance, but in the play, it is amusing without being ludicrous because Mama, who approves of the marriage, warns Sigrid and Jenny that if they laugh at Trina or make fun of her, she will reveal incidents about their own marriages which they would prefer not to have Trina know. And when Papa, along with the audience, chuckles and says he did not know these stories, Mama says she isn't telling them out of spite but only to insure Trina's happiness. Sometimes the humor is blended with sentiment, particularly in episodes which involve Uncle Chris, who terrorizes the aunts in one scene and then, in the next, wins the complete sympathy of the audience as he consoles little Arne who is suffering great pain after the operation.

The first scene sets the pace and the final scene ties all the loose fragments together to give the play unity and to end on a warm, wholesome note. Katrin starts the play by reading her first story which begins, "For as long as I could remember, the house on Steiner Street had become home." In the final scene, Mama gathers the family around the kitchen table to hear Katrin's story, and Katrin again begins, "For as long as I could remember, . . ." and the curtains close on the same episode with which the play begins. In addition to the emotional response which the audience has for Katrin's success and Mama's pride, it also has the feeling that as the curtains close, the play is beginning all over again and that the audience is almost reliving the stories it has just seen.

I Remember Mama ran during the theatrically prosperous World War II years, but it achieved popularity through its nostalgic appeal, a relief from the comedies and serious dramas dealing with the war. The acting also contributed to the successful run. Mady Christians, as Mama, dominated the stage. Her performance brought out all of Mama's courage, wisdom, and understanding. Oscar Homolka, as Uncle Chris, glowered, and bullied, and threatened, and made audiences love him. His death scene, when he revealed his admiration for Mama, his gratitude to Yessie, and his own courage to face death, was a highly emotional scene, one of the few episodes in the play which Mama did not dominate. The entire cast, in fact, seemed to be inspired by Mama, and gave excellent performances, but perhaps one other actor should be singled out. Marlon Brando, better known today for playing Stanley Kowalski in *A Streetcar Named Desire,* gave a remarkably sensitive performance as Nels, of whom Papa said, "Nels is the kind one."

The warm, sentimental appeal, the simplicity of the dialogue, and the representation of family life without overemphasis of emotion kept *I Remember Mama* running for 714 performances. Mama, also, became the principal character in a popular television serial starring Peggy Wood, as well as a motion picture starring Irene Dunne. But above all, in *I Remember Mama,* it was the lovable and wise Mama who gave the play its greatest appeal. If Mama were to summarize the audience's reaction, she might undoubtedly say, "Is good play."

Life with Father, by Howard Lindsay and Russel Crouse, based on Clarence Day, Jr.'s, sketches about his father and produced in 1939, surpasses *I Remember Mama* as an adaptation. Lindsay and Crouse have made *Life with Father* a completely integrated play which does not use rapid changes of scenery or a narrator to aid continuity or to introduce a new plot development. Their skill in selecting sketches and weaving them into a comedy which progresses leisurely toward the climax, Father's baptism, as well as their ability to supplement the original material with their own, has made *Life with Father* a popular classic in the theater. Any current discussion of the comedy includes the fact that it established the record for long-running plays in the history of the New York theater with a total of 3,224 performances. The appeal of *Life with Father* was not limited to Broadway, for the comedy played in more than two hundred cities in the United States and Canada alone.

The story is of minor importance, for there is virtually no plot, with the exception of Vinnie's determination to have Father baptized. Furthermore, the dramatic conflict consists primarily of Father's struggle to be the unquestioned master in his home. The popular appeal of the play, however, comes from the structure of the frail plot and the characterizations, for there is no other long-running play which illustrates so completely Lamb's idea of naturalizing the audience. From the very first moment of exposition to the final curtain, what little suspense there is arises not from the plot but from the anticipation of how Father will react to the secret plans Vinnie shares with the audience. The audience knows, long before Father does, that Vinnie has arranged for Cousin Cora and Mary Skinner to stay at the Day home in spite of Father's objections to overnight visitors, that Vinnie has decided he will take their guests to Delmonico's for dinner, and that she has engaged the most expensive cab the day Father is to be baptized. When Vinnie becomes ill, only the audience knows why her condition is critical, for Clarence and John, who put into her tea some of the patent medicine they were selling, do not realize they are responsible for her illness. Furthermore, when Father begins to shout and Vinnie closes the door so that Cora and Mary will not hear him, she draws the audience into the action by making it part of the family quarrel from which she has excluded her guests. This naturalization, this sharing of secrets which gives the audience the advantage over the actors, requires skillful construction, particularly since *Life with Father* has so little plot. On the other hand, the audience, awaiting the outcome with pleasurable anticipation, is delighted when the action develops just as it had expected. The entire play becomes a huge joke which the playwrights have planned and shared with the audience at Father's expense.

The playwrights' skill in using the technique of naturalization is apparent the moment the curtain rises and Vinnie is discovered instructing the new maid. In a shrewdly contrived exposition, Vinnie establishes the characterization of Mr. Day before he appears. For example, the maid has placed the cream and sugar at the center of the table where everyone can reach them, but Vinnie puts them at the head of the table with the comment, "Mr. Day sits here." After that, she tells Annie to be sure the coffee is hot, and Annie says, "Your man has coffee instead of tea of a morning." Vinnie cautions her to refer to him always as Mr. Day. Clarence enters and adds another detail to Father's characterization. He begins to read the morning paper and reports there has been another wreck on the New Haven, and Vinnie says, "I do wish that New Haven would stop having wrecks. If they knew how it upset your father. . . ." John, who is next to enter, tries to take the paper from Clarence, but Vinnie warns the boys not to wrinkle the paper. A few minutes later, Father's voice booms from upstairs demanding to know where to find the necktie he gave Vinnie to be pressed. Vinnie tells him she forgot to give it to Margaret, that he has plenty of neckties, and he is to put on another one and come right down to breakfast. By now the audience is completely prepared for Father when he yells, "Oh, Damn! Damnation!" This minor defeat is characteristic of the entire play which develops into a succession of victorious oppositions to Father's plans.

Yet in spite of these defeats, Father never loses dignity. He is a devoted husband and a good father held somewhat in awe by his family. He is never a ridiculous, blustering martinet whose wife outsmarts him but is, instead, a likable but unhappy victim of a series of feminine schemes. Moreover, several of Father's defeats make him an extremely sympathetic characterization, for Vinnie's distorted reasoning would be distressing even to someone far more self-controlled than Father. When Vinnie buys Clarence a suit which, she insists, will cost Father nothing because she has returned a toy dog she has charged which costs exactly the same price as the suit, her triumph is amusing because it reveals Father's inability to cope with her completely illogical reasoning. All of Vinnie's triumphs, in fact, add stature to the characterization of Father, for they illustrate, indirectly, his devotion to Vinnie.

Lindsay and Crouse have broadened Day's original characterizations sufficiently to make them appealing to audiences unfamiliar with the Days or with the original stories. They have re-created Father and Vinnie into more universal characters who are not limited in scope to one specific family, because they personify more familiar characters faced with typical problems of household budgets, raising a family, and hiring servants. Lindsay and Crouse have also elaborated upon the original humor, have revised and expanded the continuous arguments between Vinnie and Father,

Life with Father, Dorothy Stickney and Howard Lindsay

have accelerated the action, and have emphasized Father's defeats, but they have done so without making the characters farcical. Characters such as Cousin Cora, Mary Skinner, and even the Day children are amusing but relatively unimportant, for Father and Vinnie dominate the play.

Stories which circulated along Broadway during the long run also helped box office attendance. Some columnists took particular delight in mentioning cast changes of the four boys who represented different ages. Instead of bringing in a new cast member to replace one of the older boys who outgrew his role, so one story goes, the producers simply advanced each boy to the next older one so that by the time the play had reached its seventh year, the original baby in the cast was playing the oldest son.

The fact that *Life with Father* did not receive either of the major dramatic prizes surprised not only the public but also a number of the critics, who did not discredit William Saroyan's *The Time of Your Life,* winner of both the Pulitzer Prize and Critics' Circle Award, but who felt that *Life with Father* deserved more recognition. The public recognized the entertainment value of *Life with Father* because it enjoyed the sentimental, amusing story filled with humor that never resorted to vulgarity.

Life with Father epitomizes popular appeal in the theater with its continuous sharing of secrets with the audience, as well as the popular situation of the triumphant woman, for Vinnie triumphs in every episode. The popularity of the play brought it a record-breaking run of 3,224 performances. At this writing, no current production on Broadway even looms as a possible contender for *Life with Father's* distinction as New York's longest-running attraction.

Eight Dramas
the Critics Liked
and One Maverick

POPULARITY on Broadway from 1920 to 1950 was not limited to comedies, farces, or plays which sacrificed serious themes to emphasize humor. Audiences for the most part did prefer amusing plays, but they also supported the more serious dramas. *Angel Street,* a melodrama, and *Mister Roberts,* a serious play with comic overtones, each ran over one thousand performances. *Tobacco Road,* which ran over three thousand performances, started out as a serious play but, it must be admitted, degenerated into a show played for laughs.

Among the melodramas, *Broadway,* the George Abbott–Philip Dunning drama produced in 1926, received enthusiastic reviews from most of the first-night critics. Burns Mantle, before making his selection of plays for *Best Plays of 1926–1927,* sent the leading New York critics a list of dramas and asked them to name the ten plays they would pick if they were editing a similar volume. *Broadway* and *Saturday's Children* received the only unanimous endorsements in a total of twenty-five plays selected by the nine critics who replied to the questionnaire. Even those critics who were not so enthusiastic about the play and who thought it could never be regarded as a drama of any importance still admitted *Broadway* deserved serious consideration as an entertaining melodrama. Most critics also enjoyed Lee Tracy's performance as Roy, the young hoofer.

Broadway provided an exciting evening in the theater. It crowded plot and action with amazing rapidity into a taut melodrama; it presented a realistic portrait of the contemporary prohibition era and a story of gang warfare at a time when the newspapers were filled with stories of gangsters and hoodlums; and it combined a slight amount of diluted profanity and a more liberal amount of undiluted slang, giving the dialogue the impression of realism. The direction and production emphasized the realistic action and setting. According to Percy Hammond, the realism was carried to such an extreme that one of the night-club dancers even painted purple streaks on her bare legs to give the effect of varicose veins. Like *Strictly Dishonorable,* it avoided any preaching against the evils of crime, but it reversed *Strictly Dishonorable's* portrait of the intimate speak-easy of the 1920s by presenting a fast-paced, melodramatic story of bootleggers, hoodlums, racketeers, vindictive policemen, and chorus girls, set in a private party room of a garish night club, *The Paradise,* in New York.

Broadway, a combination of low comedy, music, and fast action, is a melodramatic version of "boy meets girl—boy loses girl—boy gets girl." Roy, the hero, is a young, none-too-bright dancer in love with Billie, an equally none-too-bright, virtuous heroine who dances in the chorus. Steve, the villain, is a night-club owner who has dishonorable intentions toward Billie which she does not suspect. Justice triumphs when Pearl, one of the dancers, and the revengeful mistress of a gangster Steve has murdered, shoots Steve, but a sympathetic detective who knows Pearl is the murderess lets her go free. At the finale, Billie and Roy team up as dance partners as well as husband and wife.

Abbott and Dunning used music effectively throughout the play. On-stage music provided background for dance rehearsals; off-stage music represented the orchestra in the main room of the club. The most effective use of music, however, came at the climax. While the off-stage orchestra played a number with gun-shooting effects, Steve shot Scar Edwards on stage without arousing suspicion by the sound of gunfire. This action automatically alerted the audience that waited knowingly for the detective to discover what it had already seen.

The popular appeal of *Broadway* is not easy to fathom just by reading the script. In the 1920s, *Broadway* had decided animation as it unfolded a combination of backstage romances, gang warfare, police investigations, and chorus rehearsals, all performed at breakneck speed. In the 1960s, however, the obvious attempts at slangy humor, and an antiquated plot comprised of a series of melodramatic situations which grade-B motion pictures and crime-detective television serials, such as "The Untouchables," have imitated and embellished, have become trite. In 1926, the staccato dialogue sounded authentic; today, in comparison with the salty dialogue in current dramas, it is mild and unrealistic. No modern stage gangster, for example, would refer to a policeman as "the son of a gun." Even the slangy humor typified in such speeches as Mazie's "I'm going to bust everything God gave her some night— all but her teeth. I'll take them and give them back to the dentist," although amusing, is outdated.

Broadway set a precedent for other plays dealing with portraits of the feverish gangster era, but it outran all its imitators. The skillful combination of music, accelerated action, gang warfare, and backstage romance woven into a series of melodramatic, popular plot situations appealed sufficiently to audiences to keep *Broadway* running for 603 performances.

Although Patrick Hamilton's *Angel Street,* produced in 1941, lacked the spectacular setting and frenzied action of *Broadway,* it impressed most newspaper critics, who wrote decidedly favorable reviews. *Angel Street* is an old-fashioned thriller with no embellishments of farce, novel setting, or new property devices to delude audiences into believing it is anything but pure melodrama. It pits a homicidal man against a virtuous heroine who is rescued at the opportune moment just as the heroines were rescued by the United States Marines in the old ten-twenty-thirty-cent tent-show thrillers at the turn of the century.

Angel Street, however, is neither hackneyed nor poorly written. It has excellent characterization, dramatic structure, and suspense. It presents no strikingly new plot variations as it unfolds the relatively simple and familiar story of a man, Mr. Manningham, who deliberately tries to drive his wife insane. While Mr. Manningham is out of the house, Inspector Rough visits Mrs. Manningham and explains that her husband is suspected of having killed a Mrs. Barlow in the very same room fiften years earlier and that Manningham's reason for returning to the scene of his crime is to find the famous Barlow rubies. Rough also tells Mrs. Manningham her husband married her to get her money to buy the house on Angel Street so that he could have free access to search for the jewels. When Mrs. Manningham is convinced that her husband is planning to place her in an institution to get her out of the way, she agrees to help the inspector find the necessary evidence to prove her husband's guilt. The inspector picks the lock on Manningham's desk and finds missing letters and an old brooch. Mrs. Manningham says the brooch originally contained some loose beads she has hidden in a vase, and when she produces the beads, they prove to be the missing rubies. In the third act, Manningham discovers his desk drawer has been rifled, sends for Mrs. Manningham, threatens her, and then starts to choke her just as Inspector Rough appears and accuses Manningham of the murder. Manningham tries to escape but is captured by deputies.

The major difference between *Angel Street* and other Victorian melodramas is the plot development. Unlike the typical mystery melodrama, *Angel Street* does not resort to sliding doors, secret panels, and unidentified characters who slink across a dimly lighted stage. The play does not build up false clues, kill off suspects, or capitalize on the blunders of strange policemen. Instead, *Angel Street* arouses suspense in a slight story singularly free from complexities by combining intellectual and emotional reactions rather than by physical action on the stage. The dramatist's use of the technique of naturalizing the audience also makes the mystery more effective. In the first act, the audience knows as much as Mrs. Manningham and Inspector Rough, and knows more than Mr. Manningham suspects. The dramatist places himself at a disadvantage, for, by not withholding information, he must develop the second and third acts with little more than a search for the evidence. This disadvantage of having the detective take both Mrs. Manningham and the audience into his confidence, however, gives the dramatist the advantage of heightening the suspense, for the audience shares Mrs. Manningham's fears and Inspector Rough's realization that Mr. Manningham may return before any definite clues are uncovered. When Inspector Rough hides off stage and the audience realizes he has left his hat on stage where Mr. Manningham is certain to see it, the situation causes an almost uncontrollable urge to shout a warning just as audiences did in the old-fashioned thrillers. At the last minute, Rough dashes in to retrieve his hat, and the audience sighs in relief; for if Mr. Manningham had discovered the hat, the audience would have lost its naturalized position in watching the evidence being uncovered.

The suspense keeps mounting until the third-act climax. After Manningham has been captured and bound securely, Mrs. Manningham asks to be left alone with her husband. The pace appears retarded as Manningham asks his wife to cut his bonds, and Mrs. Manningham mumbles to herself while she gets a razor, then seems to misplace it, then picks it up again. It is the uncertainty which makes the tempo seem too deliberately casual, for the audience is not sure if Mrs. Manningham has asked to be alone with her husband because she really has gone mad or because she wants to help him escape. Then, at the height of the suspense, Mrs. Manningham's rage finally releases her fears and she violently denounces her husband in a theatrically effective, well-written denouement. The emotional response of the audience is strong because it has shared Mrs. Manningham's terror as well as her desire to expose the villain to the same type of treatment he has given her. When Manningham is taken away and Inspector Rough says he has given Mrs. Manningham the most horrible evening of her life, she says, "Oh, no —the most wonderful," a fitting curtain speech, with which the audience agrees.

The basic characterizations in *Angel Street* may seem to be typically melodramatic. Mr. Manningham personifies an evil menace; Mrs. Manningham, the virtuous and persecuted heroine; Rough, the kindly police inspector; Elizabeth, the heroine's faithful servant; and Nancy, the brazen young servant who encourages Manningham to seduce her. The development of the characterizations, however, is not typical of melodrama. Mr. Manningham's evil is projected without resorting to snarls or sneers. His evil is far more vicious because it is a calculating mental torture which he inflicts upon his wife. Mrs. Manningham's terror is not projected by the conventional screams or shouting of an anguished heroine. In the first act, she does plead for patience and sympathy, but in the second and third acts, she conveys her fears in her bewilderment, her confusion, and her suppressed rages. Rough is neither the extremely clever Sherlock Holmes–type detective nor the dull, plodding police-man. He is shrewd, rather than cunning; efficient; and a bit whim-sical. Intelligent dialogue, free from obvious attempts to insert cleverness or humor, which would destroy the mood of mounting suspense, aids the characterizations.

Angel Street proved that a well-written Victorian thriller, if effectively produced, could please audiences and critics in the 1940s. Yet the story circulated about the play just after its opening revealed the skepticism with which Broadway regarded its chance for survival. The play had been a success in London under the title *Gaslight* and then had been tried out on the West Coast with no great success. According to Broadway gossip, when *Angel Street* opened in New York, tickets had been printed to cover only the first performance on Friday night and the subsequent Saturday matinee and evening performances. Instead of being a failure, as the management had feared, the play appealed to reviewers, many of whom felt that *Angel Street* was one of the first plays with genuine entertainment value produced that season. Obviously the producer rushed through a ticket order, for *Angel Street* developed into a hit and ran over three years to establish a record of 1,295 perform-ances.

Rain and *The Children's Hour* are melodramatic but have more serious themes and more fully developed characterizations than *Angel Street*. The successes of both plays reveal audiences' increased willingness to accept frank, realistic dialogue. In a discussion of this change in public attitude, George Jean Nathan included *Rain* and *The Children's Hour* among the twelve plays he called "the period's leading shockers." Nathan selected *Rain* not only for the profanity which was far more realistic than the dialogue in *Broad-way*, but also for the scene in which the missionary, who had tried to reform the prostitute, lost control of his emotions, and entered her bedroom. Nathan chose *The Children's Hour* because it dealt with Lesbianism and included one scene in which a hysterical child shrieked that she had seen proof of the unnatural attraction between the two women in charge of the school for girls. Both of these plays, however, had long runs because they were dramas which appealed to discerning audiences rather than to curious thrill-seekers.

Rain, produced in 1922, is the story of the missionary who tries to force the prostitute to repent but who becomes a victim of his

Angel Street, Vincent Price

own suppressed desires. In true melodrama, there is no shading
in characterization. The hero and heroine are virtuous; the villain,
evil. In *Rain,* neither Sadie Thompson nor the Reverend Alfred
Davidson are all virtuous or all evil but are, instead, two victims of
circumstances whose association leads to disillusionment for Sadie
and suicide for Davidson.

The tremendous emotional response which *Rain* aroused in audiences becomes apparent by contrasting the play with the original
story by W. Somerset Maugham, who, incidentally, was not interested in writing a dramatic adaptation. John Colton received
Maugham's permission to adapt the story and, with the collaboration of Clemence Randolph, made the characters more complex
to emphasize the tragedy as well as the probability of the situation.
The change is most evident in the characterization of Sadie, whom
Maugham depicted as an amiable prostitute, "plump, in a coarse
fashion pretty. . . . Her fat calves in white cotton stockings bulged
over the top of white boots." The adaptors softened Sadie's character, changed her appearance to that of a slim, blond girl who
"walks with the grace of a wild animal in her movements."

At the end of his story, Maugham reverts Sadie to type. Her
face is again painted. She no longer has any desire to repent her
sins or to revise her opinion of men, whom she calls, in her final
speech, "You filthy pigs! You're all the same. All of you. Pigs."
At the end of the play, Sadie is no longer the amiable Sadie of Act
I. She again uses make-up and makes the speech calling men pigs,
but it is not her final speech. When she learns that Davidson has
committed suicide, she says, "So he killed himself, did he? Then I
can forgive him. I thought the joke was on me—all on me. I see
it wasn't."

The adaptors have modified other characterizations and incidents
to supplement the original story. The most important addition is
a romance between Sergeant O'Hara and Sadie that not only makes
her a more sympathetic heroine, one whom O'Hara wants to marry,
but also provides a medium to illustrate Sadie's temporary reformation. In the original story, Maugham indicates that Sadie agrees
to return to San Francisco to serve a prison sentence because she
is frightened and wants to escape Davidson's torture rather than
because she is willing to atone for her sins. In the play, Sadie's re-
pentance is genuine, for when O'Hara arranges for her escape, she

refuses and calls for Davidson to protect her. Colton and Randolph have also made Davidson's downfall more realistic by explaining the purely spiritual marriage of the Davidsons which Maugham implied in his story. In doing so, the dramatists have created sympathy for Mrs. Davidson who, earlier in the play, has confessed to Mrs. McPhail that at one time she had hoped for a different type of marriage. Mrs. Davidson, in fact, has an effective closing speech when she comes on stage after having seen her husband's body, walks over to Sadie, and says, "I understand, Miss Thompson. I'm sorry for him and I'm sorry for you." In general, Colton and Randolph have elaborated passages of pure narrative without altering the basic plot so that *Rain* becomes an effective, convincing drama.

Audiences, however, came primarily to see Jeanne Eagels, the creator of Sadie, who is almost inseparably linked with the role. Productions of *Rain* without Jeanne Eagels have failed to capture the same wide audience appeal. When Tallulah Bankhead appeared in a revival, most of the critics praised Miss Bankhead but also referred to Jeanne Eagels in their reviews. Robert Benchley, a Bankhead fan, raved about Miss Bankhead and then added a footnote merely saying that Jeanne Eagels had previously appeared on Broadway in the role. In spite of Miss Bankhead's excellent performance, the revival was not a popular success. In the 1940s, a musical adaptation of *Rain,* called *Sadie Thompson,* with Ethel Merman as Sadie, went into production but ran into trouble almost from the start. Miss Merman objected to the songs, particularly the lyrics, and refused to continue with the show. June Havoc, who replaced her, gave a splendid performance in a very lush production, but the musical failed. Perhaps Miss Merman's astuteness in knowing how to pick the proper vehicle and songs to fit her individualized talents forewarned her of the fate of the production which, although beautifully staged, lacked integration. The songs and Polynesian dancing impeded the dramatic vigor of the plot, and the melodramatic quality of the drama intruded on the music and dancing.

Attempts to convert *Rain* into a motion picture were equally disastrous. The first version, a silent film starring Gloria Swanson, ran into trouble with the censors, particularly in Pennsylvania, where the film was so badly cut that audiences found it difficult to follow the story. The first talking picture production with Joan

Crawford no longer seemed fresh and daring, and the next version, *Miss Sadie Thompson,* with Rita Hayworth, had music and dancing but again lacked the power of the Broadway play. In its original production, Jeanne Eagels made the part come alive, fascinated audiences with her vivid performance, and virtually accomplished the impossible by making audiences accept a promiscuous heroine as an understandable character whom they did not condemn.

In 1922, *Rain* was considered to be a startling drama because it presented a new idea, the hypocrisy of overzealous religious fanatics. By treating the harlot and the missionary realistically rather than idealistically, Maugham, Colton, and Randolph still used the melodramatic conflict of virtue and vice, but, in a sense, reversed the situation, for they made Reverend Davidson by his relentless persecution of Sadie become the villain rather than the hero. This treatment, if handled with improper emphasis, could have made *Rain* become a tasteless theatrical side show. The dramatists' skill in making the story convincing and the characters sympathetic, plus the magnificent performance of Jeanne Eagels as Sadie, intrigued discerning critics and audiences who kept *Rain* running for 648 performances.

Lillian Hellman's *The Children's Hour,* produced in 1934, is more shocking than *Rain* because it deals with sex abnormality, but it presents an unsavory topic with honesty and restraint. The theme of abnormality functions as the medium to develop a second and equally important theme, the evils of vicious gossip and lies that ruin the lives of innocent victims. Miss Hellman has skillfully counterbalanced the themes, making each supplement the other so that the theme of perversion is not the predominant topic of the play.

The Children's Hour, a thorough study in evil, is based on a test case in libel fought in the Scottish courts. Mary Tilford, a malicious fourteen-year-old girl who bullies her schoolmates and lies to her teachers, resents being punished by Karen Wright and Martha Dobie, the women who run the private school she attends. To escape punishment, Mary runs home to her grandmother and tells her she is being persecuted. At first the grandmother is skeptical, but when Mary distorts something she has overheard, embellishes it with an idea she has gleaned from reading *Mademoiselle de Maupin,* and says that Miss Dobie and Miss Wright have an unnatural attraction for each other, the shocked grandmother telephones mothers whose daughters are attending the school to inform them that the school is not a proper educational institution. In retaliation, Miss Dobie and Miss Wright file a libel suit, but they lose the case. Mary's deliberate lies wreck the school, break up Karen's impending marriage, and drive Martha Dobie to commit suicide before Mrs. Tilford learns the truth.

The Children's Hour is basically a melodrama presenting the conflict of vice and virtue. Karen Wright and Martha Dobie are not women of simple virtue, for Martha confesses that Mary's accusation has made her realize she may be a potential homosexual. Miss Wright and Miss Dobie, nevertheless, are persecuted as relentlessly as any of the virtuous heroines in conventional melodramas. Mary Tilford is the symbol of vice, for she is completely evil, not only in her malice toward her teachers but also in her persecution of Rosalie, one of her schoolmates, whom she terrorizes because Rosalie has stolen a bracelet. To prevent Mary's exposing her as a thief, Rosalie, although unwilling to do so, finally blurts out the shocking lies Mary forces her to tell. Miss Hellman emphasizes the effect of the malicious slander to make audiences sympathize with the helpless teachers who are ruined by a vicious child.

Critics have not agreed on the merits of the play. The Pulitzer Prize Committee, for example, rejected *The Children's Hour* as a contender for the prize because of its unsavory story. Other critics have said the play has structural flaws but are not unanimous as to what constitutes these flaws. Yet their objections point out the elements which helped make the play a popular success. One of the criticisms of the second-act climax is that no one asks Mary to tell exactly what she has seen and heard, for if she were asked the direct question, she could not have given a satisfactory answer based solely on details in *Mademoiselle de Maupin,* and her accusations would be exposed as lies. Audiences, however, readily understand that the grandmother's embarrassment and the teachers' anger would deter them from asking a fourteen-year-old girl so distasteful a question.

Some critics believe that the play really ends midway in the third act and that all ensuing action becomes a series of anticlimaxes, each less effective than its immediate predecessor. First, Karen refuses to marry her fiancé, a physician; next, Martha commits suicide;

then Mrs. Tilford returns to make restitution; and finally Karen and Mrs. Tilford intelligently but undramatically discuss the problems they must face in the future. Yet the play's popular appeal is dependent upon these situations. Karen, suspecting that her fiancé might not believe she is innocent, forces him to admit that a doubt did exist in his mind about her relationship with Martha. Once this doubt has been voiced, audiences believe in Karen's unwillingness to rush into marriage. Miss Hellman does not explain whether Martha confesses her unnatural affection for Karen because she realizes it is true or because the horrors of her experiences in the court trial make her believe it is true, but she does convince audiences that Martha is sufficiently depressed to be driven to suicide. The drama might have ended before the final scene, in which Mrs. Tilford tells Karen she will make a public apology and then almost pleads for Karen to accept her financial aid. This weak and ineffectual offer of restitution cannot undo the harm already done, but audiences, nevertheless, are content to know that Mrs. Tilford has made such an offer once she has learned the truth. In a sense, it introduces a variation of a popular dramatic situation by giving Karen a minor triumph over Mary and Mrs. Tilford.

Even if the third act lacks the vigor of the first two, the entire play holds audience interest because Miss Hellman has handled the subject of abnormality frankly in a forceful drama which illustrates the tragedy wrought by malicious gossip and lies. Audiences appreciated this intellectual honesty and kept *The Children's Hour* running for 691 performances, an impressive figure during the dark days of the New York theater when only four plays spanned the summer season of 1935 on Broadway.

The first motion picture adaptation of *The Children's Hour*, with Merle Oberon, Miriam Hopkins, and Joel McCrea, in keeping with the Hollywood moral code of the late 1930s, changed the plot by removing any implications of Lesbianism. In spite of the revisions, the picture still presented a convincing story dealing with a malicious child whose lies almost ruin three lives. The picture ended happily with Martha remaining alive and with Karen marrying the physician. The second film version with Audrey Hepburn and Shirley MacLaine used the original plot.

In 1952, *The Children's Hour* was revived successfully on Broadway with Kim Hunter and Patricia Neal and played for a season, although it did not duplicate its former long run. The critics were not all so ecstatic as they had been for the original production, but most critics agreed that Miss Hellman's restraint in dealing with an unsavory topic had kept the play from being a shoddy, sensational drama.

Miss Hellman's restraint in writing *The Children's Hour* becomes more evident when her play is contrasted with Jack Kirkland's *Tobacco Road,* produced in 1933. Both plays have either shocked or offended theater audiences; both have been banned in several cities throughout the country. *The Children's Hour* emphasizes the topic of abnormality in dialogue which is, in itself, not offensive. The moralists, therefore, object to the theme but not to its development and agree that Miss Hellman has written a vigorous drama about an unsavory subject. *Tobacco Road,* on the other hand, develops the characterization and the story of social degeneracy in the South by means of dialogue profusely scattered with vulgarity and profanity. The moralists, therefore, object to the characterization, to the development, and to the tone of the dialogue rather than to the theme.

Newspaper critics also objected to the sordid development, faulty play construction, and general unpleasantness. Robert Garland said, "Life is just a bowl of hookworms marching through Georgia." Brooks Atkinson thought the play "clumsy and rudderless." John Mason Brown called it "feeble and unpleasant." Only Percy Hammond seemed to find something worth while when he said, "It is a vividly authentic, minor and squalid tragedy, lighted in the right spots with glowing and honest humor." Burns Mantle's reactions were almost contradictory. In his newspaper review, Mantle said *Tobacco Road* "isn't the sort of entertainment folks buy in the theater." After the play opened and seemed doomed to fail, Mantle wrote a second review in the New York *Daily News* praising the theme and Henry Hull's performance as Jeeter. Mantle's comments helped start an improvement in box office receipts. Mantle, however, did not pick *Tobacco Road* as one of the ten best plays for his 1933–1934 volume and, in *Best Plays of 1940–1941,* he expressed "no particular sense of grief" over the closing of *Tobacco Road.*

With such an array of dissenting criticisms, *Tobacco Road* would appear to be a maverick among plays critics have liked. Historians of the drama, however, impressed with the lengthy run, have considered the play more favorably as a naturalistic drama with social significance but have said little about the entertainment quality of the play. John Gassner included *Tobacco Road* in one of his anthologies because he thought it "a naturalistic comedy which could make its gravest implications acceptable as theater." Gassner's statement explains, in part, the popularity of *Tobacco Road,* for the play, to have run as long as it did, had to be acceptable as theater. If it had been merely a vulgar, sensational exhibition dealing only with episodes of utter degeneracy, it would have attracted curiosity seekers for a while but would have been linked with the type of entertainment which drew the same audiences that staggered into burlesque houses in the 1930s or the thrill seekers who attend lurid films in the 1960s. Neither of these groups could keep a play running for seven years or more on Broadway. *Tobacco Road,* of course, did draw its share of curiosity seekers, but it also drew regular theater patrons, although it repelled and disgusted many of them. It even drew support from sociologists and economists. According to Burns Mantle, societies working for the alleviation of the conditions of the underprivileged used scenes from the play to point up existing evils.

Erskine Caldwell's novel and Jack Kirkland's adaptation have the same theme, the inability of the Lesters to make adjustments to economic changes. The miserable living conditions in the back country of Georgia, the amorality of the characters, and the blasphemy and profanity are alike in the novel and the play. The plots, too, are basically the same, for in both versions the Lesters live on a barren farm with barely enough food for existence. Jeeter sends his daughter Pearl to live with Lov, encourages his harelipped daughter Ellie to seduce Lov so that he can steal a bag of turnips from Lov, and encourages his dim-witted son Dude to marry Sister Bessie. Though the novel and the play are both unpleasant in their naturalistic depiction of degeneracy, the play appears to be less offensive. In at least one public library, for example, the novel is kept in the restricted book shelves with circulation limited only to those adults who meet the approval of the librarian; in the same library, the drama is on the open stacks where anyone, even an adolescent, is at liberty to read it. When asked for an explanation, the librarian said, "There's not much danger of the play falling into the wrong hands. We usually find that people who read dramas are more mature."

Kirkland did make quite a few plot changes in his adaptation. In the novel, Dude kills his grandmother; Jeeter and Ada are burned to death; Sister Bessie is as repulsive as Ellie and has Rabelaisian adventures in a disreputable hotel; and Ada is unattractive but not unfaithful. In the drama, however, Ada confesses that Pearl is not Jeeter's daughter; Dude kills Ada; Sister Bessie's adventures in the hotel are eliminated; and Jeeter is alive but alone on the land at the final curtain. In the novel, the changing economic situations are discussed in several short passages; in the play, Jeeter, Captain Tim Harmon, the landowner, and a Mr. Payne who have come to evict Jeeter, discuss the situation in a scene which points out Jeeter's inability to make any readjustments.

Neither the theme nor the naturalistic development makes *Tobacco Road* a pleasant or stimulating drama. The overemphasis upon earthy humor, voiced in naturalistic dialogue, and the inclusion of such earthy scenes as Ellie's animal efforts to seduce Lov, detract from the tragic implications of the story. The fact that the play held the record of 3,182 performances until *Life with Father* surpassed it, can be credited to several causes. The comments of drama critics, sociologists, and reformers called the play to the attention of a variety of theatergoers. First-night critics did single out the excellence of Henry Hull's performance as Jeeter in the original cast. When James Barton replaced him, the critics again wrote reviews praising Barton's interpretation. The most important reason for the long run, however, may well have been the low admission policy, for *Tobacco Road* started during the depression era and offered theater patrons a chance to see a drama at little more than motion picture prices. After the second year, as the run continued, the cast began playing more for laughs than for interpretation of theme. With the number of stage productions in New York at a new low, particularly during the summers, the play held on at a steady pace, for the producers realized that the road companies, which were earning far more than the New York company, could advertise the long run in New York as a box office magnet. At the same time, the more extensive the road tours became, the more they proved to be added advertisements for tourists to see the New York production.

Tobacco Road did establish a record for longevity, but it does not illustrate the basic reasons for popularity. It lacks the inclusion of popular dramatic situations or even a normal love story. What it illustrates is the triumph of astute management in building up a show which might well have been a failure, by using a variety of methods to induce patrons into a theater during a period of economic depression.

There is one story in particular which explains the type of patron who was lured into seeing the play, for, in spite of innuendoes, comments from reformers, and even direct accusations from censors, the play held some degree of morbid interest for those who knew little about it except that it had a long run and drew capacity houses on the road. In a mideastern high school, far removed from most professional theatrical activity, the dramatic coach could not get her principal to buy new scenery, curtains, or even lighting equipment.

"When your plays begin to make some money," the principal said, "we'll buy what you need. Right now, we're lucky if we break even."

"I guess the only way I'll ever do that," the teacher said, "is to put on *Tobacco Road* and run it for a week."

"That's a good idea," the principal said. "There are a lot of people who'd like to see it. I'd like to see it myself."

The teacher gasped. "Do you know what it's all about?"

"No, but I'd like to. I'm thinking of seeing it the next time it comes anywhere near here."

"You just do that," the teacher said. "Then tell me how you'd feel if I asked your daughter to play Ellie."

In many respects, Sidney Kingsley's *Dead End,* produced in 1935, is even more shocking than *Tobacco Road.* *Dead End* is also a naturalistic drama which depicts the plight of the poverty-stricken. In *Tobacco Road,* the characters are amoral; in *Dead End,* however, such characters as Baby Face Martin, the gangster; Kay, the mistress; and Francey, the diseased prostitute, are immoral. In *Tobacco Road,* the dailogue is blasphemous and obscene; in *Dead End,* the dialogue spoken by the Dead End Kids is often close to the type of obscenity written on back-yard fences. The extremely obscene expressions are often distorted or spoken in a language other than English, but the general tone is undisguised. When *Dead*

End opened in New York, the censors demanded that Kingsley make deletions in the dialogue, but enough remains to indicate the original impact. Kingsley's authentic New York East Side jargon often appears unintelligible in print. It must be read aloud to clarify the rhythm of the phonetically spelled words in such expressions as "Deah was a guy at rifawm school used tuh smoke marywanna." *Dead End,* however, is far superior to *Tobacco Road* in stimulating audience sympathy and in pure dramatic craftsmanship. The theme, the evils of the New York slum districts which breed crime, has no greater significance than the theme of *Tobacco Road,* but *Dead End* is a more vigorous drama.

Kingsley has used as his text Thomas Paine's statement, "The contrast of affluence and wretchedness is like dead and living bodies chained together," and Kingsley has constructed his play as a definite study in contrasts, in both characterization and setting. He places an exclusive East River apartment in juxtaposition to squalid tenements and uses the magnificence of the back terrace and gate of the apartment house to emphasize the filth and sordidness of the street directly below it. The dialogue of Philip Griswold, the son of a wealthy tenant, is literate and cultured; the dialogue of the Dead End kids is earthy, often offensive, and, at times, shocking, Philip enjoys luxury provided by his father to satisfy his wants; the Dead End kids steal to get what they want. Kay, the mistress, represents the immoral woman surrounded by wealth and refinement; Francey, the obvious prostitute, represents the immoral woman surrounded by poverty, vice, and disease. Kay and Drina, the sister of one of the Dead End boys, provide further contrast. Kay refuses to marry Gimpty, whom she admits she loves, because she is unwilling to give up her life of luxury; Drina thinks about marrying a man she does not love so that she may provide a decent home for her brother. Kay goes on a three-months' cruise with her lover; Drina goes on strike for higher wages and is clubbed by policemen who break up the picket line.

These contrasts emphasize Kingsley's theme that poverty and the slums are responsible for crime. Gimpty and Drina, for example, who do not resort to crime, are failures. Baby Face Martin represents the treacherous criminal developed in Dead End gangs. Kingsley emphasizes his theory even more pointedly through Baby Face and Tommy. At the end of the second act, the police surround and shoot Baby Face Martin. At the end of the third act, Tommy is arrested for knifing and is to be sent to reform school where, Kingsley indicates, he may start a career that will parallel Martin's and possibly end the same way, in violent death.

Kingsley gives the play dramatic force through contrast but he makes the tenement dwellers, the Dead End kids, and the gangsters more convincing. Many of these characters are merely types, but all have some individuality and are victims of economic conditions. Since the residents of the exclusive apartment house are used principally to provide contrast, they appear only briefly and are not developed so completely. The play, therefore, presents the need for better housing, better living conditions, and social reform, but the theme and characterizations are slanted in favor of the underprivileged.

Some audiences were not pleased with an unconvincing love story between Gimpty and Kay. Most audiences, in fact, would undoubtedly have preferred that a romance develop between Gimpty and Drina. Perhaps the ending of the play is softened by Gimpty's offer to help Drina's brother Tommy. Gimpty, who has received a reward for notifying the police about Baby Face's return, tells Drina he will hire the best attorney to handle her brother's case. This situation may seem contrived, but the preceding action almost negates any possibility of setting Tommy free. The ending accentuates the tragedy of the situation, for only the supremely optimistic theatergoer would hope that Gimpty's attempt to oppose the influential Dr. Griswold could be successful.

The play's popular appeal comes not only from Kingsley's vivid development of characters but also from several vivid sequences which make a strong impact on audiences. Two of these in particular involve Baby Face Martin, who has returned to see his mother and Francey. Martin sends for his mother to meet him on the waterfront, hoping she, at least, will be glad to see him, but does not tell her whom she is meeting. When she arrives wearing a filthy housedress and looking more abject than the other tenement dwellers, Martin goes toward her. Mrs. Martin stares at him for a moment and says, "Yuh no good tramp." Although stunned, Baby Face asks, "Aren't you glad tuh see me?" She smacks his face, says, "That's how glad I am," then denounces him, refuses to take his money, calls him "Murderer," and walks away, weeping. The scene not only stirs the audience but also creates tremendous sympathy for the mother who renounces her son.

Martin's second disillusionment comes when he sends for Francey, the first girl he seduced, with whom he now hopes to relive some of the passionate moments of his youth. Francey, however, has become a prostitute and has contracted a venereal disease. As the scene progresses, the audience keeps remembering that it was Baby Face Martin who first seduced Francey and feels increasing compassion for her degradation.

Norman Bel Geddes' impressive stage setting, which realistically presented the wharf and the dead-end street at the East River, also increased the popular appeal. Bel Geddes converted the edge of the stage into a pier, and the kids dived off the stage into the orchestra pit and emerged later dripping wet as though they were actually coming out of the river. Effective lighting along the edge of the stage and footlights simulated the flow of the river and the river lights. To obtain even further realism, the management used foghorns in the lobby to announce the end of each intermission. Some critics unfavorably compared this overemphasis on realism with the old Belasco type of staging, but audiences, for the most part, were intrigued by the vividness of the stage set, which pitted a row of squalid tenement houses on one side against the luxurious back-yard terrace of an exclusive apartment house on the other.

The authentic acting also drew audiences, for Kingsley reputedly cast some of his Dead End Gang from youngsters who lived on the river front. The motion picture version helped establish the reputation for several of these boys who were brought to Hollywood to appear in the film version and who stayed to make a whole cycle of pictures dealing with the Dead End Kids. These pictures, however, degenerated from Kingsley's original social melodrama into a series of slapstick absurdities using only the same type of characters.

Probably the most interesting story to come out of Hollywood in connection with the film may have been only a press agent's release, but it does reflect the vigor of the characterizations. Samuel Goldwyn, who produced the picture, is reported to have sent a copy of the script to Claire Trevor hoping she would accept a major role along with Humphrey Bogart, Sylvia Sidney, and Joel McCrea. To Goldwyn's delight, Miss Trevor much preferred the comparatively minor role of Francey and aptly justified her choice by her excellent performance.

The Broadway production of *Dead End* impressed critics and audiences with its setting, action, and theme. It received the Theater Club Award, was one of five plays nominated for the Critics' Circle Award in 1936, and ran for 686 performances. *Dead End* also has the distinction of being one of the few propaganda plays to achieve popularity. In exposing the crime fostered by the evils of environment, particularly in the effective contrast of Baby Face and Tommy, *Dead End* projected its theme in a melodramatic play so cleverly that a great many theatergoers were too engrossed in the story and setting to realize that Kingsley was presenting a form of social preachment.

Tomorrow the World by James Gow and Arnaud D'Usseau, produced in 1943, is more definitely a propaganda play, for it denounces the evils of the Nazi regime and emphasizes the postwar problems of denazification of indoctrinated children. Like *The Children's Hour,* it also deals with a malevolent child, Emil Bruckner, the twelve-year-old son of an executed German liberal, who comes to America to live with his uncle, Michael Frame, a professor in a Middle Western college. Emil, a thorough disciple of Hitlerism, scoffs at the inferiority of Americans, disrupts his uncle's home, insults his uncle's fiancée to prevent the marriage, and murderously assaults his ten-year-old cousin before he is finally convinced that life in America is far better than life in a Hitler-dominated Germany. The major difference between Emil and Mary Tilford in *The Children's Hour* is that Mary is inherently evil, whereas Emil is malevolent only because he has been indoctrinated with evil.

As a propaganda play designed to give Americans an insight into the problems of dealing with Nazi duplicity, the play dramatizes Hitler's doctrines. Emil's uncovering the weaknesses and petty prejudices of the Frames and pitting one member of the household against the other illustrate the divide-and-conquer theory. Emil has little difficulty winning the confidence of Jessie Frame, Michael's spinster sister, when he sympathizes with her precarious position in the house, for he knows Jessie objects to Michael's marriage because she will no longer supervise the running of his home. Emil's plotting against Leona Richards, Michael's fiancée, because she is a Jewess, incorporates Nazi anti-Semitism. Emil's denunciation of his father and his resorting to physical violence against Patricia, Michael's daughter and only child in the neighborhood who tolerates his arrogance, illustrates the Nazi stultification of sentiment and the disregard for family attachments.

Tomorrow the World contrasts characters, perhaps to a lesser degree than *Dead End*. Patricia and Emil represent the difference between a likable American child and a domineering Nazi. Patricia is frank, honest, and generous; Emil is superficially subtle, dishonest, and selfish. Emil plots against his uncle to discover secret documents he can send to Germany and thus become a hero; Patricia plots to make Emil's birthday party a success. To do so, she is forced to buy all the presents and to bribe Emil's schoolmates to come to the party. In the second act, when Patricia discovers Emil prying open her father's desk, he becomes an enraged animal, follows her off stage, and strikes her with a bronze book end. In the third act, when Patricia sees Emil for the first time since her injury, she calmly expresses her disapproval with, "Emil Bruckner, you stink! Really, you're the sneakingest coward I ever saw."

Leona's reactions toward Emil contrast physical violence and verbal denunciation. In the second act, Emil lies to Leona, stubbornly maintaining he has not written obscene words about her on the sidewalk. When Leona takes a piece of chalk out of his coat pocket and again accuses him, he shouts that it is she, the Jewish prostitute, who is telling lies. Leona slaps his face, glares, but says nothing. Emil glares back and then walks away. In the third act, after Leona has prevented the infuriated Michael from choking Emil for assaulting his daughter, she shames Emil by forcing him to open his birthday gifts, by explaining how Patricia has maneuvered the party, and by revealing that she helped Patricia pay for the party because Patricia has spent all her money to buy Emil a wrist watch. This time, Leona deliberately goads Emil until she cracks his resistance and makes him cry.

The play also contrasts different types of Germans living in this country during wartime. Fred Miller, a janitor at the college, belongs to the Bund and plans to become a political leader when the Nazis overrun America. Freda, the German servant in the Frame home, is a naturalized citizen whose loyalty to the United States is unquestionable.

The plot of *Tomorrow the World* is effective drama, but the combination of propaganda exposing Nazi practices with the problem of re-educating the indoctrinated Nazi youth forces the dramatists to crowd the three acts and emphasize the problems rather than develop them step by step. Instead of disclosing Emil's complete nazification gradually, the dramatists move quickly. In the very first act Emil changes his costume from a black suit to the Nazi *Jungvolk* uniform, demands that Freda speak German, attempts to make her give the Nazi salute, and furiously slashes the oil portrait of his father whom the Nazis have taught him to hate. Emil's reformation is accomplished with equal rapidity, for it comes almost suddenly in a brief third-act sequence. Michael, who is ready to turn Emil over to the police, decides to question him once more and forces Emil to repeat the lies he has been taught about his father until the boy breaks down and asks, "Why did they hit me? Why did they lock me up in the dark?" Under Michael's persistent questioning, Emil finally says, "Please, Uncle Michael, I'm all mixed up." Michael then delivers an ultimatum. "You can be a decent member of society. . . . But if you insist on being a Nazi, we're just as tough as you are, and a lot tougher."

To believe that youngsters so completely indoctrinated as Emil are suffering from the desire to be loved, and to believe that these youngsters can be converted to the American, democratic way of life is not implausible. Since the entire play spans a period of only ten days, however, the rapid reformation becomes a hopeful solution to the problem of denazification rather than a convincing one to confirmed realists. Similarly, the romance between Leona and Michael also straddles an issue, for the dramatists deliberately avoid any discussions of religious differences and have maneuvered the romance to emphasize Emil's anti-Semitism. *Tomorrow the World,* nevertheless, illustrates effectively the dramatic techniques which can attract audiences to a propaganda play that neither minimizes nor exaggerates its challenging problem. Although the solution is optimistic, it is a humanitarian solution which the audience wants to believe. For that reason, *Tomorrow the World* ran longer than any other serious war play or propaganda drama produced during World War II. The box office draw was also aided by the excellent performances of Ralph Bellamy, Shirley Booth, and Skippy Homeier. But even with these attributes, it ran only five hundred performances, a low figure in comparison with the performance records of war comedies and farces produced during the same period.

In 1943, *Tomorrow the World* predicted problems Americans would face as an aftermath of the war; *Mister Roberts,* produced in 1948, reflected the problems idealistic American youths faced during the war. *Tomorrow the World* dramatized a problem of impending peril and a warning concerning errors which might be made in the future; *Mister Roberts* dramatized a problem of existing peril and a disclosure of errors made in the past. In *Tomorrow the World* the audience was stirred to action; in *Mister Roberts,* to contemplation. The propaganda in *Tomorrow the World* was emphasized for effect; in *Mister Roberts,* it was understated for effect.

The critics have been effusive in their praise for *Mister Roberts,* calling it "amusing," "touching," "a comedy of heartbreak," "the ideal romantic play about the war," and "magnificent." Many critics refer to *Mister Roberts,* which Thomas Heggen and Joshua Logan adapted from Heggen's novel, as a comedy, but it might also be called a tragedy with definite overtones of comedy, for it depicts the struggle of an idealistic lieutenant against a boorish, sadistic captain. Mister Roberts desires above all else to be assigned to active duty, but he is willing to sacrifice his opportunity for transfer by striking a bargain with the captain to give the crew a much needed liberty. When Mister Roberts finally does become assigned to a destroyer, he is killed. The captain, on the other hand, wants a promotion, and he is willing to sacrifice the morale of his crew and the respect of his subordinate officers to achieve his goal. At the end of the play, the captain has not received his promotion, but the audience knows he will browbeat his officers until he does become a full commander.

For the most part, the play is developed humorously. The horseplay among the crew members on board a cargo vessel, the raucous escapades of the men on liberty, and the pranks of Ensign Pulver and the Doctor are as rowdy as the action in *Sailor, Beware!* and are developed in gusty dialogue. The serious scenes between the Captain and Mister Roberts contrast with the humorous episodes, as do the scenes which depict Mister Roberts' frustration after he makes the bargain with the captain not to request a transfer. The dramatists demonstrate that an inhuman officer can be as great an enemy as an opposing navy by having Mister Roberts listen to a radio commentator discussing the victory over the German forces. The commentator says, "You and you alone must recognize our enemies: the forces of ambition, cruelty, arrogance, and stupidity . . . You must tear them out as you would a malignant growth." To Mister Roberts, this speech signifies the Captain as well as his prize palm tree, a symbol of the Captain's ambition to become a full commander, and Roberts reacts by uprooting the tree and throwing it overboard. Despite its humorous overtones, this action reveals the determination of Roberts to combat the enemy which is destroying his ideals. Similarly, the pranks of the crew, although raucous, show the struggles of frustrated men trying to escape the boredom of their imprisoned existence by revealing their cunning in plaguing the captain, their loyalty to Mister Roberts, and the unquestioned leadership of Roberts.

Mister Roberts' popular appeal can be traced in part to the changes made in adapting the play. The novel is a somewhat disjointed series of individual sketches loosely connected by the characters and the theme of life aboard the *Reluctant*. Logan and Heggen have retained the leisurely pace, the principal characters, many of the sketches, and the general tone of the novel. They have, however, unified the sketches, developed the characters in greater detail, and have heightened incidents for dramatic and emotional effectiveness.

One of the most noticeable differences between the novel and the drama is the dialogue. In both versions the vernacular is frank, often deliberately crude, and always realistic. The play does contain what John Mason Brown calls "un-Gideonized, pro-Kinsey language," but the dramatists have lessened the degree of profanity and vulgarity without sacrificing the essential realism. To ex-servicemen, the dialogue in the novel is realistic; the dialogue in the play, which shocked some audiences, often appears to be almost euphemistic.

The novel merely states that the "crew worshipped" Mister Roberts, but the drama definitely illustrates this worship when the crew conspires to help Roberts by having a name-signing contest to determine who would be most successful in forging the Captain's signature on a letter requesting transfer to active duty for Roberts. The dramatists have simplified the story of life aboard the *Reluctant* to emphasize the importance of Mister Roberts. They have eliminated irrelevant episodes in which Roberts does not appear but

Mister Roberts, Henry Fonda

have retained enough to preserve the tone of the novel. These include the crew members using spyglasses when they discover that the nurses' quarters on shore have no curtains on the shower-room windows, as well as the scene aboard ship after the liberty in which the drunken members of the crew are either dragged or hauled on deck.

Mister Roberts also uses the technique of naturalizing the audience, for the dramatists have maneuvered scenes so that the audience shares secrets with the crew, thus heightening the humor. For example, when one of the nurses visits the ship and the men begin betting on her identity, the audience knows the men have seen her in the shower room and waits with interest to discover how she will react when she learns the cause of the frenzied betting. The naturalized audience also knows that Mister Roberts has thrown the Captain's palm tree overboard. As the crew is summoned, assembled, and queried, interest grows, for the audience is certain Roberts will not admit to the act and wonders if the Captain will ever discover the culprit. Roberts never does confess, but the crew, knowing he is responsible for the deed, gives him a medal shaped like a palm tree, and the audience is content.

Some critics have objected to the humorous incidents, calling them schoolboy pranks which present a distorted attitude toward the war. Perhaps the forging of the letter or the explosion in the laundry caused by Pulver may appear exaggerated. The episode in which the Doctor and Mister Roberts concoct their own brand of Scotch whiskey by adding Coca-Cola, hair tonic, and iodine to alcohol may also appear to be little more than a burlesque scene. These incidents, however, hold audience interest in the first half of the play, provide a definite contrast for the increasing seriousness of the last act, and temper the shock when the audience learns that Mister Roberts is dead.

The play itself entertained audiences, but the excellent performance of Henry Fonda as Mister Roberts contributed greatly to the drawing power. Ideally cast, Fonda played Roberts with dignity, even in the hilarious episodes, and made the lieutenant a convincing leader to such an extent that the news of his death seemed to stun the audience as much as it stunned the men on stage. A further aid to the popular appeal in the late 1940s was the reaction of ex-servicemen who found much in the play that paralleled their own experiences. Their verbal endorsements became very effective word-of-mouth advertising.

Mister Roberts, with a total of 1,147 performances, ran more than twice as long as *Tomorrow the World* because the interlacing of comedy and drama helped popularize a serious indictment of incompetent leadership. In spite of the farcical episodes in the first act, *Mister Roberts* basically is a poignant drama which tells the story of an admirable hero whose death symbolizes one of the tragedies of war.

Laurence Housman's biographical drama, *Victoria Regina,* produced in 1935, is the least dramatic of all the plays in this chapter. It is not as well integrated as *Mister Roberts,* for it is merely a series of disconnected episodes about Queen Victoria arranged in chronological order. Unlike *Dead End* or *Tomorrow the World,* it presents no theme of social significance. It lacks the vigor and plot structure of *The Children's Hour* or *Rain.* Yet, as pure theatrical entertainment, *Victoria Regina* surpassed all other plays in this chapter by providing a brilliant tour de force for Helen Hayes, whose extraordinary performance as Victoria was responsible for the long and very successful run.

The original text and the stage production are not comparable, for Gilbert Miller, the producer, adapted the play to fit Miss Hayes's talents. Housman subtitled his thirty-episode play "A Dramatic Biography," and wrote it as a drama to be read rather than to be seen, since the rights to produce it in England were denied until the reign of Edward VIII. Housman stated that since the play could not be produced on stage, he had written the dialogue "rather more on literary than on theatrical lines."

If all thirty episodes were to be presented, the drama would probably run longer than any of Eugene O'Neill's marathon plays or even a full-length version of *Hamlet.* The unusual length of Housman's drama, however, gives him sufficient latitude to draw a complete characterization of Victoria from childhood to old age and to include a sufficient number of episodes to reveal Victoria's stubbornness, her occasional arrogance, her jealousy, her religious beliefs, her conscientiousness as a queen, her love for Albert, and her increasing dependence upon Albert. Housman has tempered the characterization with sufficient humor to portray her as a romantic and beloved queen rather than as a stuffy symbol of mid-Victorianism.

Although Victoria dominates most of the episodes, Housman has also developed the characterization of Albert to reveal his firmness, his understanding of Victoria's weaknesses, and his diplomacy. Each episode builds to a minor climax, but the play, as a whole, does not develop to a major climax. The episodes are individual units in themselves linked by chronological order and develop interest rather than suspense in their depiction of Victoria from a young girl to an aged queen.

Housman's thirty episodes have been cut to ten for the stage production, but the shorter version still presents a compelling characterization of Victoria. The first scene depicts Victoria before she ascends to the throne; the last two present her as the aged queen after the death of Albert; the remaining seven are concerned with her courtship and marriage. Several of the episodes which have been omitted are relatively unimportant; some add little to the characterization; and some do not include Victoria at all. The ten episodes selected comprise a full-length drama which presents a reasonable condensation of Housman's closet play. The links between episodes are weak, and many of the qualities which Housman has developed in full, such as Victoria's prejudices, her realization that she cannot command Albert, and her rebellion against her mother are mainly inferred.

The final scene which brings the drama to an impressive conclusion in both versions is Victoria's Diamond Jubilee. The stage is filled with Victoria's descendants and with representatives of European kingdoms. Victoria, seated in her wheel chair, is brought on stage. After she has received congratulations from those assembled, Victoria requests that the balcony windows be opened and that she be wheeled to a position where the cheering crowd may see her. When Victoria appears on the balcony, the cheering swells and does not diminish until she signals for her chair to be withdrawn. Victoria then makes the final speech, one of the most memorable in the play, in which she says it has been very gratifying to find that the people still appreciate all that she has done for them. Although the episode is impressive, particularly as Victoria is being wheeled off stage, the entire scene is little more than a tableau.

From a production standpoint, the elimination of certain episodes was a technical necessity. The producer had to cut the play to a conventional length, but, even more important, he had to give Miss

Hayes sufficient time between acts to change her make-up from the middle-aged woman to the old, gray-haired, plump-cheeked Victoria. For that reason, he omitted two important scenes between the second and third acts. When the curtain rose on the third act and revealed that Miss Hayes had changed her entire appearance and even the contours of her face so that she actually resembled the aged Victoria, the enchanted audience broke into applause before she spoke even one word. The audience was less interested in the continuity, in the literary effect, or in the dramatic story than it was in Miss Hayes's rapid changes of costume, her maturing from the very young girl in the first scene to the very old queen in the last, her marvelous tricks with make-up, and her superior skill in modulating her voice to give the effect of youth and age. Audiences came not to see the life story of Victoria but to watch the magic of Helen Hayes as she created the various facets of Victoria's character; those who were privileged to see her performance are not likely to forget it. The play does offer a vivid portrait of Victoria, but it is Helen Hayes who kept *Victoria Regina* running for 517 performances.

Prize-Winning
Plays

EIGHT long-running plays produced between 1900 and 1950 have won either the Pulitzer Prize for drama, the New York Critics' Circle Award, or both. Since prize awards are not announced until the end of the season and any play destined for a long run may already have a head start, the importance of the prize to popular appeal depends upon how much drawing power it adds to a play already established as a popular favorite.

Records show that members of committees awarding prizes do not agree on play selections, for in almost every season, dissenters object to one or both major prize awards. *You Can't Take It with You,* by George S. Kaufman and Moss Hart, awarded the Pulitzer Prize in 1937, was no exception. Critics agreed that *You Can't Take It with You* was effective theater, and that Kaufman and Hart had contrived the play with considerable skill; but not all critics believed it was the most distinguished drama of its season. Several members of the Critics' Circle nominated *You Can't Take It with You* for its prize in 1937, but the Critics' Circle Award went to Maxwell Anderson's *High Tor.*

Dramatic commentators who object to *You Can't Take It with You* call it a trivial farce with little or no plot, or a trite love story with contrived situations and an unsound economic philosophy. These criticisms are valid, for there is little or no plot. The entire play is merely a series of mildly insane antics performed by Grandpa Vanderhof and his family. Grandpa decides one day that he has had enough of the business world, stops working, and spends his time collecting snakes and stamps, attending commencement exercises, and generally enjoying life. Because someone delivered a typewriter to the Vanderhofs by mistake, Penny Sycamore, Grandpa's daughter, decides to write plays. Her husband makes spectacular fireworks, aided by Mr. De Pinna, a milkman who stopped at the house one day and stayed there. Penny's older daughter, Essie, studies dancing and makes assorted candies which her husband Ed sells. Ed also plays the xylophone and operates a printing press. Penny's younger daughter, Alice, seems to be the only normal member of the household, for she enjoys working in a business office. The play is held together by a slightly discordant, obvious love story which illustrates the boy meets girl—boy loses girl—boy gets girl formula. In Act I, Alice becomes engaged to Paul Kirby, her employer. In Act II Alice breaks the engagement; in Act III Alice and Paul are reunited. The conventional love story in the midst of hilarious antics makes Alice and Paul the least interesting of all the Vanderhofs, Sycamores, or Kirbys.

The play keeps the audience entertained even though many of the most amusing situations are obviously contrived. For example, the F.B.I. agents swoop down to arrest Ed for printing antigovernment placards the same night the Kirbys visit the Vanderhofs. What starts out as a peaceful evening ends in complete shambles when the F.B.I. arrests everybody. The following night when Mr. Kirby returns to persuade his son to go back with him, the Grand Duchess Olga, now impoverished and working as a waitress at Childs, also arrives at the Vanderhofs and impresses Mr. Kirby with her casual references to other members of Russian nobility.

Several episodes, little more than elaborated vaudeville skits or gag routines, are very funny but do nothing to advance any particular thread of the plot. The scene between Grandpa and an internal revenue agent develops into a clever lampoon of income tax expenditures because Grandpa keeps asking the income tax investigator how the money will be spent if he agrees to pay his taxes. The Grand Duchess Olga burlesques the exiled White Russians who capitalize on titles as well as the caste system among the Manhattan pseudo-socialites when she explains why her cousin, a doorman at Hattie Carnegie's, is a snob. Penny's game of mental associations develops into an impudent travesty of parlor games, psychological reactions, and discussions of sex because she starts what appears to be an innocuous game of word associations and then proceeds to give such words as bathroom and sex. Threading these sequences is a constant stream of shorter theatrical gags which include Essie's attempts to imitate Ginger Rogers, Donald's objections to making a trip to the government office every week to collect his relief check, and Ed's playing Beethoven with his own peculiar improvisations on the xylophone while Essie dances in a frenzy.

These contrived scenes might easily have resulted in a jumble of purposeless nonsense, but Kaufman and Hart have unified them with a popular central theme that emphasizes the importance of happiness and the unimportance of material wealth. All through the play, the theme, as expressed in the title, the relationship between Grandpa and his family, illustrates the real meaning of happiness.

Although Grandpa Vanderhof insists that money is not the most important goal in life, he can afford the luxury of idleness because he has an income which supplies the necessities for his family, pays for the services of a maid, and supports those members of his family who are interested in developing hobbies rather than in working at regular jobs. Several critics raise the objection that Kaufman and Hart advocate an impractical mode of living without offering a practical solution of how such thriftless existence could be possible. From the standpoint of entertainment and audience reaction, this objection means little, for the play would scarcely send audiences home determined to give up their jobs and begin living a life of leisure. *You Can't Take It with You* impresses audiences much more by showing that Grandpa and his family are happy doing what they want to do, that each member of the family respects the other's hobby, and that their many diversified interests, instead of creating a babel of confusion, blend to make the household a happy one. The play implies that people can be independent and can find happiness without conforming to monotonous routine.

The greatest appeal of the Vanderhofs is that they are funny because they take themselves seriously. Instead of laughing at the hobby, the audience enjoys the ludicrous manner in which the character develops it. Penny never realizes that any situation she dreams up for her plays, such as the predicament of the heroine who is kept in a monastery for sixteen years, is ridiculous; to Penny, the lines she writes constitute strong, forceful drama. As a result, any repressed playwright in the audience laughs at Penny's ridiculous plots and gets satisfaction in thinking that if he ever writes plays, he will do a much better job. Frustrated dancers react the same way to Essie. And most audiences are pleased that Grandpa and his family, who have an average income, are very happy; Mr. and Mrs. Kirby, who are very wealthy, are not.

The seriousness of the characters throughout the maze of mad activity permits Kaufman and Hart to end the first and last acts effectively with the family seated at dinner as Grandpa says grace, impressive in its direct simplicity. The last scene, particularly, makes a fitting conclusion to the play. Grandpa raps for silence, all heads are lowered, and Grandpa says, "Well, Sir, here we are again. We want to say thanks for everything you've done for us. . . . We've all got our health and as far as everything else is concerned, we'll leave it to you. Thank you." The entire grace is only a few sentences longer, but the tone retains the same sincerity and simplicity. The importance of the grace is not the religious connotation but the reverent, universal appeal which does not single out any specific denomination or group, but, instead, permits each member of the audience to interpret it in the light of his own beliefs.

At one performance, this quiet scene was anything but impressive. *You Can't Take It with You* played at the Booth Theater while *Idiot's Delight* played at the Shubert, with the stages for both theaters back to back. The final scene of *Idiot's Delight* represented an air raid, with sirens screaming, planes zooming overhead, gunfire, and general pandemonium. The shows were timed so that Grandpa could finish his final prayer and the curtain come down before the air raid started. One night the shows were off schedule, and before Grandpa could finish, the air raid began in the Shubert Theater, and the sounds of bombing and zooming planes wrecked the quiet serenity of Grandpa's prayer.

The amiability rather than the nonsensicality of the slightly insane Vanderhofs made the characters sympathetic rather than ludicrous. Audiences enjoyed Grandpa, who was a humorous rascal and a lovable grandfather who brought contentment to all members of his family as well as to all people who came to his home, with the exception of the poor income tax collector and the F.B.I. agents whom he bedeviled. And when Tony Kirby told his father, "I wanted you to see a real family . . . a family that loved and understood each other," the audience knew what he meant, for the happiness in the Vanderhof home proved to be contagious and spread through the audiences, who kept the play running for more than two years with a total of 837 performances.

Both *You Can't Take It with You* and *State of the Union,* the Howard Lindsay–Russel Crouse comedy produced in 1948, integrate a plea for tolerance and democracy with a love story and sufficient humor to make them theatrical entertainment rather than social preachments which use the stage as a soapbox. They differ completely, however, in development. Kaufman and Hart unify a maze of humorous lines and situations into a loosely constructed drama by means of a frail plot; Lindsay and Crouse use humorous lines and situations to bolster a strong plot in a sturdily constructed drama. *You Can't Take It with You* offers an economically unsound theme; *State of the Union* offers a sound criticism of political intrigue.

State of the Union's winning the Pulitzer Prize in 1947 stirred up no heated controversy. Some critics did not approve of the selection, but their objection to the prize award was an objection to all plays produced during a season in which the Critics' Circle did not make an award.

State of the Union is an indictment of American political leaders and their machinery for building up a popular Presidential candidate. The hero, Grant Matthews, a wealthy industrialist and a liberal, must abandon his own convictions or else make compromises and defend the opposing views of the party leaders if he wishes to be a candidate for President. His mistress, Kay Thorndyke, a newspaper publisher, encourages him to conform to party policy and to capitalize on the weaknesses of minority groups to encourage votes. His estranged wife, Mary Matthews, would prefer to have him lose the nomination rather than lose his integrity. The conflicting influences of the two women make Grant realize that he cannot further his political ambitions without sacrificing his own beliefs.

The play reveals how hopeless it is for a Presidential nominee to bolt the party and how little choice the average citizen has in selecting the proper candidate. With such a timely theme, particularly in 1945 and 1946, when the nation was already beginning to talk about the next election, the play, if written by ardent propagandists intent solely on exposing political corruption, might have been a serious drama filled with political tirades and involved arguments which would have little or no entertainment value. Lindsay and Crouse, however, have definitely avoided involvements. They do not state how Grant's ideals differ from the party platform, do not attempt to thrust on the audience any definite solution for the problem of political corruption, and do not resort to a melodramatic conclusion in which Grant proves that he can triumph over the experienced politicians. Instead, they have kept the serious speeches to a minimum and have contrived a polished, smoothly written comedy which develops its theme through humor and excellent characterizations that are not stereotyped. Jim Conover, the party leader, is an impressive political figure who has the suave manners of a clever politician rather than the obvious tactics of a theatrical political boss. Spike is a shrewd newspaperman rather than a ruthless, hard-drinking reporter who would sacrifice anything to get a good story. Grant is neither the typical philandering husband nor radical crusader but is a likable hero with human failings. Nor is Mary Matthews the typical stage wife who lacks the physical attractiveness of the mistress. Grant turns to Kay because Mary is too clever and too willing to deflate his ego when he becomes obsessed with his own importance and because Kay flatters him into believing he really is the important political figure he would like to be.

The dialogue is filled with lines which satirize arguments between capital and labor, the prejudices of political leaders, the foreign policy, and the disagreements among labor organizations. The gag, always a popular device if well done, is used in clever curtain lines. At the end of Act I, Kay tells Grant that for the next few weeks she will be in New York while he will be with his wife, and Spike says, "Politics makes strange bedfellows." At the end of Act II, Kay asks Conover if there is any real difference between the Democratic and Republican parties, to which Conover says, "All the difference in the world. They're in and we're out." This type of gag is also sprinkled profusely throughout the play, such as Mary's observation when Grant refuses to drink before making a speech, "That's the difference between Grant and me—I'd rather be tight than president"; or Nora's comment that although a Democrat had slept in the room now occupied by Matthews, "he wasn't a Roosevelt Democrat."

State of the Union is never dull or uninteresting, but the serious moments lack the effectiveness of the funnier episodes. In general, when Mary is involved in the action, the play picks up decided interest, for Lindsay and Crouse have contrived a number of sequences which permit her to indulge in humorous antics, such as the scene where she becomes disgusted with her dinner party and gets drunk; the following scene when she tries to remember what happened and keeps drinking cup after cup of black coffee; or the final episode in Act I when she discovers that Kay and Grant have been together again and immediately prepares makeshift sleeping quarters on the floor which Grant assumes are for her, but to which Mary relegates Grant as she quickly appropriates the double bed for herself. One of Mary's best lines, "Everybody here tonight was thinking of the next election. Well, it's time somebody began thinking of the next generation," according to George Jean Nathan, was paraphrased from a speech by Glenn Frank. From the audience's point of view, it was one of the most effective speeches in the play, regardless of its source.

Rumor has it that Lindsay and Crouse wrote the role of Mary with Helen Hayes in mind, but when Miss Hayes felt she needed a year's rest before undertaking a new show, they rewrote the script to build up the role of Grant. Ralph Bellamy, established as a box office draw after his long run in *Tomorrow the World,* and Ruth Hussey, well known to audiences for her motion pictures, gave excellent performances as Grant and Mary and helped the play become a sell-out comedy. Their replacements toward the end of the run proved to be equally effective and kept *State of the Union* on Broadway for 765 performances.

The play appealed to audiences also because it capitalized on the popular situation of having the right woman emerge triumphant, although the playwrights emphasized Mary's victory by having Grant lose the nomination. The ending did suggest that Grant might still be considered a popular candidate, but the realistic audience knew that unless Grant compromised with the politicians, such a suggestion was little more than a pipe dream. *State of the Union,* nevertheless, proved that political discussions could have popular appeal if they were developed humorously without complications of involved arguments rather than developed as social preachments. As a result, the play entertained audiences with its good acting and clever lines. Perhaps the political satire had, as one critic suggested, masculine appeal, but the domestic triangle intrigued both men and women.

Mary Chase's Pulitzer Prize play, *Harvey,* produced in 1944, and Tennessee Williams' Critics' Circle Award winner, *The Glass Menagerie,* produced in 1945, provide an interesting contrast between prize plays selected in the same season. Both plays deal with characters who try to escape from reality by living in a world of fancy. *Harvey*'s record of 1,775 performances more than tripled the run of 561 performances for *The Glass Menagerie.*

Harvey tells the story of a harmless drunkard, Elwood P. Dowd, and a large, white, invisible rabbit that he calls Harvey. Elwood's sister Veta and her daughter, embarrassed by his actions and his chattering with the invisible Harvey, arrange to have Elwood treated at a sanatorium. Before the play is over, both the psychoanalyst and Veta believe they also have seen Harvey, and Veta decides not to permit Elwood to undergo any treatment, for she prefers that he remain as he is—friendly, harmless, and happy. Most of the critics refer to *Harvey* as a fantasy, for it is supposed to deal with a fairy spirit found in old Celtic mythology. The basis for both the fantasy and the original title of the play, *The Pooka,* are explained when Wilson, an attendant at the sanatorium, checks the word *pooka* in an encyclopedia and discovers that a pooka is "a fairy spirit in animal form. Always very large. . . . Very fond of rum-pots, crackpots."

Harvey is not a play for the literal-minded, for it is an incongruous combination of fantasy and farce which develops into a confusing maze when any attempt is made to analyze the plot. The complexities become even more apparent in determining the exact status of Harvey. Some critics refer to Harvey as an invisible rabbit; others, as a rabbit seen only by Elwood; still others, as an imaginary rabbit. It is not true, for example, that Elwood is the only person who sees Harvey. Veta tells Dr. Henderson she has seen the rabbit, and Dr. Chumley, the psychoanalyst, says he knows Harvey is not merely

Harvey, Frank Fay and friend

a hallucination. Furthermore, the stage directions specifically explain that Harvey crosses the stage and enters Chumley's office. In the Boston tryout, an actor dressed in a rabbit's costume played the scene, but Brock Pemberton convinced Miss Chase that the rabbit should not be visible. In the New York production, the effect of Harvey's crossing the stage was attained by having a door open, then a pause for ten seconds, and then a door across stage open. If Mary Chase had kept Harvey completely invisible and had not inserted the scene where Harvey crosses the stage, the play might have been a delightful fantasy in which even the literal-minded audience might have accepted the idea that Elwood could persuade others to believe in his pooka. Dr. Chumley's theory that he could get rid of Harvey by curing Elwood's alcoholism also doesn't stand up under analysis, since Dr. Chumley, who is not an alcoholic, believes that he also has seen the rabbit. Some of these incongruities might be overlooked if *Harvey* kept audiences entertained throughout all three acts. The first act holds little interest until Elwood enters, and the third act bogs down in confusion until a worldly-wise taxi driver makes Veta realize how completely different Elwood will be if he undergoes treatment. When Elwood is on stage, however, he sustains interest with his charm, his observations on life, and his one-sided conversations with Harvey. In many respects Elwood's philosophy of life is similar to Grandpa Vanderhof's in *You Can't Take It with You,* for both men avoid the routine struggle for material wealth. Elwood is even more financially secure than Grandpa Vanderhof and is free to indulge in his idiosyncrasies without economic worries. Just as Grandpa finds contentment in leisure and hobbies, Elwood finds solace in drinking and in Harvey, both of which create for him a happy dream world. Elwood's comments on life, if considered apart from the play, reveal a strong plea for kindliness and understanding among men, but this philosophy gives the farce an incongruous undertone. If the audience were to accept Elwood seriously, he would become a pathetic figure who refuses to face reality and who finds escape only in insobriety.

Audiences for the most part did not take Elwood or the play seriously. They enjoyed watching Frank Fay as Elwood chattering with Harvey as well as seeing Josephine Hull fluttering through the role of Veta. Their performances did a great deal to help the play become a popular favorite. By the time replacements began stepping into the cast, *Harvey* was well established as a long-running success. The tremendous popular appeal of the play was also due, in part, to the booming World War II years when *Harvey* played on Broadway. The comedy amused audiences who crowded the New York theaters in search of humor and escapism.

The fact that *Harvey* received the Pulitzer Prize does not mean it appealed to audiences for its literary distinction. The Pulitzer Committee selects the American play produced in New York which represents the "educational value and power of the stage, preferably dealing with American life." Audiences did not come to see *Harvey* for the educational value they might find in the characterization of an amiable alcoholic who is more desirable than his sober companions. They supported the play because it provided entertainment, and good entertainment at that, in a well-acted farce that avoided war themes and gave them an opportunity to laugh at sobriety.

The Critics' Circle does not select plays on the basis of educational value but awards its prize to "the best play written by an American playwright and produced in New York." *Harvey* was among those plays considered by the Circle, but *The Glass Menagerie* received the majority of votes. The basic philosophy, the desire to escape from reality, is the same in both *Harvey* and *The Glass Menagerie,* but in *Harvey,* the overtones are humorous enough to entertain audiences and the farcical development does not demand sympathy for Elwood. In *The Glass Menagerie,* the humor is ironic, and the serious development induces sympathy for Tom, the son, who finds refuge from his mother's nagging in going to the movies, in drinking, and finally in running away just as his father had done years before; sympathy for Laura, the crippled daughter who tries to escape from her shyness into a world of illusion; and sympathy even for Amanda, the mother, who plans for the future in terms of the past. The hopelessness of Amanda's schemes to find a gentleman caller for Laura, of Laura's struggles against her mother, and of Tom's inability to convince Amanda of his frustration are depicted with pathos.

The slight plot of *The Glass Menagerie* is developed in seven episodes largely concerned with the preparation for a gentleman caller and his visit. Amanda has nagged Tom into bringing Jim home to see Laura, but the plan ends in disillusionment, for the gentleman is already engaged. Laura goes back into her world of unreality, Tom runs away from home, and Amanda continues to make plans which will never materialize. Tom also acts as narrator to open and close the play with his reminiscences and to integrate the action between several episodes. Unlike Katrin's short speeches in *I Remember Mama,* which link the episodes, Tom's lengthy monologues strain for artistic phrasing and become theatrical devices which often fail to hold audience interest. The fault is not with the actor, as some reviewers have indicated, but with the basic script. The lines read well but lack dramatic force because the narrator states in elaborate phrasing what is about to happen. When the scene is played, the much simpler dialogue which does not strain for poetic tone is far more effective.

If Edward Dowling had presented *The Glass Menagerie* as Williams first wrote it, the play might have been, at best, an artistic failure. Dowling eliminated a screen device Williams had originally planned for the play. Williams included the device in his first published text and explained that his purpose in using it would have been to heighten the effect by projecting pictures or titles on the screen. The device, however, would not have highlighted the scenes or have created a favorable emotional response, for the titles would have made the dialogue redundant. For example, in the script, immediately after "WHAT HAVE YOU DONE SINCE HIGH SCHOOL?" was flashed on the screen, Jim was to say, "What have you done since high school?" More important, such pictures as BLUE ROSES, GLAMOUR MAGAZINE COVER, or such titles as "AFTER THE FIASCO," "TERROR," "LOVE," and "HA," not only appeared to be as obsolete as silent film titles injected into a talking motion picture but also became progressively more annoying. If the screen device had been kept in the play, it would have been as irritating to the audience as it is to the reader. More recent printings of the play have deleted the screen titles as well as the explanation of the device.

The development of the slight story, which is little more than an elaborated incident, is secondary to the development of the mood and characterization. For this reason, some theatergoers interested only in plot said they frequently found they had difficulty concentrating on the action. Williams subtitled his drama "A Memory Play," and emphasized the mood through the narrator, whose reminiscences opened and closed the play. The characterization, the acting, and the direction had greater interest for most audiences because Williams developed his three principals in detail and provided excellent roles for Edward Dowling as Tom, Julie Haydon as Laura, and, most important of all, Laurette Taylor as Amanda.

The script does not indicate the extent to which Jo Mielziner's imaginative set, Julie Haydon's sensitive performance, and Paul Bowles's haunting incidental music contributed to the audience's enjoyment. Nor does it point out Edward Dowling's and Laurette Taylor's contributions in making the play a popular success. By eliminating the screen device and by his expert direction Dowling avoided pseudo-artistic effects to gain maximum audience appeal. He was responsible also for having Williams write a new scene so that Amanda could be off stage to make a costume change indicated in the script, for which Williams had provided no time allotment.

Laurette Taylor's performance unquestionably made the greatest contribution to the long run. Other actresses who played Amanda never received the same ecstatic reception from the public or from the critics, some of whom were almost brutal to Gertrude Lawrence's performance in the motion picture version. Helen Hayes toured successfully in an overseas production of *The Glass Menagerie* and in performances at the New York City Center, but the original triumph of the role is linked with Laurette Taylor. An older generation of theatergoers came to see the actress who had charmed them in *Peg o' My Heart*; the younger generation came to see a renowned actress making a sensational comeback; and Miss Taylor captivated both groups with her performance. She portrayed Amanda in her own fashion and, in spite of the annoying, nagging characterization, made Amanda a woman for whom audiences felt sorry even if they did not sympathize with her. Miss Taylor's contributions were not limited to acting. She is reported to have changed dialogue in rehearsals and during performances, even to the point of deliberately ad-libbing for effect. Regardless of what tactics she used, Laurette Taylor impressed audiences who were privileged to see her in *The Glass Menagerie*.

The Critics' Circle Award must also be considered in appraising the commercial success, for the producers hoped the play would win a major prize. *The Glass Menagerie* first opened in Chicago and played to unprofitable business for three weeks in spite of good reviews and constant newspaper comments praising the play and

Laurette Taylor. Then receipts started to pick up and the play developed into a hit, but at the end of the thirteenth week, although box office business was excellent, the producers moved the show to New York with the definite purpose of having it open on Broadway in time to be a contender for the drama prizes. *The Glass Menagerie* opened March 31, 1945; two weeks later it became the seventh play to receive the Critics' Circle Award, and the first Critics' Circle winner to run over five hundred performances. Both the prize and the critics' enthusiastic praise, unfortunately, built up the play to such an extent that some audiences who expected to see a more spectacular drama were somewhat disappointed in the sensitive, quiet, memory play telling its story of frustration. Perhaps this explains why the Pulitzer Prize winner, *Harvey,* which lacks the basic congruity but which emphasizes humor, ran at least three years longer than *The Glass Menagerie.*

Although Williams has written two longer-running plays, many critics as well as theatergoers have called *The Glass Menagerie* his best play. In the twenty-year period since its opening on Broadway, *The Glass Menagerie* has been presented by amateur groups, colleges, little theaters, and stock companies all over the United States. The New York revival marking the twentieth anniversary of the play in the summer of 1965 was scheduled for a limited run. Critics again wrote favorable reviews for the play as well as for the performances of Maureen Stapleton as Amanda, George Grizzard as Tom, Piper Laurie as Laura, and Pat Hingle as the Gentleman Caller. One or two critics made references to the original production and to Laurette Taylor's performance, but the new generation of theatergoers who had never seen Miss Taylor or the Edward Dowling production were intrigued with the play. The producers, instead of closing *The Glass Menagerie* at the end of the limited run, extended the engagement and advertised the sale of tickets through October. For the last weeks of the run, the original cast changed completely with Jo Van Fleet playing Amanda; Farley Granger, Tom; Carol Rossen, Laura; and Hal Holbrook, the Gentleman Caller.

The heroine in *Street Scene,* Elmer Rice's most popular play, like the characters in *The Glass Menagerie,* is also a victim of frustration. Rice's drama, produced in 1928, received very favorable newspaper reviews and won the Pultizer Prize for 1929, but this award failed to please dissenters who condemned *Street Scene* for its lack of distinction and for its stereotyped characters. One critic, for example, called the play entertaining but "theatrical rubbish." Yet the very elements which raised the greatest controversy gave *Street Scene* its greatest audience appeal.

Success did not come easily to the play. Veteran producers who read the script turned it down because they thought it lacked popular appeal. After William Brady finally put the show into rehearsal, the director resigned and Rice replaced him. When the play opened to excellent reviews, skeptical ticket brokers were still not interested in buying blocks of seats they usually ordered for hit shows, but the public endorsed the play and kept it running for 601 performances.

Street Scene tells the kaleidoscopic stories of the people who live in a tenement house and presents a variety of short episodes to dramatize their sordid lives. As the play progresses, it resolves principally into the story of the Maurrant family. Mrs. Maurrant is having an affair with Sankey, a bill collector, and Mr. Maurrant, aware of what is happening, returns home unexpectedly, finds the lovers, and kills them. In the last act, Maurrant is trapped by police; and his daughter, Rose, and her younger brother, Willie, move out of the neighborhood.

The play includes a variety of character types such as a malicious gossip, an adulterous wife, a jealous husband, a rabid radical, a spinsterish social worker, an obvious trollop, a frustrated schoolteacher, and a group of curiosity seekers who visit the slums. Rice has made these people a cross section of Swedes, Italians, Jews, and native-born Americans. The stage set represents the street in front of a tenement house, and the tenants shout from the windows or sit on the front steps and chatter. Each family is involved with its own domestic problems, but as the play develops, the tenants acquire a degree of individuality and the story of the Maurrant family becomes predominant. The play is convincing to audiences because these character types are familiar. Rice, in fact, has created some of the characters so sharply that they have become almost representative symbols of specific types. For example, social workers insist that Rice's unhappy image of Miss Simpson, the investigator from the charities, has unfavorably influenced public opinion. Quite recently, a professor recruiting students for a school of social work made specific reference to *Street Scene* and told prospective applicants that Miss Simpson did not represent a true picture of the modern social worker.

One or two critics have called the Maurrant episode "lurid," "discordant," and an intrusion on the realistic setting and atmosphere. It is doubtful that audiences would agree with these objections, for Rice presents the illicit romance between Anna Maurrant and Sankey objectively to emphasize his theme, the oppression of the tenement dwellers. He makes the story of Anna the tragedy of a woman who seeks escape from carping neighbors, from morbid surroundings, and from a domineering husband. Without the triangle of Anna, her husband, and her lover, *Street Scene* would be little more than a series of episodic sketches—realistic, perhaps, but with no tangible plot to hold audience interest.

Much of the popular appeal, in fact, comes from the melodramatic plot development, which grows in intensity until it reaches a taut climax. Rice makes the events leading to the murder become the means of blending the characters and their casual dialogue into a single plot. At first the women who live in the same house gossip about Anna's affair. Bit by bit Rice adds sufficient evidence to convince the audience that Anna has a lover and that her husband is aware of her relationship with Sankey. When Maurrant tells Anna he will be out of town the next day, the audience suspects he is plotting to trap the lovers. Tension mounts when Sankey comes to the apartment, for the audience is certain Maurrant will return. And when he does come back on stage, looks up at his apartment, and sees the shades drawn, the emotional impact of the play reaches its height, for the audience knows what is happening in the street and in the apartment, while Frank Maurrant only suspects what is happening, and his wife and Sankey are completely unaware of the impending danger. Sam's futile attempts to prevent Maurrant from entering the house and to warn Mrs. Maurrant emphasize the tension. In fact, audiences almost have the impulse to shout warnings, but Rice checks any such reactions by making Sam the spokesman for the audience as he shouts hysterically while Maurrant runs up the stairs. Even before Maurrant fires the two shots, the marshal and Mrs. Jones are alerted to action, and immediately after the two shots, the street becomes a surging crowd of excited onlookers.

In the third act, the police capture Maurrant; Sam offers to help

Rose but she makes several speeches which seem strangely placid for a girl whose mother has just been murdered. As Rose leaves, new tenants arrive to examine the vacated apartment, the women who live in the house begin to gossip about Rose just as they gossiped about her mother, and the play ends as it began, a pictorial representation of a street in a tenement district.

One critic refers to Rose's speeches as "pseudo-significant"; another feels that Anna's death has not moved the dramatist sufficiently, but if Rice had pleased these critics, he would have written a melodramatic conclusion to which still other critics would have objected. By underwriting the last act to preserve the realistic conclusion, Rice emphasized the effects of the environment upon the characters. He created understanding for Anna's motives (even though audiences did not condone her immorality), understanding for Frank's actions, and sympathy for the unfortunate daughter. If Rice had eliminated or even de-emphasized the love triangle, he would have written a more realistic drama that pleased critics, but a social indictment that would not have appealed to audiences.

Rice has often preached against the evils of society in his plays, but every time he has overstressed his ideas, the plays have failed. *Street Scene,* too, has its share of Rice's theories, as in Anna's pleas for tolerance: "People ought to be able to live together in peace and quiet, without making each other miserable," "Everybody wants a kind word now and then," and "A person should get more out of life than just looking after somebody else." Too many of these speeches might have resulted in the same audience apathy which caused Rice's other propaganda plays to fail. In *Street Scene,* however, they relate so closely to the plot that the audience concentrates on the love triangle and not on Rice's criticism of tenement houses and their occupants.

The enthusiastic audiences who supported the play were less interested in the indictments of society or the preachments against the slums than they were in Rose's desperation to reconcile her parents, in Mrs. Jones's malicious gossiping, or in Anna's futile efforts to avoid suspicion. *Street Scene* provided audiences with a stimulating theatrical experience because it intrigued them with its novel setting, with the constant parade of extras who streamed across the stage to provide the proper atmosphere, with the mounting tension in the second and third acts, and with the love triangle.

A musical version of *Street Scene,* presented on Broadway in 1947, veered sharply from conventional musical comedy as well as from the pattern set by such adaptations as *Oklahoma!* and *Carousel* which included chorus routines and shifted settings to give the variety of scenes musical comedy audiences expected. *Street Scene* followed the original stage play, perhaps too closely, and retained the same combination of melodrama and realism Elmer Rice had used in his drama. Kurt Weill's score was closer to opera than to musical comedy and had one number, "Moon-Faced, Starry-Eyed," which might have become a popular tune. Most of the critics praised Kurt Weill's music, Langston Hughes's lyrics, Elmer Rice's play, and the superior cast headed by Anne Jeffreys as Rose, Polyna Stoska as Anna, and Brian Sullivan as Sam. Several critics were sufficiently impressed with *Street Scene* as an opera to compare it favorably to the Gershwin–Heyward *Porgy and Bess.* Yet, in spite of excellent reviews, *Street Scene* was not a popular draw and closed after 148 performances. Several historians of the drama have said they felt the musical *Street Scene* was ahead of its time, for audiences in 1947 were not ready to accept serious musical drama as popular fare. *Street Scene* has been revived by the New York City Opera Company and may, the historians feel, have a longer run in some future revival than its original 148 performances. It is doubtful, however, that any revival of the musical version will ever have the popular appeal of Rice's Pulitzer Prize play with its record of 601 performances.

Marc Connelly's *The Green Pastures,* adapted from Roark Bradford's *Ol' Man Adam and His Chillun,* and produced in 1930, is one of the few Pulitzer Prize winners to meet with almost complete approval from critics, who have called it one of the better-written dramas in the history of the American theater. The only controversy has been over the Pulitzer Committee's failure to acknowledge the importance of Bradford's stories, which Connelly converted into the most successful morality play produced in New York.

Bradford's collection of thirty-three tales, subtitled "Being the Tales They Tell about the Time the Lord Walked the Earth as a Natural Man," presents Biblical stories as they might be interpreted by Negroes in the Deep South. In its amusing but often anachronistic modernization of the stories, the book records the simple faith of these Negroes. Although the stories are dramatic in themselves, they are disconnected episodes which have a tenuous unity only through their Biblical connection and through the characterization of "De Lawd." A great many show people doubted that the stories could be dramatized effectively. Alexander Woollcott reported that Irvin Cobb had been asked to write an adaptation but had refused because he said he couldn't see a play in them. Marc Connelly accomplished the seemingly impossible task of retaining Bradford's concepts of De Lawd, of Heaven, and of the miracles, but he deleted stories, added new scenes, and made at least three important changes which converted the original sketches into an integrated, reverent drama with a unifying theme.

In the first place, Connelly creates a substantial framework for the stories by opening the play with a scene in a Sunday school. Mr. Deshee, an elderly preacher, is reading portions of the first five chapters of Genesis to a group of children. When he finishes, he asks, "Now, how you think you gonter like de Bible?" Within seconds, the children are asking Mr. Deshee to explain how the world began, how the Lord decided where he wanted the earth, what the angels did in Heaven, and whom God resembled. The scene becomes a prologue for the ensuing action which dramatizes the stories of the Bible as visualized by Mr. Deshee and his class. To emphasize this idea, Connelly includes an additional Sunday-school sequence after De Lawd has left Adam and Eve in the Garden of Eden. Instead of disrupting the visualization of the Biblical tales, Connelly uses only the voices of Mr. Deshee and his pupils as they discuss the events which precede the next scene.

Connelly's second innovation is the addition of several scenes in De Lawd's private office, which include the episode where Gabriel takes his trumpet, polishes it, places it to his lips, and is admonished by God, "Now watch yo'self, Gabriel"; the sequence in which God decides the moon is overheated because too many angels dance around it on Saturday night; the discussions between God and Gabriel about the evils of mankind; the interview between God and the patriarchs who recommend Moses to be God's missionary on earth; and even a gossip session in Heaven between two angels who clean God's office. These scenes preserve the tone established in the Sunday-school sequence, provide necessary transitions between stories, and emphasize the importance of Connelly's third innovation, the unifying theme which links the episodes and heightens the impressive conclusion. Bradford's stories end as simply as they began, but Connelly's adaptation builds to a climax. Throughout the play, God has expressed his displeasure with man's sins and corruption and has tried to find a solution to the problem of redeeming mankind. In the final sequence, God tells Gabriel he had learned about mercy through suffering. Then, as God looks out into the audience, he hears a voice off stage describing Jesus as he carries the cross up the hill. This conclusion differs from Bradford's final story but preserves the mood by which Connelly has transformed the simple and amusing little stories into a distinguished drama.

The episode in which Hezdrel, an apocryphal character created by Connelly, talks to God, provides further unity, for according to the stage directions, Hezdrel is played by the same actor who plays Adam. Moreover, when the curtains open, he is standing in the same position as Adam in the third scene.

Connelly has also added dignity to the characterization of the Lord. Bradford begins with the story of the fish fry and introduces God on the first page of the text. Connelly waits until the second scene to present the fish fry, but he uses the episode to create an impressive entrance for God. As the scene begins, the angels and cherubs create the atmosphere Mr. Deshee has described to his Sunday-school pupils. After the Archangel enters and presents Sunday-school diplomas to the cherubs, the youngsters chatter and the choir sings until Gabriel appears and announces, "Gangway! Gangway for de Lawd God Jehovah." For a moment, the stage is silent, and then God enters. He is the most impressive figure on stage, the symbol of dignity. As God speaks, the choir responds, and then God announces, "Let de fish fry proceed." This entrance still does not lead into Bradford's first story, for Connelly has added a humorous episode in which a little cherub tries to use God's coattail as a trapeze and is reprimanded by an angel for playing too rough with God. Again God does not proceed to taste the custard, which Bradford mentioned in the first paragraph, until he has requested the choir to sing. This elaboration of a short paragraph to gain dramatic effect typifies Connelly's revisions. He has also changed Bradford's dialogue to heighten the effect and to emphasize the benign dignity of God. Bradford, for example, in describing the Lord's meeting with Adam, has De Lawd say he must give

Adam a family because single men "runs around wid women all night." Connelly does not resort to the anachronistic reference to provide humor. Instead, he has God tell Adam that he must have a family, and Adam asks, "Lord, jest what is a family?"

There have been minor objections to Connelly's adaptation because he created episodes which some critics felt were too sophisticated to represent the simple faith of the Southern Negro. The most obvious example is the cabaret scene in Babylon which does not deviate too far from Bradford's accounts of King Nebuchadnezzar's feast or Salome's dance, but the sequence does have a more sophisticated tone than the rest of the play. The objections to Connelly's adaptation, however, are overbalanced by the approval which most critics have given *The Green Pastures* as a modern morality play and as a drama which deserves the Pulitzer Prize.

Although the play itself appealed to audiences, the staging, and the performance of Richard B. Harrison as De Lawd proved to be invaluable assets to the audience's enjoyment. The producer introduced several innovations which enhanced the drama. He used a choir both off stage as transitional music and on stage as part of the play. At times, the choir seemed to be singing directly under the stage, and the voices swelled into the theater to create a majestic transition between scenes. Second, the scenic effects were kept to a minimum to emphasize the very simplicity of the drama. For the sequences in which the Lord walked the earth, the producer installed a treadmill so that De Lawd could remain in the center of the stage while props, such as flowers and bushes attached to the treadmill, moved past. But above all, Richard B. Harrison's performance as De Lawd gave the play its greatest appeal. Some sources refer to Harrison as a Negro preacher; others, as a lecturer; and still others, as a former Pullman porter. Before consenting to play the role, Harrison went to the Episcopal Diocese of New York to discuss the possibility of his appearing in the drama and was assured he could bring distinction to the part. His dignified performance apparently impressed the cast as much as it did the audience. During the run of the play, the actors were reputed to have come to him with their problems, to have asked him to settle disputes, and to have treated him with the same reverence they showed him on stage. According to columnists in other cities, Pittsburgh, for example, when Harrison walked through the districts where many

Negro families lived, he was greeted with "Good morning, Lawd," just as he was greeted on stage. It was Harrison's performance, combined with the excellent production of Marc Connelly's distinguished adaptation, which gave *The Green Pastures* a run of 640 performances. When Harrison took ill and left the cast, the show closed. Or, as Ward Morehouse aptly said, "When he died, the play died with him."

A revival of *The Green Pastures* in the 1940s failed, not only because it lacked Harrison's presence in the cast but also because an overemphasis upon stage sets destroyed the simplicity. A more recent television production, however, seemed to capture some of the spirit of the original presentation.

The approval given *The Green Pastures* as a Pulitzer Prize play is exceeded by the approval given two long-running dramas produced after the establishment of the Critics' Circle Award. *A Streetcar Named Desire,* produced in 1947, and *Death of a Salesman,* produced in 1949, have more in common than their distinction of winning both the Pulitzer Prize and Critics' Circle Award. Both plays deal with characters who have come to the end of their resources and whose sham defenses against reality cause their downfall; both present the futile struggle of people doomed in the first act.

Arthur Miller's *Death of a Salesman,* the prize winner for 1949, begins in the present but dramatizes by well-integrated flashbacks the past events which have led to Willy Loman's downfall. As the play progresses, Willy develops into a tragic hero who arouses sympathy. Tennessee Williams' *A Streetcar Named Desire,* the prize-winning play in 1948, does not dramatize the events which have led to the downfall of Blanche Du Bois. As the play progresses, she becomes an unfortunate heroine who arouses interest, often the same type an audience might have in a psychopathic case study.

A Streetcar Named Desire is the story of Blanche Du Bois, who becomes an alcoholic and a seducer of young boys after her husband, a homosexual, commits suicide. When the authorities force her to leave the town where she has taught in the high school, Blanche comes to the French Quarter in New Orleans to live with her sister and brother-in-law, Stella and Stanley Kowalski. Her pretenses of purity and her condescending airs antagonize Stanley, who learns the truth about Blanche and prevents her from marrying his friend Mitch. The night Stella gives birth to her baby, Stanley

A Streetcar Named Desire, Jessica Tandy and Marlon Brando

comes home from the hospital, gets drunk, and attacks Blanche. In the final scene, Stella, who refuses to believe what Blanche has told her about Stanley, has Blanche committed to an institution for the insane.

The unsavory story combines the frustration in *The Glass Menagerie* with the seduction in *Rain* and the moral decadence in *Dead End*. Williams has used a plot filled with sensationalism, but he has made several scenes theatrically effective in their realism. These include the sequence in which Blanche first reveals that she is an alcoholic when she discovers a whiskey bottle, pours a half tumblerful, and belts it down; the scene in which Stanley tells Stella he has learned the truth about Blanche and then scatters the contents of Blanche's trunk to convince Stella that Blanche has lied about her financial condition; and the moment of terror when Blanche smashes a bottle and clutches the broken top to prevent Stanley from attacking her. Although these scenes are effective highlights in themselves, they do not prevent the play from becoming static. Blanche's pretense of gentility, her deliberate coyness with Mitch, and her affectations are, to some critics, merely portraits of an interesting case study photographed from different angles.

The conclusion of the drama is somewhat confusing. Audiences assume that Blanche is insane because she hears strange noises and sees distorted images, but a literal-minded audience can never be certain whether these are caused by her alcoholism or by her insanity. Even when Blanche has dressed herself in her tawdry finery and babbles about her admirer who is taking her away on a trip, Williams indicates in the stage directions, "Blanche has been drinking steadily since Mitch left." The uncertainty is increased after Stella admits she does not know whether she is doing the right thing in sending Blanche to an institution but adds, "I couldn't believe her story and go on living with Stanley." A few moments later, when Blanche struggles with the matron, Stella again says her decision was prompted by the story of Stanley's attack and not by Blanche's increasing mental disorders. The action throughout the play gives definite proof that Blanche is an alcoholic but insufficient proof, in the light of Stella's uncertainty, that Blanche's mental condition is worse than it was in the opening scene.

To some audiences, Blanche's actions also are somewhat confusing. By making her a deliberate liar, Williams creates a doubt that even when Blanche is revealing the secrets of her sordid past, she is telling the complete truth. The motivation for her behavior is always narrated. There are no incidents to show why Blanche, revolted by an abnormal husband, would have become promiscuous and degenerate. Some audiences, therefore, are confused by the lack of evidence to explain Blanche's behavior, but this confusion does not detract from the dramatic impact that *A Streetcar Named Desire* has made upon audiences. Some critics have explained that the drama effectively portrays the conflict that exists in every man between his animal desires and his attempt to be civilized. This struggle is dramatized not only through the conflict between Blanche and Stanley but, more important, also through the struggle within Blanche herself. The inner conflict, the critics feel, creates and explains the confusion in the characterization.

In spite of the obvious flaws in characterization and the narrative development, *A Streetcar Named Desire* is impressive theater. In the last three scenes, particularly when Blanche screams hysterically at Mitch, when her emotional conflict with Stanley reaches its height, and when she is led to the sanatorium, the play becomes compelling drama.

When the play first opened, most of the critics wrote ecstatic reviews, although one or two dissenters did object to the production. In retrospect, several of the critics who were at first most enthusiastic have somewhat reversed their original appraisal and have written adverse comments pointing out weaknesses in the play. The fact remains, however, that these critics were sufficiently impressed on opening night to write enthusiastic reviews, and their original keen interest in the play paralleled the reactions of most audiences. The important factors in determining what makes a long run are not the technical or literary values of the play. Any drama which can fill the theater for a two-year run must have some appeal even for those audiences that thought of Blanche as a psychopathic case study. There were, however, a great number of theatergoers who felt that they did understand the heroine, could feel compassion for her, and, even in some cases, could identify their personal conflicts with hers. Any play which can arouse this type of audience reaction deserves recognition as effective theater.

Neither Williams' plot nor its development, however, would have attracted audiences for 855 performances, the longest run of any of Williams' plays. Much of the credit belongs to Elia Kazan, who directed the production and whose technique of building scenes to reach an emotional climax gave the play much of its intensity; to Jessica Tandy, whom critics hailed as a second Jeanne Eagels for her performance as Blanche; to Uta Hagen, who played the role superbly in the road company before replacing Miss Tandy in the New York cast; and particularly to Marlon Brando, whose performance as Stanley catapulted him to fame. Audiences that had seen him play Marchbanks, the young poet in *Candida,* or Nels in *I Remember Mama,* were doubly surprised by his vigorous performance as Stanley. One of the great actresses of the theater, in a remark made during an interview, bemoaned the fact that Brando's performance in *A Streetcar Named Desire* had ruined the talent of a young man whom she thought might have become one of the great actors on the American stage.

Brando intrigued audiences, but not as Williams had intended in the script. Anyone who reads the play without having seen Brando's performance would assume that Williams had tried to picture Blanche as a doomed woman because she did not understand the plight of her husband; that Stella's marriage to Stanley, as Blanche ridicules it, is degrading; and that Stanley's attack upon Blanche represents his crudeness, his vulgarity, and his animalism. Theater audiences, however, often reacted otherwise. A great many men sympathized with Stanley, thought Blanche was a nagging female who was jealous of her sister's normal marriage, and were delighted to see Stanley spoil Blanche's chance of marrying Mitch. The reactions of some women to the play were even more surprising. They, too, were intrigued by Brando's performance, and their comments as they left the theater, particularly after matinee performances, were often about Stanley. Some women said they thought Blanche had goaded Stanley into attacking her; others said they thought Blanche's reaction to Stella's marriage was ridiculous and that they could certainly understand why Stella would have married Stanley, especially if he looked and acted like Brando. From the standpoint of dramatic technique, the audience should have been sympathetic with the plight of a woman who told lies all her life and then, when she finally told the truth, found that no one would believe her. That she did arouse compassion in some audiences is undeniable, particularly with those who felt that she was an unfortunate heroine and who understood and sympathized with her conflict not only with Stanley but also with herself. Yet a great many theatergoers who were as tired of her whining and affectations as Stanley was remained impassive to her downfall. Other theatergoers who felt that Blanche's ridiculing of Stella's happy, normal marriage was incited by jealousy also remained unsympathetic. On the other hand, most audiences understood Stanley's actions, particularly as portrayed by Brando and later by Anthony Quinn. Their performances emphasized Stanley's virility, made his crudeness and vulgarity more realistic than Blanche's neurotic fluttering and decadent gentility, and helped keep the play running for more than two years.

Audience reaction to *A Streetcar Named Desire,* nonetheless, is passive for those audiences which are unable or do not wish to identify themselves with Blanche. Arthur Miller's *Death of a Salesman,* which is also the tragedy of an individual doomed by the world of illusion he has created, arouses a more active audience reaction. Even an impartial audience cannot disassociate itself from the story of Willy Loman's failure as a salesman and as a father, for Willy's struggle to be a success is universal. Miller has made no compromise in portraying Willy's weaknesses both as an unfaithful husband and as a liar, and yet he has made audiences sympathize with Willy's conflict because much in Willy's life may parallel the audience's experiences, either real or vicarious. Willy's determination to die so that his family may survive, and Biff's rebellion against his father, which emphasizes Willy's failure as well as the realization that Biff's life need not end as tragically as his father's, makes audiences understand how futile Willy's false standards and objectives have been.

Death of a Salesman is one of the few prize-winning dramas which most critics have praised in such superlatives as "majestic," "soaring tragedy," and "superb." In newspaper reviews, in *Variety,* which rates commercial value, and in anthologies which include plays selected for literary merit, *Death of a Salesman* is called "eloquent," "relentless," and "distinguished." The story is basically a simple one. Willy Loman has struggled all his life as a salesman. He has built up grandiose delusions not only of his own success but also of his sons' ability to become even more successful. During the first act, the audience knows that Biff, the older son who idolized his father, now resents him, but the audience does not learn the cause of Biff's resentment until the second act when a flashback reveals that Biff found his father in a hotel room with a strange woman. Willy asks for a change in jobs, is fired instead, and, in desperation, commits suicide so that his family will get his insurance.

Although the play deals presumably with the last two days in the life of Willy Loman, it integrates two separate plot developments. The first is the story of the past which reveals by flashbacks the strong attachment between Willy and his sons, and also the development of Biff's resentment toward his father. The second is the story of the present which includes the effective interview between Willy and the smug young executive who fires Willy when he asks to be taken off the road and given an office job; the ironic scene in a restaurant when Willy's sons arrange to meet him but decide instead to spend the evening with two girls they have picked up; and the episode in which Biff discovers that Willy is planning to commit suicide. The story of the past reveals the development of Willy's delusions; the story of the present gains impact through integration with episodes from the past and reveals the growth of these delusions which have destroyed Willy's ability to face reality. The two stories are blended into a climactic scene in which Biff calls his father a failure and then makes Willy realize he is responsible for Biff's failure. While Biff is telling Willy that they both are "a dime a dozen" and that he cannot live up to the lies Willy has tried to make him believe, Biff suddenly breaks down, throws his arms around his father, and sobs. The scene reaches its effective climax as Willy discovers that the strong attachment between him and Biff still exists.

The emotional power of this scene is almost equaled by the final sequence, which represents the funeral attended only by Willy's family and Charley. When Biff insists that Willy "had the wrong dreams," Charley defends Willy's philosophy, saying that no one must blame Willy, for all salesmen dream of success. It is then that Linda, Willy's wife, kneels at the grave and asks Willy to forgive her because "I can't cry . . . Help me, Willy . . . I can't cry."

Some reviewers have questioned the motivation of Biff's resentment toward his father because Miller does not include any incident to show that Biff's affection for his mother would cause him to become antagonistic when he discovers his father with the strange

Death of a Salesman, Arthur Kennedy, Lee J. Cobb and Cameron Mitchell

woman. Most audiences agree with the critics who believe that Biff grows contemptuous not because he is attached to his mother but because he is disillusioned in his father whom he has idolized. When Willy tries to explain the situation and tells Biff he will understand about these things when he grows up, Biff calls him a liar, and continues to shout at Willy, "You fake. You phony little fake," as he rushes off stage.

Miller has depicted Willy as a failure who induces sympathy but who does not command respect. Willy's struggle for security is impeded by his own incompetence, his false pride, and his wrong conception of success, and yet Willy does illustrate the tragedy of the little man, not as a salesman, but as a father. His suicide, although motivated by his delusions, demonstrates his willingness to sacrifice himself to provide for his family and to atone for his responsibility for Biff's failure.

The emotional power in *Death of a Salesman* appeals to audiences, but the characterization has equal audience interest. Willy represents the misguided little man who has failed to learn that success is not accomplished by wishful dreams or by inflated ego. Miller emphasizes the fallacy of Willy's philosophy in a scene which contrasts Willy's illusions of his sons' success and Charley's realistic acceptance of his son Bernard's achievements. Charley has told Willy that Bernard is going to argue a case before the supreme court, and Willy is astonished that Bernard has not even mentioned it. Charley says, "He don't have to—he's gonna do it." Miller has also drawn convincing characterizations of Biff, who realizes his own shortcomings; of Happy, who has inherited Willy's false conception of success but who lacks Willy's gentleness; and of Linda, the loyal wife whose devotion to her husband appears at times to be greater than her love for her sons.

Death of a Salesman is an excellent drama to epitomize the long-running plays produced before 1950. It illustrates the growth and development of realism in the drama and presents with compassion rather than with clinical realism the story of a man who is doomed. It depicts the struggles of the little man against the economic system without becoming a rabid propaganda play which violently denounces the capitalistic system. *Death of a Salesman* has further distinction as a literary play, for in spite of its complex structure and integration of past and present sequences, it moves clearly from scenes of realism to episodes of reminiscences. It has the distinction of being the first contemporary drama up to 1950 selected for distribution by a book club, a further indication that the play appealed to the reading public as well as to theater audiences. The fact that *Death of a Salesman* received both the Pulitzer and Critics' Circle Prizes and also achieved a popular run of 742 performances would seem to indicate that by 1950, theatergoers had developed an awareness of good drama and that a play with definite literary distinction could become one of the most popular dramas on Broadway.

1950
to
1965

More
Popular Fare

By the end of 1950, Broadway producers were optimistic about new playwrights on the theatrical horizon, technical innovations in production and staging, and the increased public support for better-written American drama. Critics pointed out that long-running plays in the 1940s, such as *The Glass Menagerie, Detective Story,* and *Death of a Salesman,* were far superior to the popular fare of the 1910s, and that audiences were developing a more literary appreciation for drama. Some critics predicted that plays in the 1950s and 1960s would reflect an even greater popular interest in significant dramas.

Such optimistic views, however, have only partially materialized. The long runs on Broadway show that audiences still support escapist fare as well as the prize winners. Economic conditions have had a strong influence on shortening runs and increasing failures. Rising production and labor costs have sent admission prices up and the number of new productions down. Critics have endorsed fewer plays each season; and only one play produced since 1950, *Mary, Mary,* has run for more than fifteen hundred performances. Since the late 1950s, editors of books about the best plays of the season have found the limited number of new shows often fails to provide the ten or twelve plays they select annually as the most distinguished productions of the season. To keep their quotas, they have included musical comedies and off-Broadway productions.

The number of theaters available for stage productions increased when television producers did not renew options on such theaters as the Hudson, Mansfield, or Ziegfeld. Producers found it easier to keep productions running without fear of having the show closed if receipts dropped below a specified gross, but the practice of keeping plays running during unprofitable weeks with the hope that attendance would improve, as the producers had done with *Abie's Irish Rose* in the 1920s and with *Tobacco Road* in the 1930s, became too expensive an operation to be practical.

Producers could not afford to gamble on mediocre scripts in the hope that a profitable run would develop, and, as a result, most long-running plays produced since 1950 were better written than those which critics had called "claptrap" in the 1910s. Several comedies, however, which sustained long runs in spite of hackneyed plots, owed their popular success to pre-sold theater parties, a practice which grew steadily in the 1950s. By allowing groups to buy out an entire performance and then resell the tickets to raise funds for charities, schools, etc., astute managers were able to break even or at least to recover some of their production costs, even if the critics wrote poor reviews. Theater parties did not necessarily insure long runs, for if the play did not appeal to audiences, box office sales were almost negligible, and as soon as the pre-sold performances were over, the managers closed the show.

The heavy advance theater party sales for *The World of Suzie Wong,* produced in 1958, insured the management of capacity houses for several months. When the theater parties ended and attendance began to drop, the management resorted to two-for-one tickets and the play continued to near-capacity houses but with lower box office receipts until it established a run of 501 performances. Interest in the show before the opening ran high. Paul Osborn had adapted the play from a best-selling novel by Richard Mason, and advance publicity capitalized on the public's familiarity with the title, if not with the story. As a matter of fact, a surprising number of theatergoers, for some odd reason, bought tickets because they thought *The World of Suzie Wong* would be a musical production.

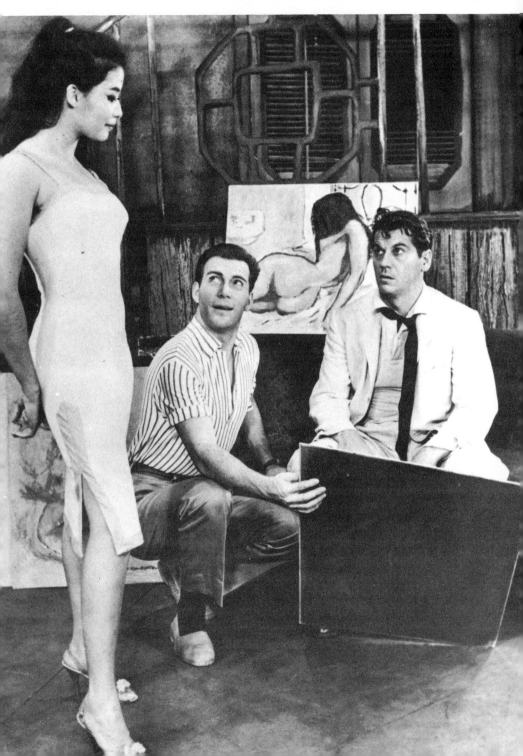

The World of Suzie Wong, France Nuyen, William Shatner and Ron Randell

Press agents issued frequent stories referring to the cast, with particular emphasis on the role of Suzie to be played by France Nuyen, a beautiful Eurasian actress who had appeared as Liat in the motion picture *South Pacific.*

The World of Suzie Wong opened to mixed criticisms ranging from "tender" to "tearjerker." Some critics linked the play with the early Belasco production of *Madame Butterfly;* others called it a modern version of *East Is West* because *The World of Suzie Wong* tells the love story of a Chinese girl and a white man, but the similarity in stories is slight. In *East Is West,* Ming Toy is a virtuous heroine; Suzie Wong is a prostitute in Hong Kong who spends most of her money to support her illegitimate child. Robert Lomax, a young painter, comes to Hong Kong, falls in love with Suzie, but does not have an affair with her. Suzie temporarily abandons soliciting to become the mistress of another white man, Ben Jeffcoat. After Ben leaves her and returns to his wife, more misfortunes befall Suzie. Her house collapses and her baby is killed in the ruins. The slight similarity between *The World of Suzie Wong* and *Madame Butterfly* is Ben's leaving Suzie as callously as Pinkerton leaves Cho-Cho-San. The basic difference is that audiences sympathize with Madame Butterfly because she really loved Pinkerton but have little sympathy for Suzie because she knows from the start that her affair with Jeffcoat is purely a commercial one and that she receives more money from being Jeffcoat's mistress than she did previously. At the final curtain, Lomax, reasonably confident that his paintings have commercial possibilities, plans to marry Suzie who, of course, has been in love with him all along.

The World of Suzie Wong also resembles other Belasco plays in heavy sentiment, with actors speaking unconvincing lines as stilted as the dialogue in *The Music Master.* The humor, too, is reminiscent of older plays but is more updated in its references to sex. A typical scene concerns the prostitute who starts to cry because she forgot to collect from her last customer. The hotel manager who rents rooms to the girls has a running gag when he consistently tells Lomax that he is not running a brothel because brothels are illegal in Hong Kong. Just as obvious is the sailor who stumbles into Lomax's room, finds Kay Fletcher, the nice girl who wants to marry Lomax, mistakes her for one of the prostitutes, and begins to take off his uniform. Suzie's jealousy of Kay piques her into making barbed comments, some of which are occasionally funny, about Kay and virgins. The comic scenes provide obvious humor but they are never too effective because they are not funny enough to build to a humorous climax, and the serious scenes are not tense enough to make audiences need the contrast of comic relief.

The World of Suzie Wong, however, resembled Belasco plays more directly in its technical production. Jo Mielziner's excellent sets entranced audiences. The street scene particularly, with its colorful banners, gaudy street decorations, and brilliant costumes, seemed to reproduce the authentic atmosphere of a crowded area in Hong Kong. One episode, a rainstorm, was so realistic that audiences almost felt the dampness.

Along with the technical production, the Oriental setting and cast gave *The World of Suzie Wong* further popular appeal. In 1958, Broadway had two other long-running plays with Oriental casts. The Rodgers and Hammerstein musical *Flower Drum Song* dealt with a Chinese family and included an almost entirely Oriental cast. Leonard Spigelgass' *A Majority of One* concerned a Japanese business magnate whose household servants were played by Orientals.

France Nuyen as Suzie helped account for some of the play's popularity. Critics referred to her loveliness; audiences were familiar with her performance in the motion picture *South Pacific;* and during the run of *The World of Suzie Wong,* columnists kept linking her name with that of Marlon Brando. The principal factors which kept *The World of Suzie Wong* running on Broadway for fifteen months, nevertheless, were the combination of pre-sold theater parties and the subsequent use of two-for-one tickets.

Anniversary Waltz, by Jerome Chodorov and Joseph Fields, produced in 1954, drew mixed notices, some better than the reviews for *The World of Suzie Wong,* others far worse. In plot and characterization, *Anniversary Waltz* has little to raise it above the level of mediocrity. It is more literate and perhaps funnier than such comedies as *Separate Rooms* or *Kiki,* but it is less entertaining than *My Sister Eileen* or *Junior Miss,* the two earlier, long-running comedies written by Fields and Chodorov.

Anniversary Waltz tells the story of Bud and Alice Walters, who are celebrating their fifteenth wedding anniversary. Bud gets drunk and tells Alice's parents that he and Alice had lived together before the wedding. The Walters children overhear the conversation; and when Debbie, the thirteen-year-old daughter, appears on a TV program, "Juvenile Jury," she blurts out the truth about her parents. The station goes dead for a moment and a new program comes on, but not before Bud loses his temper and kicks the TV screen. Bud walks out on his wife and family, stays away for a week, and then returns very penitent only to find that Alice is ready to walk out on him. The play ends on an obvious but totally unsatisfactory reconciliation when Alice learns she is pregnant. An analytical audience leaves the theater discontented, for Fields and Chodorov have written the play as though the Walters lived in an isolated world. They leave unanswered the question of how the friends of the Walters family will react to the TV announcement or how the Walters will live down the story. The writers have contrived, however, to make Bud, who has severed connections with his business partner, return to the firm because the partner knows he needs Bud's help to sell a large advertising account.

Most of the humor is based on Bud's violent temper, his dislike for television, and his insistence that he will not have a TV set in the house. In Act I, Alice's parents send a set as an anniversary gift. At the end of the act, after Bud has upset Alice's parents with the story of the premarital relationship, Alice refuses to come to bed and sits down to watch the late show. Infuriated, Bud rushes over, kicks the set, and ruins it. In Act II, Bud's partner sends a second set, and again, when Bud hears Debbie on the program, he rushes over, kicks the set, and demolishes it. In Act III, Bud sends Alice a third set in atonement for his actions. The audience is somewhat surprised when the play ends without Bud's losing his temper and kicking the screen once more. In another outburst of temper, Bud breaks down the bedroom door Alice has locked, but this off-stage action seems anticlimactic to his capers with the TV screens. When Debbie comes home from the television studio and Bud is ready to whale some sense into her, Alice and her parents interfere and defend Debbie, even to the point where Alice delivers an ultimatum that if Bud doesn't leave Debbie alone, she and the children will leave the house. This edict enrages Bud sufficiently to make him reverse the situation by walking out on his family. The whole episode may seem well contrived, but most men in the audience would sympathize with Bud and would probably have the same desire to beat some sense into the whole family.

That *Anniversary Waltz* achieved a run of 615 performances cannot be credited to rave notices. One or two favorable reviews called the play "witty," "at last the theater has good reason to be thankful for television," and "ecstatically funny," but, on the whole, the reviews were negative and referred to the play as "mechanical" and "repetitious."

To its advantage, the play had expert performances by Kitty Carlisle, making one of her infrequent appearances on Broadway, as Alice, and by MacDonald Carey, a popular leading man in the movies, as Bud. Even if the television gags became repetitious, they did present a timely satire, for *Anniversary Waltz* was one of the few commercial successes produced in the 1953–1954 theatrical season and was one of the first plays to ridicule television productions successfully. Brooks Atkinson said, "Maybe it supplies the needs of the times." In that respect, it did fill a niche, for it gave audiences the opportunity to attend the theater in a season when only a dozen or so productions managed to stem the tide of rising prices and poorer productions. But as a play written by experienced dramatists, *Anniversary Waltz* was a distinct disappointment and is now an outdated comedy.

Neil Simon's *Come Blow Your Horn*, produced in 1961, owes its success indirectly to television, for Mr. Simon's experience writing TV routines for Sid Caesar, Phil Silvers, Garry Moore, and other stars undoubtedly helped him create one of the most popular comedies produced in the 1960–1961 season. Although the gross receipts listed in *Variety* indicate that *Come Blow Your Horn* did not draw capacity houses for much of the run, the play earned a substantial profit and ran well over a year before the management used two-for-one tickets to bolster the box office receipts. Some critics called the comedy "old-fashioned" or "not much of a play," but most of them admitted it had quite a few humorous moments. One critic even prophesied correctly that *Come Blow Your Horn* might well turn out to be the surprise hit of the season. Audiences seeking entertainment, and not a drama with a serious message, found the play highly diverting.

The story deals with Mr. Baker, a glass fruit manufacturer, whose older son, Alan, has set up a bachelor apartment to avoid parental interference with his playboy activities. As the play opens, Alan's younger brother Buddy decides to move in with him. Instead of objecting to this invasion of privacy, Alan welcomes Buddy and even gets him a date with one of the girls in the same building. By the third act, Buddy has become a carbon copy of Alan, and Mrs. Baker has threatened to leave her husband and move in with the boys. Alan has fallen in love with a nice girl whom he wants to marry and has become disgusted with Buddy's Bohemian adventures. Mr. Baker is ready to throw both boys out of the business but changes his mind when Alan gets two excellent orders for the firm and introduces his father to his fiancée, who knows how to manage both father and son.

The slight plot is secondary to the characterizations and dialogue filled with obvious jokes and repetitive gags. For example, Mr. Baker calls Alan a bum. When Alan asks, "Why am I a bum?" Mr. Baker says, "Are you married?" Alan says, "No," and his father says, "Then you're a bum." From then on, the reference to bum becomes a running gag. There is no denying that the play is contrived. Things work out too smoothly in the last act. Mama and Papa reconcile, and Papa even forgives his sons when the big orders come in, but the play does provide excellent entertainment. It makes no pretense of being anything but an amusing comedy sprinkled with funny lines and situations, and unlike *Anniversary Waltz,* leaves no questions about possible outcomes unanswered.

Although the family name is Baker and the characters speak with no particular accent, the audience knows the story deals with a Jewish family blustering its way through arguments and confusion. Papa Baker fancies himself to be an abused man when he is, in reality, a domineering husband and father. He refuses to listen to arguments, delivers ultimatums which the audience knows will not be carried out, and plays most of his scenes in a mood of resigned anger. Mama Baker, in spite of her whining and fussing, is a more sympathetic character. She is constantly worrying over the quarrels between her husband and sons and has a running gag line of her own, "I'm nauseous." Her funniest scene comes in the second act when she tries taking telephone messages and gets them confused. Mama answers the phone, then asks the person to wait while she hunts frantically for a pencil she can't find, and then asks the man to speak quickly so that she can write the message down as soon as she hangs up before she forgets it. The call has been from a buyer who wants to cancel a pickup date Alan has arranged because his wife is coming into town. Mama starts to hunt for a pencil and mumbles, "They don't have Alka-Seltzer, they're gonna have a pencil?" Before she can find a pencil, the phone rings again. The girl whom Alan has asked to meet the buyer is calling because she has forgotten the name of the hotel. Mama gets the message confused, gives the girl the name of the hotel, and hangs up. Again Mama starts looking for the pencil and again the phone rings. Alan is calling to ask if anyone has tried to reach him, but by this time, Mama has forgotten the first two messages. The audience, having heard all three calls, knows that nothing but confusion will result, but the anticipation of trouble is only half the fun, for Mama's routine is the equivalent of a riotous vaudeville or television monologue.

Alan is the least colorful of the three principal characters but is amusing as the sophisticated Manhattanite who reforms when he sees Buddy going through the same phase of sowing wild oats. In the third act, Alan has decided to marry Connie Dayton; and as the entire family leaves the apartment, clearing the way for Buddy to have a rendezvous with a weird character he has met in Greenwich Village, Alan's parting line is a repetition of the running gag, "So long, bum."

Excellent performances by the original cast made the principal roles highly diverting. Audiences enjoyed Lou Jacobi's performances as the irate father, particularly when the outraged Mr. Baker refused to speak to his sons and talked about them as though they were not in the room. When Buddy tried to plead with his father and touched his arm, Lou Jacobi delighted audiences as he said with indignant surprise, "A father you're shoving?" Pert Kelton regaled audiences as the anxious mother without resorting to Jewish mannerisms or dialect, especially in the telephone scene. Hal March, who romped through the playboy role for most of the long run, made Alan a likable character in spite of his philanderings in the first two acts. March's established reputation as a television star also helped at the box office. During the Broadway run, the astute management kept public interest aroused by running clever cartoon advertisements in most of the newspapers and varied the ads from week to week to call attention to the type of gag lines which were to entertain audiences at *Come Blow Your Horn* for 677 performances.

Sylvia Regan's *The Fifth Season,* produced in 1953, was just as contrived as *Come Blow Your Horn* and was even more localized in setting. Miss Regan's play, which dealt with the garment industry in New York, owed its popular success to Menasha Skulnik, a popular star in the Yiddish theater, who appeared as Max Pincus, half the firm of Goodman and Pincus, a wholesale dress company. Critics thought little of the comedy but enjoyed Skulnik enough to predict that his entertaining performance would keep the show running.

In the first act, business is at a low ebb for Goodman and Pincus until Lorraine, the head model, induces Miles Lewis, a prominent store owner, to visit the shop and buy a line of dresses. Mr. Lewis, however, is more interested in the models than in the merchandise and runs up a fabulous bill which puts Pincus and Goodman on the verge of bankruptcy. In the meantime, Johnny Goodman has become involved in an affair with Lorraine, has alienated his son, and has almost lost his wife, who is determined to get a Reno divorce. To salvage the business as well as the personal life of his partner, Pincus tries to convince Mrs. Goodman that he, and not Johnny, has been having the affair with Lorraine. Pincus is also ready to marry Mrs. Klein, a wealthy widow, whom he hopes will invest enough money to keep the firm solvent. At the last minute, the partners get the upper hand over Mr. Lewis, who pays his back debts and promises to buy more dresses at much better terms for Goodman and Pincus if they do not tell his wife about his escapades; the Goodmans reconcile; a new customer is on his way to buy a complete new line; and Max Pincus is free to marry Miriam Oppenheimer, the bookkeeper.

In the script, the two partners have roles of approximately equal length, but Pincus has the best lines. At times his dialogue seems rather prosaic, particularly when Pincus says to Johnny, "I thought we were friends. Now I see we're not friends—we're just friends," but as Skulnik emphasized the words with his own peculiar intonations and gestures, they became very funny. Pincus also has five out of six curtain lines which depended upon Skulnik for their humor. For example, Pincus says that when he got into the elevator and the operator asked him where he was going, he said, "When you are down, where else can you go but up?" It is possible to visualize the humor if the line is read aloud with the proper inflection at the end of the sentence. The curtain line in Act II, however, requires more than mere vocal inflection to be humorous. Johnny has called Lorraine for a date instead of calling his wife. The next morning, Mrs. Goodman berates Johnny and walks out. Johnny asks, "Pinkie, what did I do?" and Pincus answers with the tag line of a popular Yiddish joke, "Johnny, did you call a wrong number." To some audiences the joke falls flat, for the line means nothing without the build-up. To audiences aware of any variation of the joke, however, the line is doubly effective, for it is the punch line in the story of the very dignified woman who makes a phone call and asks to speak to a member of the New York Social Register. In some variations it is New England Society or the British nobility; one version even referred to the White House. To the woman's dismay, she hears a feminine voice with a decidedly heavy Yiddish accent say, "Oi, lady, did you call a wrong number!"

In New York, the play appealed to audiences familiar with the locale, for the Broadway theater area is adjacent to the garment center which runs along Seventh Avenue. The characters, the business transactions, and the idiomatic dialogue meant more to Broadwayites than it did to out-of-town theatergoers. The title, for instance, is an old standby in the garment industry and refers to the off-season, or, as one character explains, for the benefit of the audience, in the garment industry there are five seasons—spring, summer, winter, fall, and slack.

Skulnik, of course, was the biggest draw for audiences that had seen him in the Yiddish theater as well as for Broadway theatergoers who knew him by reputation but who had never seen him perform on the English-speaking stage. The role of Max Pincus admirably suited his talents. He was entertaining when he acted worried, when he played the bashful suitor, and when he uttered such ridiculous lines as, "I know bookkeepers who don't know three times eight is twenty-five," and made them sound plausible, or when he explained why he preferred not to marry the twice-widowed Mrs. Klein because she took him to the cemetery to show him the graves of her first two husbands.

The plot of *The Fifth Season* was hackneyed, but Skulnik's performance, the inclusion of new styles in a brief fashion show, and the localized interest in the garment industry had enough popular appeal to entertain New York audiences for 654 performances.

Although Leonard Spigelgass' *A Majority of One,* produced in 1959, has better-written dialogue than *The Fifth Season* or *Anniversary Waltz,* it probably will never be designated as one of the literary plays of the 1950s, for it presents an almost unbelievable story made plausible by the ingratiating performances of Gertrude Berg and Sir Cedric Hardwicke. The plot, at first glance, seems utterly ridiculous. Mrs. Jacoby, a Jewish widow from Brooklyn, goes to Japan with her daughter and son-in-law, a member of the United States Diplomatic Service. While on shipboard, she meets Mr. Asano, a Japanese merchant to whom she is aloof because her son has been killed by the Japanese during the war. When Mr. Asano tells her that both his son and daughter have also been war victims, she is less hostile and soon becomes quite amiable with Mr. Asano. Her son-in-law, Jerome Black, thinks Mr. Asano is being friendly in order to get Mrs. Jacoby to intercede for him in a trade agreement which the United States is trying to arrange with Japan. At her daughter's suggestion, Mrs. Jacoby stops seeing Mr. Asano, but when the mission in Japan fails, primarily because Mr. Asano seems to dislike Jerome, Mrs. Jacoby visits Mr. Asano. In a very delightful scene, she renews her friendship, gets a little drunk on saki, makes a simple suggestion which Mr. Asano says may be a valuable signpost for making Jerome's mission a success, and even gets a proposal of marriage. Mrs. Jacoby's children are distressed not only over her visit but also over the possibility of such an impractical marriage, even though Mrs. Jacoby does not accept the proposal. After Jerome receives word that negotiations with Mr. Asano will be resumed the following morning, the Blacks are contrite and plead with Mrs. Jacoby to stay in Japan, but she is determined to return to Brooklyn. In the last act, Mr. Asano comes back to New York as a delegate to the United Nations and visits Mrs. Jacoby. At the final curtain, there is every indication that Mrs. Jacoby and Mr. Asano will solve the problems that impede their marriage.

Even though the plot seems farfetched, the play is neither ridiculous nor absurd. Audiences may never believe that such a romance could develop, but they never lose interest in the story nor in its basic plea for tolerance. A Brooklyn widow, very much like Mrs. Jacoby, when asked how she liked the play, said, "To me it could never happen, but it would be nice if it did." Her attitude may not be typical, but it does illustrate the persuasive powers of Gertrude Berg and Sir Cedric Hardwicke to make even skeptical audiences almost hope for a happy ending.

Some critics have called *A Majority of One* a modern version of *Abie's Irish Rose,* but the mixed religious background is the only similarity of the plays. *Abie's Irish Rose* lampoons the entire problem of mixed marriages; *A Majority of One* presents the problem seriously. Spigelgass never ridicules the religious ceremonies or foreign expressions he inserts into the action. Mr. Asano, for example, explains the Japanese rituals in his home to Mrs. Jacoby; but at the same time, he also makes certain that the food he serves her is prepared in accordance with Jewish dietary laws. In the third act, Mrs. Jacoby blesses her candles on Friday night and then explains to Mr. Asano what her prayer signifies. Since each character tries to understand the customs and even the vocabulary of the other, the play gets the same reaction from audiences, who develop a better understanding of both characters. Mr. Asano asks why Mrs. Jacoby has referred to herself as *mishugeh,* which he pronounces "My sug-ah." Jerome explains that the Yiddish word means scatterbrained, and Mr. Asano says that if Mrs. Jacoby is "my sug-ah," it is a delightful thing to be. On the other hand, Mrs. Jacoby learns the Japanese word *nakado,* meaning marriage broker, and from then on uses it instead of the Yiddish word *shadchun.* At the end of the play, Mrs. Jacoby raises her wine glass and toasts Mr. Asano with the Japanese word *Kompai,* and he responds with the Hebrew *L'Chaim.* It is this mutual respect, this attempt to appreciate another mode of living, which gives the play its appeal, for audiences, aware of the implausibility of the marriage, are interested in seeing how two charming people with different religious backgrounds attempt to find mutual understanding.

A basic principle in argumentation is to admit the logic of the opposition rather than try to disprove it with false reasoning. In *A Majority of One,* the marriage between Mrs. Jacoby and Mr. Asano is obviously impractical, but instead of forcing the plausibility of such a marriage on audiences without adequate preparation, Spigelgass has Mr. Asano tell Mrs. Jacoby's family their objections are very reasonable but adds that he could give them arguments against the marriage which they had not even considered. He then enumerates further reasons why such a marriage should never take place. This reverse psychology eliminates any chance of the audience's thinking, "But it couldn't work," for once Spigelgass has established the validity of the opposition, he proceeds to develop the affection Mrs. Jacoby and Mr. Asano have for each other and suggests that they might possibly work out their problems. The play, therefore, becomes a variation of the popular *Romeo and Juliet* family feud situation as well as a variation of the Spewacks' popular formula, boy-meets-girl.

Most of the humor depends upon the stars' performances, but there are funny lines which gain effectiveness through repetition. For example, early in the play, when Mrs. Jacoby talks about the motion picture *The Law and Jake Wade,* with Robert Taylor, she says, "I think Robert Taylor is Jewish," which brings a laugh from the audience primarily because of Miss Berg's twinkle and knowing look. But in the next act, the Japanese houseboy talks about the same picture and says, "You know, Jacoby-san, I think Robert Taylor Japanese," which brings an even bigger laugh, aided, of course, by Mrs. Jacoby's startled look.

The principal reason for the play's popularity, however, is that it provided Gertrude Berg with a tour de force that enabled her to indulge in the type of dialogue and situation which made her radio program "The Goldbergs" a popular favorite for years. Mrs. Jacoby does not look out the window, as Molly Goldberg did, and shout, "Yoo-hoo, Mrs. Bloom," but she does indulge in Molly's habit of giving advice whether anyone asks her for it or not. She says to Essie, the neighbor, who has been experimenting with filter-tip cigarettes, "The best filter tip is—don't smoke." When Mrs. Jacoby returns from her visit to Mr. Asano's home and her daughter keeps plying her with questions, Mrs. Jacoby insists upon talking about the dinner. Alice says impatiently, "Mama, we're not interested in the menu," and Mrs. Jacoby says just as firmly, and in typical Molly Goldberg tradition, "If you want to hear the rest, you have to hear the menu." *A Majority of One* also gives Gertrude Berg the chance to indulge in Molly-type philosophical stories. When she tells Mr. Asano a long-winded, homespun yarn about covering a couch and finally twists the story to explain how the same principle would help Mr. Asano's business, he is impressed and tells her she may have given him the clue which will improve diplomatic relations between Japanese and United States industries. Again, this sounds farfetched in synopsis, but as Gertrude Berg tells the story, she makes it convincing enough not only to impress Mr. Asano but also the audience. Finally, in almost every play, Miss Berg usually has one scene which permits her to be indignant, to reprimand someone, and to emerge triumphant. *A Majority of One* is no exception, for at the end of the second act, she scolds Alice and Jerome, tells them that in spite of their talk about prejudice and tolerance, they are far more bigoted than they suspect, and then proves she is a better diplomat than Jerome by showing that she has arranged for Mr. Asano to reopen negotiations.

Miss Berg's tour de force on its own would not have carried the play without the excellent costarring performance of Sir Cedric Hardwicke. He made the almost impossible role of Mr. Asano believable, provided the proper reserve to contrast with Miss Berg's warm, almost effervescent personality, and helped make the romance credible. With less ingratiating performers, *A Majority of One* might have meant little at the box office, for Orthodox Jewry could well have been opposed to the story of intermarriage, particularly with an Oriental, and American families with war casualties might have been just as opposed to presenting the Japanese in a favorable light, but Miss Berg and Sir Cedric Hardwicke made audiences willing to overlook their prejudices, if only for one evening, and kept the play running for 556 performances.

Casting Rosalind Russell as Mrs. Jacoby in the motion picture version of *A Majority of One* astonished a great many people, both in and out of show business, who had expected Gertrude Berg to appear in the film and who also thought Rosalind Russell would not be convincing as a Jewish woman from Brooklyn. Miss Russell surprised the critics with her competent performance. No one was surprised, however, when Rosalind Russell starred in the stage version of *Auntie Mame*, produced in 1956. When the book first appeared, most readers agreed that the story was ideal for Miss Russell either as a motion picture or as a play. The Jerome Lawrence and Robert E. Lee adaptation of Patrick Dennis' novel proved to be a tour de force that capitalized on Miss Russell's ability as a comedienne and provided her with the opportunity to be involved in impossible farce situations, to wear a variety of costumes that made the play virtually a one-woman fashion show, and to hurl barbed innuendoes and vicious jibes at breakneck speed in almost every sequence. The novel carried Auntie Mame through a series of adventures that ranged from the very farcical and the burlesque to episodes tinged with seriousness. In the play, Lawrence and Lee unified the adventures and made Mame a warm, sympathetic woman in spite of her hilarious antics.

Both the novel and the play tell the story of Mame Dennis, whose brother has died and has left his son in her custody. He also has designated the Knickerbocker Bank as trustee to make certain Mame raises Patrick according to the terms specified in his will, and Mr. Babcock, the bank's representative, soon places young Patrick in a private school where he will be away from her influence. Mame loses her money in the stock market crash of 1929 but regains a fortune when she marries Beauregard Pickett Burnside, a Southern oil magnate. For a while Mame finds happiness traveling around the world with Beauregard, but on one of their European tours, they climb the Matterhorn, and Beauregard, a camera fiend, insists upon climbing higher and higher to get a better camera shot of Mame, and falls off. Two years later, the widowed Mame returns to find that Lindsay Woolsey, a publisher, is maneuvering to have her write her memoirs and has hired Agnes Gooch, a mousey but efficient stenographer, and Brian O'Bannion, an amorous Irish poet, to assist her. Mame gets rid of O'Bannion, but not before he has seduced Agnes. When Patrick, who has developed into a conceited prig, introduces Mame to his fiancée, Gloria Upson, a snob from Connecticut, Mame instantly dislikes her. After she meets Gloria's parents, Mame strategically plans a dinner party for the Upsons, to which she invites Vera Charles, a famous actress, as well as other characters who have drifted in and out of Patrick's life. Just before dinner, Woolsey arrives with galley proofs for Mame's memoirs, and everyone except the Upsons becomes engrossed in the manuscript. Patrick, leafing through the galleys, is surprised to find that he is a principal character in the book and says he has forgotten about the number of times he unzipped Vera and put her to bed when she was drunk. The outraged Upsons are even more furious when Woolsey announces that Mame is donating all book royalties to establish a home for Jewish refugees which will border on the Upson estate, a very restricted area in Connecticut. To the surprise of no one in the audience, Gloria breaks the engagement. In the final scene, Patrick and his wife, Pegeen, an interior decorator Mame had hired to refurnish her apartment before the Upson dinner, bring their son Michael to see Mame. Before the scene ends, Mame is charming Michael with stories of the Orient, is preparing to take him abroad with her, and is talking to him just as she did to Patrick in Act I. When the curtains close on *Auntie Mame,* the audience feels, just as it did at the final curtain of *I Remember Mama,* as though the play were beginning all over again.

In the novel, Mame is a bizarre woman whose affection for young Patrick is, at times, just another passing phase. By eliminating some of the ludicrous episodes in the adaptation, Lawrence and Lee have strengthened the characterization so that Mame wins audience sympathy almost from the start. Her attachment for Patrick begins raucously but deepens as the first act develops. After Mame loses her money in the stock market, she gets a walk-on role in a very bad play starring Vera Charles, but she wears bracelets that jangle every time she moves her arms, and her tintinnabulous gestures ruin the scene. Immediately after the performance the entire cast deserts her and she is sitting alone on stage when Patrick appears and gallantly tells Auntie Mame he thought she was wonderful. Then, emulating the dialogue in the play, he calls her Lady Iris, asks to escort her home, and offers her his arm. Auntie Mame responds with "Chahmed, Lord Dudley," and hugs him. This scene gives added impact to a later episode when Patrick, realizing that Mame has saved him from making a fool of himself by marrying Gloria, says, "Thank you, Lady Iris," and Mame answers, "Chahmed, Lord Dudley."

Most of Mame's dialogue is brittle and hilarious, such as her curtain line in the Macy department store episode after she has been fired. As she leaves the stage, she calls out to Beauregard, who wants to buy two dozen pairs of roller skates, "Get 'em at Gimbels." Several of Mame's pointed remarks, however, have serious undertones. Gloria tells Mame the Upsons live in the most restricted community in Connecticut, and Mame says, "I'll get a blood test." When Mame breaks up the engagement and Mr. Babcock tells her she has ruined his plans for Patrick's future, she says, "I doubt very much that

Patrick will allow you to . . . make him an Aryan from Darien!—
and marry him off to a girl with *braces on her brains!"*

The play was definitely a tour de force for Rosalind Russell, who
enchanted audiences as she zoomed through the role. The supporting cast, although excellent, was overshadowed by the frenetic
actions and dialogue of Auntie Mame. Peggy Cass, however, in
the brief role of Agnes Gooch, the drab secretary, made her presence felt the entire time she was on stage, and got a few raucous
laughs, particularly after her date with Brian, when she stumbled
into the house, her clothes disheveled, and yelled, "I've *lived*. Lived.
Now what do I do?"

After *Auntie Mame* had run about fifteen months, Greer Garson
took over the starring role and was in turn replaced by Beatrice
Lillie, but in spite of Miss Garson's charm and beauty, Miss Lillie's
talents as a comedienne, and both their excellent performances,
the initial success of the play belonged to Rosalind Russell, who
eventually starred in the motion picture. Her brittle performance,
the popularity of the novel, the fast-paced action, and the lavish
production—all helped *Auntie Mame* achieve a run of 639 performances.

Never Too Late, by Sumner Arthur Long, like *Auntie Mame,*
may never be called great drama, but it is good theater. It has not
been designated as one of the best plays of its season, but it did
regale audiences and kept moving at a fast pace.

According to the program notes, Mr. Long got the idea for his
play when he saw a middle-aged woman "obviously pregnant and
beaming about it." Mr. Long began wondering how her husband
had reacted when he first learned the news and decided he had the
basis for a plot. The play had a summer tryout at the Cape Playhouse in Dennis, Massachusetts, in July, 1962, with the title *Cradle
and All.* When the comedy opened on Broadway in November,
1962, the reviews were very favorable, although one or two dissenters used such terms as "creaky" and "popular." Perhaps the plot
does resemble the "popular fare" of the 1920s, but George Abbott
directed the contrived story to give it his usual fast-paced tempo.

The play becomes involved in mounting absurdities as it unfolds
the complications in the lives of Mr. and Mrs. Lambert when Mrs.
Lambert, a woman in her middle fifties, discovers she is going to
have a baby. It takes a bit of doing to reconcile her husband and

Never Too Late, Paul Ford and Maureen O'Sullivan

her married daughter to the idea, but Mrs. Lambert soon learns to handle both of them. In the first scene, she is little more than a household drudge, running up and down stairs, catering to her husband, her daughter, and her son-in-law. But once she learns about her condition, and, at the same time, finds that she need not be concerned about saving her husband's money because she discovers he is far wealthier than she had suspected, she goes on a spending spree beginning with frivolities and new clothes and branching out into remodeling the house by putting a bathroom on the first floor to save her from running up and down steps. The play becomes sheer farce when Mrs. Lambert, to her husband's dismay, arranges to buy lumber from a rival concern because she says they are offering her a better price than her husband's company. Mr. Lambert tries staying home to check on bills and stop some of the extravagances because, as he says, he makes more money by stopping it from going out faster than it is coming in.

As Mrs. Lambert revels in her new emancipation, her daughter is forced into becoming the household drudge and finds she no longer has time to make herself look presentable. Realizing that her husband is no longer attentive, she decides to make him aware of her presence, calls him at work, says, "Charlie, go to hell," and hangs up. She explains to her mother that for the rest of the day Charlie will be thinking only of her. Mrs. Lambert thinks this is a good scheme, for she has had a squabble with her husband over expenses; so she, too, calls her husband, gives him the same treatment, and hangs up. In the third act, both men, completely upset by their wives' rebellion, have gone to a bar and come home drunk. Mr. Lambert antagonizes his neighbor, the mayor of the town, who threatens to give an important contract to a rival firm. Charlie is shrewd enough to pretend that he has been the troublemaker, patches up all differences with the mayor, and saves his father-in-law's business. Mr. Lambert then gives Charlie a better interest in the firm, agrees to hire a servant, and all ends happily for everyone concerned.

The plot embodies variations of two popular dramatic situations. The first, the triumphant woman, gets a novel twist, for Mrs. Lambert capitalizes on her pregnancy to get whatever she wants. In the first act, when her husband balks at her extravagances, she feigns dizziness or sick spells and emerges triumphant. Later, when her

husband is less docile, she follows her daughter's example and re-
bels. But regardless of the situation, after the first scene, Mrs. Lambert triumphs at all times. This pleases the women in the audience
and does not seem to antagonize the men.

The second popular situation, the obstacles to love, also has a
novel approach, for the play deals with two romances that are not
variations of the boy-meets-girl theme. Middle-aged people who
have not shared the Lamberts' experience in preparing for a new
baby still understand their arguments, their problems, and their
reconciliations. The troubles of the son-in-law and his wife have
equal popular appeal for the young married couples in the audience
who readily understand the arguments about having a family and
the difficulties in getting along with the in-laws. Most of the audience may sympathize with the older Lamberts, but the problems
of the younger couple have enough universality to be amusing to
the middle-aged and to be extremely convincing to younger people,
thus giving *Never Too Late* audience appeal for two different age
groups.

In spite of the popular dramatic situations, the success of the
play depended a great deal upon the excellent performances of
Paul Ford, Maureen O'Sullivan, and Orson Bean to save it from
lapsing into absurdity. Audiences who remembered seeing Paul
Ford as the somewhat thickheaded, opinionated officer in *The Teahouse of the August Moon* found the role of Mr. Lambert somewhat
similar. In both comedies, Ford managed to play an unsympathetic
character sympathetically so that audiences, by the end of the last
act, felt at least a little sorry for him. Ford was convincing in showing how difficult it would be for a middle-aged man with a married
daughter suddenly to find that he is to be a father again, that his
wife is remodeling his home, and that money he has saved for years
is suddenly being spent on the type of luxury which he has never
wanted. And yet the fact that he loves his wife is always evident.
When Maureen O'Sullivan appeared wearing a ridiculous-looking
hat, Paul Ford stared at the hat disapprovingly but said nothing.
And when Miss O'Sullivan said, "You don't like it," he didn't say
yes or no but, "Keep it anyway." His resignation was the same for
almost all of the bills which she ran up.

Miss O'Sullivan made the wife more realistic than a mere silly
spendthrift. As the woman in her early fifties, she was dowdy in the

first scene and wore a hair style that added years to her appearance, but she emerged as a middle-aged beauty after she learned about her pregnancy, and, as the play progressed, she became more sprightly and more youthful in her actions, if not entirely in her appearance. Miss O'Sullivan endowed the role with the proper loveliness, made the glowing, expectant mother perfectly convincing, and got sympathetic response from all women in the audience, who approved of her extravagances. She even made the slight silliness of Mrs. Lambert's business transactions seem plausible rather than farcical and acted as a perfect buffer between her husband and her son-in-law.

Charlie, as played by Orson Bean, was not merely a wisecracking son-in-law who triumphed in the last act. Instead, Bean made Charlie a likable young man, somewhat confused, who emerged in the final scene as a sensible son-in-law who made Mr. Lambert realize he did have executive ability and was able to make decisions. Bean's experience as a comedian made him the ideal foil for the Lamberts and gave him the opportunity to deliver ridiculous lines with perfect timing to get some of the biggest laughs in the show.

Even though *Never Too Late* is "popular fare," it is more believable than such an absurd farce as *Anniversary Waltz,* is less contrived than *Come Blow Your Horn,* and is not restricted in locale as *The Fifth Season.* Above all, it proves that a large segment of the theatergoing public in the 1960s still wants pure entertainment. *Never Too Late* epitomizes this type of popular fare in that it combines a light story, excellent performances, and popular situations. Its sole purpose is to entertain, and audiences find that it gives them a relaxing evening in the theater, the chance to laugh at absurdity, a play with no serious message, and a story they can forget as soon as they leave the theater.

Theater columnists credited the excellent business on Broadway during the summer of 1964 to the New York World's Fair. In fact, the number of productions playing during the summer was greater than it had been in years. *Never Too Late* profited from this influx of visitors, for it appealed to people who wanted a relaxing evening in the theater. At the close of the Fair in 1964, *Never Too Late* continued drawing audiences with Dennis O'Keefe, Martha Scott, and Will Hutchins as replacements for Paul Ford, Maureen O'Sullivan, and Orson Bean. When box office receipts began to drop, the management resorted to two-tickets-for-one. In the spring of 1965, Arthur Godfrey replaced Dennis O'Keefe, and Maureen O'Sullivan returned to play her original role. The management, anticipating drawing power from the new cast, eliminated the two-tickets-for-one, but gross receipts did not increase. Any hope of keeping the show running through the 1965 Fair season was abandoned, and the production closed April 24, 1965, with a total of 1,007 performances.

Barefoot in the Park and *Any Wednesday* also profited from visitors to the World's Fair in 1964. Reports from the road tryouts indicated that *Any Wednesday*, by Muriel Resnik, might be successful, but skeptics considered the leading man's withdrawal from the cast before the New York opening as a sign of trouble. When the play opened on Broadway February 18, 1964, with Sandy Dennis and Don Porter, however, it became an instant hit.

The slight story deals with Ellen Gordon, a curious combination of childlike innocence and worldly sophistication. Ellen is the mistress of John Cleves, a prominent tycoon who has a rendezvous with her every Wednesday in her out-of-town apartment. Cleves connives to make as many expenditures as possible tax-exempt. On Ellen's birthday he gives her a diamond necklace with the initials of his company attached, thus making it a deductible item. He has even set up Ellen's apartment as business property charged to his firm.

Into this love nest stumbles Cass Henderson searching for Cleves. Henderson, who got the address from Cleves's new secretary, soon becomes aware of Ellen's relationship with Cleves. He tricks Ellen into allowing him to stay, but when Mrs. Cleves arrives, also having learned the address from Cleves's secretary, Henderson pretends to be Ellen's husband, hoping this deception will make Cleves agree to a business proposition. Mrs. Cleves insists that the young couple have dinner with her and her husband, and when they all return to Ellen's apartment, the atmosphere is tense. They try playing a few parlor games, but Cleves is a poor sport. His wife tries to smooth over the difficult moments; and Ellen makes a slip which gives Mrs. Cleves a clue to her husband's infidelity. She leaves the apartment but returns unexpectedly, discovers that her suspicions are correct, and is ready to get a divorce so that Cleves may marry Ellen.

In the last act, Ellen is unhappy over the prospect of her marriage. Mrs. Cleves, on the other hand, seems quite radiant. When she is alone with her husband and says she will take over Ellen's apartment, Cleves shows renewed interest in his wife. She suggests that he might call on her any Wednesday, just as he has done with Ellen.

Cleves, however, loses not only his wife but also his mistress, for Ellen decides not to go through with the marriage. She has also rejected Henderson's proposal of marriage. Finally the remorseful Ellen calls Henderson at his hotel and leaves a message that she hopes will bring him back. Henderson does not get the message, for he is already knocking at the door, ready to propose again and to give the play a happy ending.

With only one set and four characters, the play acquires an intimacy that would make any additional visitor to this love nest an intruder. Although Cleves's secretary never appears, nor is her voice heard on the telephone, the constant references to her errors in sending both Henderson and Mrs. Cleves to the hideaway apartment, as well as Cleves's exasperation as he growls to her on the phone, makes her almost as real as if she were on stage.

The popular appeal is not inherent in the basic plot, for audiences could readily dislike three of the characters. Ellen, in spite of her charm, is immoral; Henderson, although likable, is a willing conniver who would help deceive Mrs. Cleves; and Cleves is selfish, ruthless, and unfaithful. The only sympathetic character should be Mrs. Cleves, the long-suffering wife, for she is an attractive, urbane woman who has devoted her life to keeping her husband contented and to running her household properly. Yet what might have been a mildly amusing comedy with unsympathetic characters emerges as a delightful comedy that never loses interest because the characters are intriguing. Ellen is not the typical mistress nor is she an aging Lolita. Instead, she is a somewhat ridiculous and yet naïvely appealing young girl caught in the mesh of a romance with a glamorous older man. In the last act, the audience knows that Ellen and Mrs. Cleves have been treated shabbily. The audience's growing dislike for Cleves produces a growing empathy for the women. The fact that the mistress and the wife desert Cleves gives the play further audience appeal by illustrating the popular situation of not only one but two triumphant women. Moreover, Ellen's decision to marry Cass Henderson is not unexpected. In the second act, when Henderson watches Cleves playing the games, he reacts more kindly toward Ellen, and the audience begins to realize that he is a wholesome, sentimental young man. In the last act, when Ellen lies down on the couch, puts her head in Henderson's lap, and sobs out her dismal love story, the audience anticipates that Ellen would be far happier with Henderson than with Cleves. Even when Ellen sends Henderson away, the audience suspects he will return. And the final curtain comes down on the right touch of romance that almost makes the audience forget the overtones of immorality that have dominated the plot.

Perhaps the popular appeal of the triumphant woman, as well as the frothiness of the plot which, in past years, would have been called "typical summer entertainment," attracted World's Fair visitors, but *Any Wednesday* kept running after the Fair had closed and spanned another theatrical season. Sandy Dennis' performance as Ellen undoubtedly helped the original box office impetus, for she received glowing reviews from the critics. She also won the Tony Award, the *Variety* Critics' Poll, and the approving nod of Henry Hewes, editor of *Best Plays*. Before the end of the season, however, *Variety* printed a second review, this time not so kindly disposed toward Miss Dennis. At this writing, Barbara Cook has replaced Miss Dennis and the play is still doing profitable business, although not playing to capacity houses.

Ellen and Corie, the madcap young wife in Neil Simon's *Barefoot in the Park,* are very much alike, for both heroines are pixies, rather immature and amusing. *Barefoot in the Park* opened October 23, 1963, and became one of the biggest sellout shows of the season.

The plot is a slight variation of the boy-meets-girl formula in that boy gets wife, boy loses wife, boy gets wife. In the first act, Corie and Paul Bratter, newlyweds, move into a sixth-floor walkup apartment after a six-day honeymoon, and trouble seems imminent. The apartment is bare, the skylight has a broken pane which seems obvious only to the audience, and the radiator is not working. Corie has selected the apartment without showing it to Paul, and when he staggers in, breathless from his long climb up the stairs, he cannot work up any enthusiasm for the four walls. The bedroom is merely a large closet with no room for a clothes rack, and the bathroom has only a shower. Paul would rather have a tub. Corie's mother, Mrs. Banks, soon arrives, and she, too, staggers into the apartment almost in a daze. Like Paul, she is bewildered by the lack of conveniences, but she offers no adverse criticism. Paul goes out to buy liquor, and when he returns, Mrs. Banks is ready to leave but promises to come to dinner on Friday evening. Paul then tells Corie what he has learned about the weird assortment of tenants who live in the building and makes particular reference to a Victor Velasco who lives on the roof. A few minutes later Velasco knocks on the door and explains that he would like to use their bedroom window to get onto the roof because he is trying to avoid the landlord. He also wheedles an invitation from Corie for dinner on Friday.

Scene One of Act II takes place on Friday evening. The curtain rises on a beautifully decorated apartment. The skylight, however, still has the broken pane. Velasco soon takes over the arrangements for the evening, and Mrs. Banks, who tries to be a good sport and not spoil the fun, allows Velasco to take her and the Bratters to a restaurant for an exotic dinner that she knows will not agree with her. The impoverished Velasco has no hesitancy in making certain that Paul will be paying the bill.

The second scene takes place at 2 A.M. Mrs. Banks is anxious to get home, but again Velasco takes over and insists upon driving her home. After they leave, Paul and Corie begin arguing. Corie wants life to be a continuous honeymoon while she indulges in such antics as walking barefoot in the park in midwinter, an act Paul thinks is utterly nonsensical. Paul insists that he must have time to concentrate on his law practice. Corie grows more and more exasperated until she finally demands a divorce, and Paul, goaded by her nonsensical arguments, agrees to go through with it, even to drawing up the settlement terms. At the end of the scene, Paul tries to sleep on the living-room couch, which is anything but comfortable, and snow begins to fall through the broken skylight.

In the third act, Corie still plans to go through with the divorce until she learns that her mother has not been home all night. She rushes up to Mr. Velasco's apartment but returns almost immediately followed by her mother who is wearing Velasco's bathrobe and slippers. Mrs. Banks explains to her shocked daughter that she and Velasco had fallen in the mud, Velasco had broken his leg, and she had passed out. When she awoke, she was lying on Velasco's floor. Fortunately, Velasco hobbles on stage to confirm Mrs. Banks's story. Velasco leaves, but not before inviting Mrs. Banks to return for a simple dinner in his apartment. Mrs. Banks offers Corie a little sage advice on how to preserve her marriage and then goes back to Mr. Velasco's apartment. Within seconds, Paul staggers back. He is militant, drunk, and sick enough to come down with a bad cold, for he has been walking barefoot in the park to impress Corie. The contrite Corie suddenly seems more mature as she realizes that she and Paul are very much in love. Instead of ending with the typical embrace, however, Simon uses a gag situation. Paul climbs out on the roof, begins to totter, yells to Corie that he is getting sick, and Corie rushes out to lead him back as the curtain falls.

In addition to the four principal characters, the cast includes a telephone serviceman and a delivery man. Both are used in Act I primarily to establish the running gag—the effect of the long climb up the six flights of stairs. The telephone man also appears in the last act. He has seen the eager young bride in Act I, and now he watches in desperation, almost in fright, as Corie and Paul either bicker or completely ignore each other. At times, he is forced into the role of interlocutor to relay messages from Corie to Paul. More important, he gets a laugh with every line.

Neil Simon has made his characters sympathetic, affable, and amusing. There are no real heroes or villains, just nice people involved in ridiculous situations. Mike Nichols, who directed the play, has made several episodes resemble the clever routines he performed with Elaine May. The characters are serious even in their most ludicrous moments. They speak the funny lines earnestly and make the obvious gags seem part of the normal conversation. The audience begins to laugh in the first episode and continues laughing as the tempo accelerates. As a result, there appear to be no deliberate pauses in action to allow audiences to finish laughing at one gag before the actors introduce another.

In many respects the play resembles a series of television comedy sketches filled with gag routines. The performers' expert timing, the deliberate plugging for laughs, and the audience's ability to see an entire stage instead of just a camera close-up enhance the comedy and make the gags more effective on the stage than on the screen. In television, the running gag, to be effective, must be exaggerated or crowded into the limited span of a half-hour or hour program. On stage, however, the same gag may develop at a more leisurely pace for maximum effect. In *Barefoot in the Park,* for example, each entrance, with the exception of Corie's and Velasco's, becomes a running gag that might easily have been overworked. The entrances, however, are maneuvered with dexterity, with sufficient time intervals, and with amusing variations of the same breathless reaction to make each entrance become more hilarious than the preceding one.

Many of the quips are frothy and soon forgotten, but several have subtle undertones that audiences remember. For example, when Mrs. Banks tells Corie how to make her marriage successful and then casually adds, "Like two out of every ten couples," the audience impact is excellent. The happily married women enjoy thinking that they are better off than their married friends; unhappily married women are consoled with the thought that they are not alone in their misery. The line, in fact, illustrates a current theory advanced by some psychiatrists that melancholy people are happier when they read a melancholy poem or story, for they realize that other people may have emotional problems similar to theirs.

Although Corie and Paul have the longest roles, Mrs. Banks, particularly as played by Mildred Natwick, dominates the scenes. Miss Natwick won the approval of Henry Hewes for the outstanding female performance other than the lead in his *Best Plays* and won also the nomination as runner-up in the *Variety* Drama Critics' Poll. The road company starred Myrna Loy, who also dominated the action with her effective portrayal of Mrs. Banks. Instead of being a typical mother-in-law or typical long-suffering widow, Mrs. Banks is a good sport, wise enough to know when to advise her daughter and when to let her work out her own problems. In contrast to the current vogue of television commercials satirizing the older woman who meddles or the petulant daughter who tells Mama she would rather do things for herself, the characterization of Mrs. Banks as a modern mother-in-law who has good, old-fashioned sense is refreshing.

The familiarity of the plot may account in part for the popular appeal. The audience knows that lovers' quarrels will lead to a reconciliation; the audience also suspects that the broken skylight will mean trouble. Even the simulated romance between Mrs. Banks and Velasco appears plausible, because Velasco explains in the last act that he must now eat simpler food and live a less strenuous life, and Mrs. Banks realizes that she has slept on the floor without her bedboard and has slept well.

In less capable hands, *Barefoot in the Park* might have been an exaggerated farce with overacting that played down to audiences. Mike Nichols' direction and the expert acting by Mildred Natwick, Kurt Kasznar, Elizabeth Ashley, and Robert Redford never let the play descend into unbelievable absurdity.

At this writing Mildred Natwick and Kurt Kasznar are still giving superb performances that draw audiences to the theater. Penny Fuller and Anthony Roberts are excellent cast replacements as Corie and Paul.

Barefoot in the Park undoubtedly profited from summer visitors in 1964 and 1965, but its compelling humor has kept the play running longer than Mr. Simon's earlier success, *Come Blow Your Horn,* because the action and direction give *Barefoot in the Park* an accelerated tempo that never slackens; and the audience leaves the theater exhausted from laughter.

Comedies
the Critics
Liked

ONE of the frothiest comedies to be rated among the best plays of its season is *Affairs of State* by Louis Verneuil, produced in 1950. The plot, an updated version of *Cinderella* with slight traces of *State of the Union,* deals with Washington political maneuvers, but the author has superimposed innocence on what might have been a French comedy of sex. The story concerns George Henderson, now filling out the unexpired term of a senator who has died. Although he needs the support of Philip Russell, aged seventy, to be re-elected, George is having an affair with Philip's forty-year-old wife, Constance. Philip, concealing the fact that he knows about the affair, throws his support to another candidate and tells George, who is baffled by the turn of events, that a romance with a married woman at this time would kill any chances of political advancement and further suggests that George enter into a marriage of convenience until after the election. George and Constance are aware of the hopelessness of the situation and decide the ideal girl for such a marriage would be Irene Elliott, Philip's twenty-eight-year-old niece, who seems to be completely lacking in sophistication. At first Irene appears stunned at the proposal, but after George explains that she would be a wife in name only and that she would be paid for time, Irene becomes practical, demands a guarantee of three years' salary and a substantial allowance for buying the proper clothes. Two months later Irene is poised and dressed in the height of fashion, and charms important visitors in her home. While strangers are present, she is the adoring wife; but when she is alone with George, she is an aloof, businesslike companion. Constance, suspecting that Irene has fallen in love with George, confesses to Irene that she is the other woman in George's life and that after the election she will divorce Philip and marry George. Irene seems undisturbed by the news, but after Philip tells her that an Undersecretary of State is ill and that George would be a logical replacement, she is particularly charming to the Secretary of State and maneuvers the conversation so that he finally says he would like to see George in his office the next morning. George knows that if he divorces Irene and marries Constance, he will lose the appointment, and Constance, realizing that she can never marry George, reconciles with Philip. By the end of the play, George admits he has fallen in love with Irene, and Irene is willing to be more than a wife in name only.

That the play ran for 610 performances is not difficult to understand, for Verneuil has included at least two popular situations. For the women, he has allowed the virtuous Irene to triumph over Constance. He has naturalized the audience by revealing early in the play that Constance wants to divorce Philip and marry George. Before the play is half over, the audience knows that all four principal characters are aware of the true situation, but that each suspects the others do not know. The fun, therefore, comes in watching Philip's maneuvering to get George married without arousing the suspicions of Constance or George. The emancipation of Irene from the mousy little schoolteacher to the sophisticated, smartly dressed Washington hostess is enough indication to theaterwise audiences that George will fall in love with Irene and marry her. The suspense, therefore, rises, not from anticipating how George will get rid of Constance so much as from speculating how long it will take George to realize that Irene is the right girl for him.

Unlike *State of the Union*, which discusses some of the problems of picking political candidates, *Affairs of State* concentrates almost entirely on the love story and keeps political intrigue to a minimum, including just enough comment to make plausible the fact that if

George divorces Irene, he will ruin his career in Washington. The marriage of convenience and the sex angle, which could have been developed with leers and innuendoes, are glossed over by emphasizing the Cinderella story of Irene, the political career of George, and Irene's efficiency as a helpful wife. Even when George is ready to break down the barrier, Irene maintains a wily aloofness. As a result, the play, which might have been a bedroom farce, is an innocent comedy that sophisticated audiences accept as frothy and unsophisticated audiences enjoy as romance.

Many of the lines induce smiles rather than chuckles, but at times the dialogue sparkles. Probably the most effective line is in the third act. George gallantly offers to decline the appointment to the State Department, but Constance tells him he cannot sacrifice his career for the love of a woman. "A king of England can do that," she says, "but *not* an American Undersecretary of State."

Excellent acting, particularly Celeste Holm's performance as Irene, helped make the play a commercial success. Miss Holm, for whom Verneuil wrote the play, fairly glowed as the drab little Cinderella who changed into a glamorous heroine. After she left the cast, June Havoc replaced her and also gave an excellent interpretation of the role.

Still another version of the Cinderella story is *The Solid Gold Cadillac* by Howard Teichman and George S. Kaufman, produced in 1953. This time, however, Cinderella is neither young nor beautiful but is an older actress who outwits smart businessmen. Before the curtain rises, Fred Allen's voice coming over the loud-speaker announces, "This is a fairy story—the story of Cinderella and the four ugly corporation directors. Once upon a time—" and the play begins with the stockholders' meeting. The directors are maneuvering to push through their elections and a dividend cut without opposition until a dumpy little woman rises, is recognized by the chair, and then brings up the question of directors' salaries. The embarrassed executives hastily look up the records and find she is Mrs. Laura Partridge, who owns ten shares of stock. Before she can be stopped, Mrs. Partridge makes a motion that the salaries are too high. When it appears that the motion might not be seconded, she counters with a proposal that a committee be formed to study salaries. The chairman hastily adjourns the meeting and the four directors offer Mrs. Partridge a job with the corporation to keep her contented. She raises their offer from one hundred dollars a week to one hundred and fifty, gets a private office and secretary, and then discovers she has no duties. To keep herself occupied, she writes letters to the stockholders on a personal basis. The directors find the mailing costs are mounting and take away Mrs. Partridge's secretary, but Cinderella discovers that the directors have pulled a fraudulent business deal, and again she bludgeons them into getting what she wants. From then on the play seesaws between Mrs. Partridge's rise and fall in the corporation. She is sent to Washington to inveigle Mr. McKeever, former head of the company and now an important figure in Washington, into giving orders to the company; but instead, she gets him to resign from his position, becomes involved in a scandal, and loses her job. At the last moment, Mr. McKeever discovers that Mrs. Partridge's letters to the stockholders have influenced most of them to write proxies made out in her name, thus giving her control of the company. One of the directors says it is a purely technical control and asks Mrs. Partridge if she understands. She says, "This means just one thing. Gentlemen, you're all fired." And so Cinderella and her Prince Charming, Mr. McKeever, become directors of the company. In the last scene, when an elderly woman gets up to ask a question, Mrs. Partridge shouts, "Oh, no. That's how I got my start! The meeting is adjourned!"

In many ways, the comedy is almost a deliberate lampoon of early melodramas such as *The Lion and the Mouse,* for Mrs. Partridge triumphs over big business just as Shirley triumphed over Mr. Ryder. *The Lion and the Mouse* appealed as a love story, but *The Solid Gold Cadillac* is purely the comedy of a dumpy little lady who wins control of a big company with only a slight hint of a possible romance. When McKeever suddenly leaves Washington accompanied by Mrs. Partridge and they are forced to spend the night in Philadelphia, the story breaks into the newspapers. The second act begins with a curtain showing various headlines that range from "McKeever Case Rocks Capital" to "Tycoon Follies Girl in Love-Nest Scandal." Audiences may read a more definite romance into the play than Teichman and Kaufman have indicated, but the basic plot involves no further love angle. As a compromise to public taste, however, the authors have included a romance between Miss Shotgraven, Mrs. Partridge's secretary, and Mark Jenkins, a mail-order clerk. The motion picture version built up a romance between Judy Holliday as Mrs. Partridge and Paul Douglas as McKeever, but Broadway theater audiences were content with the humorous business tactics of the actress and the tycoon.

As in almost all of Kaufman's plays, the humor ranges from the obvious gag to the clever situation. Particularly amusing is the scene in which Miss Shotgraven begins to cry, and Mrs. Partridge asks if she is in trouble. Miss Shotgraven nods and Mrs. Partridge asks if she has told the man about her condition. The bewildered secretary asks, "What condition?" then realizes the implication, and is shocked that Mrs. Partridge could think such a thing. Mrs. Partridge calmly replies with one of the funniest lines in the play, "Well, in my day, when a girl said she was in trouble, she was in trouble."

Much of the play's success should be attributed to Josephine Hull, ideally cast as the supposedly scatterbrained Mrs. Partridge, who entranced audiences with every line from the scenes in which she aped McKeever's profanity to those in which she promoted Miss Shotgraven's romance. During the run of the show, Miss Hull suffered a heart attack and was replaced by Ruth McDevitt. Weekly grosses dropped, but the play had sufficient audience appeal to achieve a run of 526 performances, for the entertainment value did not depend entirely upon Miss Hull. Loring Smith's performance proved to be a perfect foil for Mrs. Partridge. In his first scene, he rushed around the room and shouted at the telephone, while his secretary, superbly played by Vera Fuller Mellish, conveyed messages to him without saying a single word. Even when she brought in the newspaper while McKeever was going through a series of exercises, she silently squatted up and down beside him holding the paper for him to read. Loring Smith's best scene came after he learned that Mrs. Partridge was an actress. To impress her, he delivered an oration, "Spartacus and the Gladiators," especially written for the play by Marc Connelly, which Smith made fantastically absurd by accompanying each exaggerated intonation with a ridiculous gesture.

Fred Allen, whose dry, nasal voice was familiar to all radio listeners, also contributed to the popular appeal. In his role of off-stage narrator, Allen set each scene, making the most of such gags as, "Prince Charming was bald as a honeydew and fifteen pounds overweight, but he also had fifteen million dollars, which did not make him any less charming." Even the less hilarious comments seemed funnier than they appear in the text, thanks to Allen's voice.

Although Louis Kronenberger did not select *The Solid Gold Cadillac* as one of the ten best plays of the year, John Chapman included it among the "Golden Dozen" plays he synopsized in *Theater '54,* and John Gassner included it in his fourth volume of *Best American Plays,* which also included George Axelrod's *The Seven Year Itch,* produced in 1952. Louis Kronenberger did not select Axelrod's comedy as one of the ten best plays of the year, but he did predict that *The Seven Year Itch* would run on Broadway for two years. His wise prophecy proved to be an understatement, for the play ran 1,141 performances, or almost three years.

The Seven Year Itch offers no message or theme and has a plot with few complexities. Its sole purpose is to provide entertainment as it tells the story of the Shermans who have been married for seven years. Mrs. Sherman and the children are spending the summer in the country; and Mr. Sherman, who has stayed in town, is ready for a last fling. The girl in the apartment upstairs tips over a tomato plant which crashes onto the couch where Sherman had been sitting just a few minutes before. He starts to yell, sees the girl, forgets about the accident, and gets involved in an affair. After spending the night with the girl, he rushes off to the country to be with his wife.

The play is one of the few long-running comedies in which the wife never learns about her husband's infidelity. *The Seven Year Itch* might have been just another routine comedy dealing with immorality, but Axelrod has subordinated the familiar story and has emphasized fantasy by having his hero indulge in a series of reveries in which he imagines how events may happen. As the play progresses, the humor arises from the difference between Richard's daydreams and the episodes in reality. As Richard visualizes the first meeting, he sees the girl in a seductive evening gown, and he is wearing a black patch over one eye. As they sit on the piano bench, he plays brilliantly and then starts to make impetuous love. In reality, the girl first appears in a checked shirt and dungarees. She goes back to her apartment to get a bottle of champagne, returns wearing a cocktail dress, and again Richard is inspired to make his daydreams come true, but all he can play is "Chopsticks."

Instead of the beautiful love scene he had visualized on the bench, he fumbles for the girl, making them both lose their balance and fall off.

When Richard is not an active participant in the daydreams, he becomes a bystander commenting on the proceedings, as he does when he imagines his wife is out with Tom McKenzie, a novelist. Every time Tom quotes a line, Richard sneers about the line coming right out of Tom's books.

There are no innuendoes in the play. Every situation is made perfectly clear through dialogue or daydreams which require little mental effort from audiences other than listening and laughing. Axelrod, however, has included enough gags to make the action flow smoothly and quickly. In the third act, for example, Richard imagines that when his wife learns about his infidelity, she shoots him. As he is dying, he pleads for a cigarette, but his wife says, "A cigarette! You know what Doctor Murphy told you about smoking!" Most of the gags dealing with sex are funny but unsubtle. Richard, a publisher of paperbacks, is planning to reprint Hawthorne's *The Scarlet Letter*. He says the company had taken a poll, found that 80 per cent of the people didn't know what the title meant, and decided to change the title to *I Was an Adulteress;* but a second poll showed that 63 per cent didn't know what the new title meant. Richard also says his company ran into trouble on its plan to use a lurid cover with Hester in a low-cut dress, for if the neckline were cut too low, where could they put the A?

Occasionally, Axelrod deviates from the subject of sex, as in the episode between Richard and Dr. Brubaker, a psychiatrist, whose book Richard will publish. The scene progresses into a battle of wits, for Richard lies on the couch, tells Brubaker his problems, and tries to maneuver Brubaker into giving him free advice, while Brubaker keeps reminding him that his fee is fifty dollars an hour. For the most part, however, the play deals with Richard's concern over his sex life, his married life, and his fear that his wife will discover he has spent a night with the girl whose name, incidentally, is never mentioned in the play.

The Seven Year Itch has been included in several anthologies, not as a major literary contribution to the American theater but as a clever satire on a familiar theme brought up to date through psychological reveries. It enjoyed a long run because it presented a sex play without offending audiences, provided a continuous stream of gags and reveries which gained in effectiveness as they contrasted with reality, and gave Tom Ewell, as Richard, an excellent opportunity to entertain audiences with a whole series of impersonations from the amorous man-about-town to the frightened husband. The comedy might not have had so much popular appeal if Axelrod had presented the girl as a wronged heroine, but he contrived the situation to have the girl, rather than Richard, break off the affair because she had no desire to become involved with an older, married man. By having her walk out on Richard, and by having Richard rush off to meet his wife, Axelrod sent the audience home contented.

F. Hugh Herbert's *The Moon Is Blue,* produced in 1951, like *The Seven Year Itch,* spends three acts discussing sex. *The Moon Is Blue* will never win any prizes for literary distinction, but critic John Gassner thought enough of its value as well-written entertainment to include it in his *Best American Plays.* The plot concerns a young girl who allows herself to be picked up, goes to a man's apartment, emerges unscathed, and ends by marrying him, which is virtually a synopsis of the earlier long-running play, *Strictly Dishonorable.* The small cast of four characters resembles the cast of three in *The Voice of the Turtle,* for Patty's father appears only briefly in one scene and most of the play deals with the three principals. According to reports, Herbert originally had five characters but eliminated one in the tryouts. What remains now is the story of Patty O'Neill, not quite twenty-one, who allows herself to be picked up by Donald Gresham. Patty informs him almost immediately that she is a virgin and intends to remain that way. Donald agrees that if she comes to his apartment, there will be "affection, but no passion." The scene shifts to the apartment, and the play sustains its humor and pace through a series of two- and three-character scenes because the dramatist has used Lamb's theory of naturalizing the audience. Every time Patty gets into a compromising situation, the audience enjoys watching the bewildered character on stage misjudge the circumstantial evidence. For example, Patty spills ketchup on her dress, takes it off, and wears Don's bathrobe. Don, who has gone out in the rain to meet Cynthia, his former fiancée, returns dripping wet, and Patty insists that he change his wet clothes. After Don has put on pajamas and a robe, Patty goes into the bedroom to put on her dress. Her father arrives, takes one look at Don, hears Patty call out, "Wait! I'm not buttoned up yet," misunderstands the situation, and without saying a word, hits Don in the eye and knocks him out. Earlier in the play, David Slater, Cynthia's father, a middle-aged playboy, has proposed marriage to Patty and given her six hundred dollars which he had won in a gin game so that Patty wouldn't have to worry about finding a job for several months. Patty is reluctant to accept the money, but under Slater's persuasion, finally agrees to take it. Don returns just as Patty is kissing Slater in gratitude, misjudges the whole scene, and once again the audience enjoys the situation of mistaken circumstances. In the last act, Patty returns to see Don. When they hear Slater at the door, she hides in the bedroom, but Slater tries to make a phone call, hears Patty's voice on the extension, and misinterprets her presence in the bedroom. In all of these scenes, the more involved the situations become for the actors, the more amusement there is for the audience.

Earlier plays which dealt with promiscuous heroines, such as *Born Yesterday* and *The Women,* were amusing but often shocking to many theatergoers. *The Moon Is Blue* with its virtuous heroine who withstands all onslaughts and even brings out the male instinct to protect her is more closely allied to *Strictly Dishonorable,* except that in Sturges' play, the innocent heroine makes the audience believe she does not fully realize exactly how involved the affair might be. Patty O'Neill, on the other hand, knows exactly what involvement she does not want until Don says she has been advertising her innocence. Patty asks what is wrong about that, and Don says, "People who advertise are anxious to sell something," which makes Patty realize she has been talking too much. Instead of keeping silent, she immediately switches the topic and keeps right on getting everybody confused. At one point, her ability to chatter and make everything the men do seem wrong causes Slater to ask why "young men are always cautioned against bad girls. Anyone can handle a bad girl. It's the good girls men should be warned against."

With only four characters in the play, Herbert succeeds in making the action move swiftly by his amusing characterizations. Patty, the slightly rattlebrained chatterbox, babbles on and on. Don, the bewildered hero, doesn't know exactly what to think, half the time believing that Patty is innocent, and the other half suspecting she might be willing to have an affair with Slater, the amiable alcoholic, who admits he should never try to raise a daughter. Even when he proposes marriage to Patty, he doesn't make the audience consider the idea too seriously.

These amusing characterizations gained effectiveness through excellent acting. The winsome appeal and charm of Barbara Bel Geddes as Patty made the delightful but somewhat addled heroine completely believable; Barry Nelson gave Don the right touch of masculinity and bewilderment; and Donald Cook played the lecherous older man without losing audience sympathy.

In addition to delightful performances, the play capitalized on popular dramatic situations. The heroine emerged triumphant, for in the last scene, when Don talks about the future, Patty tells him to stop shilly-shallying and say, "I love you." Furthermore, all through the play the audience, aware of all the facts, had the advantage of watching all three men in the cast misjudge Patty's involvements. Even the familiar plot which held no surprises was counterbalanced by the characterizations and continuous humor which helped keep *The Moon Is Blue* on Broadway for 924 performances.

Jean Kerr's delightful *Mary, Mary,* produced in 1961, is almost a sequel to *The Moon Is Blue,* for it might be one way of explaining what could have happened ten years after Patty and Don Gresham were married. The triangle of Patty, Don, and Slater in *The Moon Is Blue* parallels that of Mary, her husband Bob, and a motion picture star, Dirk, in *Mary, Mary.* In both plays the garrulous heroines are endowed with utter frankness. Mary, for example, keeps talking to Dirk, admits she has been talking too much, but babbles on. When Dirk tries to interrupt, she goes right ahead with her flippancies until Dirk says, "You really ought to learn when to shut up," which is another version of Don's comment in *The Moon Is Blue* when he tells Patty to stop talking about her virtue. The fact that Barry Nelson and Barbara Bel Geddes, who played the lovers in *The Moon Is Blue,* originated the roles of husband and wife in *Mary, Mary* makes the similarity between the two plays even greater.

Mary, Mary, however, is by no means a carbon copy of *The Moon Is Blue,* for the play evolves on its own and presents an

Mary, Mary, Barry Nelson and Barbara Bel Geddes rehearsing

amusing comedy which offers no great surprises but which does offer a pleasant evening's entertainment. As the play begins, Bob is divorcing Mary and is planning to marry Tiffany. His attorney is having trouble figuring out Bob's income tax and has asked Mary to help explain deductions which he and Bob cannot remember. The moment Mary appears, the audience knows she will triumph over Tiffany, but the fun comes from watching Mary and Bob trying to avoid a reconciliation. Dirk Winston, a famous motion picture star, brings Bob a manuscript, meets Mary, and is impressed. Before the play is half over, Dirk makes love to Mary, arouses Bob's jealousy, and asks Mary to take a trip with him. That night Mary thinks Bob is out of town and spends the night in their apartment, but a snowstorm has blocked all the roads and Bob returns. When they are almost at the point of reconciliation, they quarrel, and Bob walks out. The next morning, Tiffany discovers the bed in the living room has not been slept in and suspects the worst. She is not disturbed, but Bob, upset by the meeting of Mary and Tiffany, hunts around in his desk drawer, pulls out two bottles which he thinks contain aspirin and vitamin pills, and swallows three pills. A few minutes later, Tiffany discovers he has taken sleeping pills by mistake. As Bob gets progressively drowsier, Tiffany goes to the drugstore for an antidote, and Dirk again asks Mary to leave with him. In an effort to stop her, Bob finally locks her in the closet and throws away the key. Tiffany comes back, says she has decided Bob is not the man she should marry, and she, the attorney, and Dirk leave. Bob sleepily tries to unhinge the door to let Mary out, but Mary, who has duplicate keys in her purse, opens the door from the inside. Within minutes she and Bob have reconciled and Bob contentedly falls asleep.

The play is brittle, rather than deep, and the audience knows the ending in the first act. The comedy, nevertheless, holds interest because Jean Kerr has peppered it with gags that not only are amusing in themselves but also help develop the slight action. In the third act, for example, Mary and Bob hunt for cigarettes and finally find a crumpled pack under the cushion in the armchair. They grab the cigarettes, light up, exhale, and then say, "Mmm— that's *real* coffee." They both laugh, but Tiffany, who does not see the point, asks for an explanation. Bob tells her about the television announcer who became confused while giving a cigarette commercial and said, "Mmm—that's *real* coffee." Tiffany still does not laugh, but when Bob goes into the kitchen, she asks Mary how long it takes before husband and wife build up such intimate family jokes. Bob has explained to the attorney that although he thinks Mary is as beautiful as a lovely piece of white porcelain, he could never tell her because, "She would have said 'white porcelain—you mean like the kitchen sink?' " In the last act, when Bob is practically asleep, he does tell her and Mary starts to quip, "White porcelain. You mean—," catches herself, and says, "Oh, that's very sweet."

Some of the jokes seem to be inserted to smooth over necessary lapses of time, but they almost always build to a good laugh. Bob does not want to publish Dirk's book about Hollywood. On the other hand, Mary finds the book highly diverting and says she could turn to any page at random and find something that would delight the reader. She proves it by reading Dirk's explanation of how Hollywood starlets learn to smile without using facial muscles so they won't develop wrinkles. The line in itself is amusing but becomes even funnier as Mary deliberately mugs to illustrate the point.

Several times Tiffany says that divorced men who remarry usually make the same mistake twice. For that reason, she is anxious to meet Mary. Jean Kerr, however, definitely contrasts the women, for the moment Mary appears, the audience detects differences rather than similarities, and finds ample reason why Bob should stay married to Mary. Tiffany is bossy, brittle, and well aware of her good looks. Mary is winsome and unsure of herself. By explaining that she always hoped to be as attractive as her sister, she makes the audience realize she is unaware of her charm and is far more desirable than Tiffany.

The play combines several popular dramatic situations from a variation of the boy-meets-girl theme to that of mistaken judgment when Tiffany suspects what the audience knows is not true. The situation of the triumphant woman is all too obvious, for the audience expects Mary to reconcile with Bob and would find any other ending a distinct disappointment. These situations helped the long run, for the popular appeal is more inherent in the smooth flowing action, the slick production, the witty gags, and the excellent acting. A better indication of the play's appeal is the fact that the motion picture version with Debbie Reynolds opened at Radio City Music

Hall and ran concurrently with the stage version on Broadway, which outlasted the film's run in Manhattan and the subsequent runs in neighborhood film houses. *Mary, Mary* finally closed with a total of 1,572 performances, making it the longest-running play produced since 1950.

Barbara Bel Geddes, Barry Nelson, and Michael Rennie gave the comedy its original box office impetus, but the comedy survived a great many changes in cast. Michael Rennie was replaced by Michael Wilding, Edward Mulhare, Michael Evans, Tom Helmore, and Howard Morton. Julia Meade, Nancy Olson, Inger Stevens, Diana Lynn, Patricia Smith, and Mindy Carson have all played Mary. Barry Nelson's replacements include Scott McKay, George Grizzard, Tom Poston, Murray Hamilton, and William Prince.

Mary, Mary is still too recent a production to be included in anthologies other than the *Best Plays* series, but editors in later anthologies will undoubtedly include it as a representative comedy of the early 1960s.

No Time for Sergeants, by Ira Levin, adapted from Mac Hyman's novel and produced in 1955, like *Mary, Mary* was a *Best Play* and received favorable reviews as well as instant public approval. The story is a deliberate burlesque of Army customs and procedures, but the emphasis is on farce and contrived situations rather than on satire or plausibility. *No Time for Sergeants* does not censure the Army as *Mister Roberts* does the Navy, for the play lacks a serious theme and dramatic undertones. Instead, it tells the adventures of Will Stockdale, an amiable hillbilly who is drafted, obeys all orders, even takes pride in being assigned the odious task of latrine orderly, and completely baffles his superiors, including Sergeant King, who has tried to get Will drunk only to find that Will, raised on moonshine, can outdrink all other Army men. Will becomes buddies with Ben, who wants to join the Infantry, and, for most of the play, concentrates on helping Ben get transferred. He and Ben become involved in an airplane maneuver and fly into the area where an atom bomb is tested. Their plane catches fire and they parachute to safety, but the army officers think they are dead. They return to their post in time to hear the General ask an assembled audience to stand at attention with the flags at half-mast in honor of the two dead heroes. When the officers discover that

Ben and Will are still alive, the play goes from the farcical to the ridiculous. General Bush and General Pollard hustle Ben and Will into a large car with all shades drawn and drive them into the forest. There the Generals ask them to sign transfer papers to another division so that the whole incident can be hushed up. Will, however, balks until he and Ben get medals, which are hastily appropriated from the Generals' uniforms. Then Will suggests that the Generals stand at attention while the medals are presented. General Bush agrees to do anything to get rid of the men, but General Pollard refuses. At the strategic moment, the radio plays "The Star-Spangled Banner" and the whole company, including both Generals, stands at attention.

The play begins with Will's making a speech telling the people in his home town how he got his medal. The action then flashes back to the story Will is telling, and the play ends as Will concludes his speech. The fact that John Chapman selected *No Time for Sergeants* as one of the best plays in *Theater '56,* as did Louis Kronenberger for *Best Plays of 1955–1956,* indicates the farce has some reading merit. The comedy may be a lot of fun for audiences and readers, but it is far from wholly satisfactory as a logical play, for it leaves unanswered too many questions. How did Will and Ben manage to escape injury if they were in a bombing area? Wouldn't the news of their escape have been discovered? And, since the play deals with Will's story, wouldn't some newspaper reporter have picked up the whole incident? There are no logical explanations in the obviously contrived and ridiculous plot, for the sole purpose of the play is to provoke laughter whether the situation is plausible or not.

In contrast to *Mister Roberts, No Time for Sergeants* is a decidedly weak comedy. Surprisingly enough, it lacks not only the seriousness of *Mister Roberts,* but the bawdiness as well. The language is simple, almost juvenile, particularly when Will is on stage. Women in both plays are scarce. In *Mister Roberts,* the nurse, the only woman in the cast, appears in only one scene which is a significant episode in the lives of the sailors. The women in *No Time for Sergeants* are limited to very minor walk-on roles in two episodes and do nothing to further the frail plot. *Mister Roberts* has a humorous first act and a second act in which the seriousness of the situation becomes more and more apparent in spite of the humor. *No Time for Sergeants* has a humorous first act with several satirical episodes. The second act, however, deals primarily with the escapades of Ben and Will in the plane and the resultant confusion. The humor becomes grotesque and the ridiculousness of the situation causes an emotional letdown. In *Mister Roberts* audiences remember the humor but also the bitter ending; in *No Time for Sergeants* audiences have an evening of fun but forget the whole story when they leave the theater.

The play owed much of its original popular appeal to Andy Griffith, whose convincing performance as the hillbilly, whose authentic Southern drawl and whose ability to make even the most ridiculous lines sound natural, gave the comedy much of its energy. When Griffith was on stage—and fortunately he was on for most of the play—he dominated the scenes, made the action secondary, and enabled the play to provide an evening's entertainment which began at a rapid pace but gradually bogged down.

No Time for Sergeants ran almost two years with a total of 796 performances, a high figure in comparison with the general run of shows, but a shorter run by almost a year than *Mister Roberts'* total of 1,157 performances. During the World War II years, *No Time for Sergeants* might have run much longer, but, by 1957, toward the end of the New York run, the humor of army situations had worn thin and audiences were less inclined to see a dated comedy.

The Happy Time, Samuel Taylor's adaptation of a novel by Robert Fontaine, produced in 1950, deals with family life in the 1920s, but it is not as dated as *No Time for Sergeants.* The plot combines sentiment reminiscent of several sequences in *I Remember Mama* with overtones of sex characteristic of French comedies. Yet the combination blends into an enjoyable play about a French-Canadian couple, their adolescent son, and a curious household of relatives. Fontaine had previously made a dramatic adaptation of his novel which was never produced, but Taylor wrote an entirely new play.

The setting is the Bonnard home in Ottawa in 1920. Papa, who is French rather than French-Canadian, is a violinist and leads the orchestra in a vaudeville house. Maman Bonnard is a Scot. Bibi, their twelve-year-old son, has inherited his father's love for music and his mother's quiet charm. Other members of the household include Grandpa, an old roué; Papa's brother Louis who drinks almost incessantly; Felice, his wife, a shrew; and Uncle Desmonde, Papa's dapper younger brother who boasts about his conquests with women.

In many respects, the play concerns Bibi's problems during his adolescence. When Papa brings home Mignonette, a beautiful actress who has lost her job, to work as a maid, she enchants not only Uncle Desmonde but also young Bibi. This angers little Sally, the American girl who lives next door and who is infatuated with Bibi. Uncle Desmonde has given Bibi a copy of *La Vie Parisienne* which prompts Bibi to hide Mignonette's nightgowns so that when she walks from the bedroom to the bathroom she will look like the women he has seen in the pictures. In the last act when Bibi confesses, the audience is aware of the fact that he does not realize the implications of his prank. *La Vie Parisienne* gets Bibi into further trouble, for he takes it to school and trades it for baseball pictures. One of the boys traces a picture from the magazine but draws the head of the geometry teacher on the voluptuous body. When Bibi returns from school, he tells his father that the principal not only has blamed him for drawing the picture but also has made slanderous remarks about the entire Bonnard family. In one of the most amusing scenes in the play, Papa and his two brothers pay a surprise call upon the principal to defend the family honor. At first the principal is inclined to treat the visit casually; but when the Bonnards grow angry, he begins to insult them. Uncle Desmonde is at the point of punching him, but the principal gets out of his chair. As he does, *La Vie Parisienne,* which he has hidden in his lap, falls to the floor. The brothers change their tactics and soon build up the story that the principal is the man they have seen at the burlesque house sitting in the first row and applauding for the girl who tosses garters into the audience. It takes little time to convince the principal that he could be a victim of circumstantial evidence just as he has victimized Bibi for something he did not do.

In the last act Mignonette quarrels with Desmonde because she believes he has stolen her nightgowns, and Sally admits that she lied to the principal and told him Bibi had drawn the picture. At the final moment, Bibi is talking to his father, his voice begins to change, breaks, and Bibi asks in fright, "Papa! What happened here?" The curtain comes down before Papa can answer.

The humor comes largely from the contrast of French sophisticated farce with the wholesome story of a happy family life. Half the play deals with sex, including Desmonde's conquests, Grandpa's final fling with a gay widow, and Papa's efforts to explain the facts of life to Bibi. The other half deals with Maman's resignation in coping with her family, her happy but complicated married life, and Sally's infatuation for young Bibi. A scene with risqué overtones is followed by a sequence involving simple problems of domestic life. The scenes which reveal Bibi's efforts to understand adult actions are humorous, never offensive, and particularly appealing to adult audiences. Quite often the humor is broad, especially when Bibi innocently repeats a remark which displeases Maman and he cannot realize that he has said anything wrong. For example, Grandpa has explained to Bibi that growing up is a matter of using "the glands and the heart and the mind together correctly." Later, when Papa jokingly offers Bibi a cigar and he says he will wait until he is a man before he smokes one, Maman asks him, "When will that be?" Bibi innocently replies, "It is a matter of the glands," which shocks Maman. Then, to add to the humor, Bibi asks, "I said something?"

The Happy Time has two sequences in which adults discuss the subject of sex with Bibi. The first is a scene between Grandpa and Bibi; the second and even more effective sequence occurs late in the play when Papa discusses love. In a few short sentences, he summarizes the happiness in his own marriage and makes Bibi realize that although much of what he has heard may not be clear, they will again discuss the subject when Bibi is older. The entire scene is written with candor but without offense. It is, in fact, sentimental, for when Papa has finished and Bibi has gone out of the room, Maman, who has been listening at the door, comes on stage and kisses Papa. What distinguishes these talks from similar episodes in other long-running plays is the manner in which both older men speak simply and directly instead of playing the usual embarrassed parent who hedges about discussing the subject of sex. Moreover, both men tell Bibi just enough to make him realize that he is not yet old enough to understand a more detailed discussion.

The Happy Time became a hit on Broadway for a variety of reasons. The comedy presents a different version of a happy family life from, for example, *You Can't Take It with You*, in that all the

Bonnards lead more normal lives. The unhappily married Uncle Louis and Aunt Felice provide a definite contrast to the blissful existence of the Bonnards. Although the play deals with sex, the French comedy angles are interlaced with sentimental scenes to make the play appealing rather than shocking. Furthermore, the play's racy aspects are not overwritten or given sly inferences which could have made some of the episodes far more suggestive. The love affair of Desmonde and Mignonette relies on the popular boy-meets-girl formula, for Desmonde meets Mignonette, falls in love, almost loses her, and then gets her. Even more important, the audience always knows more than the actors, particularly in the matter of the nightgowns; for in Act II, Scene One, the audience sees Bibi stuffing the nightgowns into the window seat. Then, in the third act, when the entire Bonnard family discusses the missing nightgowns, only the audience and Bibi know where they are hidden. When Mignonette accuses Desmonde, who pleads innocence to no avail, the scene becomes even more humorous, for again the audience knows that Desmonde would be the logical suspect and that no one would guess Bibi was guilty. All these attributes combined with excellent performances, particularly that of Claude Dauphin as Papa, made *The Happy Time* an enjoyable, relaxing evening's entertainment and had enough popular appeal to give the comedy a run of 614 performances.

The Fourposter and *Two for the Seesaw,* two comedies with small casts are tours de force for both the playwrights and the actors because each play has only two characters on stage. *The Fourposter* by Jan De Hartog, produced in 1951, deals with the married life of Michael and Agnes, and, perhaps, a fourposter bed. As the play begins, Michael carries Agnes over the threshold on their wedding night. The scene develops into a series of quarrels and embarrassing situations as the young couple prepare for bed. Michael finds on the bed a little pillow embroidered with the words "God Is Love." Agnes reminds him that the pillow was a gift from her mother; Michael reminds her that the bed was his father's. When Michael has turned down the gas, Agnes insists she still smells gas; Michael says she is smelling his breath. After Agnes has sniffed to make certain, Michael embraces her and the lights black out. The next scene takes place one year later. Agnes is obviously pregnant and Michael is concerned about getting the doctor in time.

Agnes seems undisturbed, but when she tells Michael he had better go for the doctor, he rushes out, runs back in, pushes the bassinet over to Agnes, and runs out.

Ten years elapse between the first and second acts. In the opening scene, Michael, who has become infatuated with another woman, talks about leaving Agnes, but she cleverly wins him back. The second scene occurs seven years later. It is four o'clock in the morning and Michael and Agnes are waiting up for their son to return home. Michael is furious not only because of the late hour but also because he has found a whiskey bottle in Robert's room. When they hear Robert coming in the front door, Michael goes out brandishing a riding crop and insisting that he will teach Robert a lesson. A few minutes later he returns looking dazed. Agnes asks him what he told Robert, and Michael says, "Good morning." Agnes thinks that after Michael had raised all that fuss, surely he could have said a little more, but Michael says, "I couldn't. He was wearing a top hat."

Five years elapse between the second and third acts. The opening scene is their daughter's wedding night. Agnes announces that this is the first day of their daughter's marriage and the last day of hers, for she has found a new romance. Before long, Michael convinces Agnes that he needs her now more than ever. The last scene takes place twelve years later. Michael and Agnes are preparing to move. They have their usual quarrels, but the major discussion concerns the pillow "God Is Love," which Agnes wants to leave on the bed for the next couple. Michael believes it would be the worst thing for a groom to find on his wedding night because it would show the man that he is trapped in a world dominated by women. Agnes, nevertheless, tries various schemes of hiding the pillow each time Michael goes out. Finally, after Michael has taken out all the luggage, he throws back the bedcovers, puts the pillow on Agnes' side of the bed, puts a bottle of champagne on his side, smooths the spread back in place, picks up Agnes, and carries her out of the room.

With the exception of the pillow, De Hartog does not resort to props such as telephones or even letters to keep the action moving, nor does he allow the play to lapse into dull arguments. Instead he gives the plot movement by keeping the scenes comparatively short and by building each sequence to a minor climax. The lapse in years between acts and even between scenes adds progression, and the domestic quarrels of the couple keep the audience interested in the slight story.

The Moon Is Blue and *The Voice of the Turtle,* the earlier long-running plays with small casts of four and three characters, respectively, often settled into long sequences with only two characters on stage. *The Fourposter* could also have had a larger cast by introducing the son or daughter in one or two scenes, but such an innovation would have detracted from the play, for once the audience has grown accustomed to the two-character development, it never loses interest. Furthermore, by making the bedroom the setting, De Hartog gives the comedy an intimacy which the couple shares only with the audience. Any third character on stage would be an intruder who would spoil the audience's secret feeling of participation. Undoubtedly the small cast helped make *The Fourposter* an economical production which could sustain a long run. Several recent articles about show business, however, reveal the fact that regardless of the number of actors on stage, the backstage costs remain the same. During one of the out-of-town engagements, a theater critic wrote that although *The Fourposter* had only two people on stage, the touring company, including the road manager, stagehands, property men, etc., totaled eleven.

The popular appeal of *The Fourposter* did not lie in the economy of cast salaries, the technical perfection of the production, or even the rapid changes of properties and costumes. It was, rather, the story and the acting which kept the play running for 632 performances. De Hartog's use of the bedroom never shocked or offended audiences; the story merely revealed the problems and quarrels of an average couple. When Michael threatened to break up the marriage, the audience did not take the threat seriously, for it knew Agnes would handle the situation as well as she had handled other problems in the past. Similarly, when Agnes decided to leave Michael, the audience again knew that this quarrel, like all others, would end in a reconciliation. The play had further appeal as a love story about a happy marriage because Hume Cronyn and Jessica Tandy, who originated the roles of Michael and Agnes, were happily married in real life. The bedroom setting, therefore, became more intriguing to some audiences. One woman said she felt as if she were looking in on the private life of the Cronyns rather than at the stage story of Michael and Agnes. She saw the play a second time with cast replacements and said that she still liked the production but that it no longer had the same intimate appeal. Capable cast replacements, however, did keep the comedy running in New York for almost a year after the Cronyns took the show on tour.

The concluding episode in *The Fourposter* had just the right touch of humor to add audience appeal, especially in Michael's placing of the bottle next to Agnes' pillow. The final action of Michael carrying Agnes out of the room, just as he had carried her into the room in the first scene, gave the play a happy ending and sent the audience home contented with the story, the development, and the final outcome.

Two for the Seesaw, William Gibson's comedy produced in 1958, resembles *The Fourposter* in two respects. It has a cast of only two characters and it uses a bed as a principal prop. Otherwise, there is no similarity between the plays in plot, in dramatic technique, or even in dialogue. *The Fourposter* tells the story of a happy marriage; *Two for the Seesaw* is the story of an illicit romance. *The Fourposter* develops its story in simple dialogue without resorting to off-color innuendoes. *Two for the Seesaw* is filled with profanity, blasphemy, and earthy language. *The Fourposter* uses one set with changing properties; *Two for the Seesaw* requires a complicated set which contracts to reveal two rooms or expands to one room. There are no telephone conversations in *The Fourposter,* but at least two scenes in *Two for the Seesaw* are based entirely on phone calls. A bed is used as a principal stage prop in both plays, but in *The Fourposter,* the bed symbolizes the happy married life of Michael and Agnes; in *Two for the Seesaw,* the bed is primarily a necessary piece of furniture. Rumor has it that during the early tryouts on the road, one scene showed the two characters getting into bed, turning out the lights, and then continuing the scene for a few minutes in the dark; no such episode exists in the final version.

The story concerns Jerry Ryan, a lawyer from Omaha, who is divorcing his wife. Gittel Mosca, a dancer, has drifted through several unhappy affairs. Jerry is reserved, cultured; Gittel is earthy, uninhibited. In spite of their different backgrounds, they become involved in a turbulent affair which takes them through several crises including Gittel's illness and Jerry's studying to pass the

Two for the Seesaw, Dana Andrews (replacement for Henry Fonda)
and Anne Bancroft

New York bar examinations. Ultimately they both realize the affair cannot continue and Jerry returns to his wife.

The play develops the idea that the affair gives Gittel and Jerry new outlooks on the future. Jerry, for example, learns from Gittel the meaning of generosity, for she has given willingly of herself, not just physically but also emotionally when she encourages him to study for the bar examinations, tries to help him forget his marital troubles, and tries to make him see the joy of living. Gittel, on the other hand, learns from Jerry that she must have more self-respect and must make other people do things for her rather than her always doing things for them.

William Gibson's *The Seesaw Log* gives a running account of the problems he and the producer faced in getting the proper actors for the play. Gibson states quite frankly that Henry Fonda's acceptance of the leading role made the production possible, but as Gibson's account progresses, he intimates that Fonda felt he was not right for the role. Gibson does admit that the man's role was the more shadowy of the two and that as he rewrote the scenes, he tried to build up the man's part to make the role more convincing for Fonda. In the final production, however, Anne Bancroft as Gittel ran away with the show. Many critics, nevertheless, were impressed with Fonda's performance, and their glowing praise of the acting and the play gave the production the impetus to set out on a long run. As soon as his contract had terminated, Fonda left the show to be replaced by Dana Andrews. Before the play completed its run of 750 performances, Darren McGavin also appeared as Jerry and Lee Grant followed Anne Bancroft as Gittel.

Particularly appealing to New York audiences was the performance of Miss Bancroft, an Italian by birth, who gave a most convincing portrayal of the Jewish heroine. Her gestures, her Bronx accent, and her vitality dominated the stage. Miss Bancroft's flamboyance emphasized Gittel's coarseness and earthiness, but, at the same time, her ability to make Gittel a warm, compassionate woman built audience sympathy for what might easily have been an unsavory heroine. Although Henry Fonda may have been dissatisfied with his role, he gave Jerry a quiet reserve and built up audience sympathy for a more unsympathetic character than Gittel. Jerry's motivation for leaving his wife, his attachment for Gittel, and his final reconciliation with his wife were never as clearly defined as Gittel's actions and her infatuation for Jerry. Fonda, nevertheless, made Jerry a believable character whose actions audiences understood even if they did not always approve.

What might have been just another play about a predatory man and a promiscuous woman becomes a humane drama because Gibson has written several sequences which show the ability of Gittel and Jerry to cope with misfortune. Theirs is not merely a casual affair, for when Gittel becomes ill, Jerry is as solicitous of her as if he were her husband. And when Jerry becomes discouraged about studying for the bar examinations, Gittel encourages him, as a wife might, to continue. Throughout the play the humor, which is often earthy and bawdy, is balanced by sentiment. Although the telephone conversations constitute a fair portion of the dialogue, they are realistic and do not distract audiences that know an entire scene must, of necessity, be limited to the telephone.

Even the intricate stage set, which one or two critics thought overmechanized the production, fascinated New York audiences. The lights were dimmed during scene changes but the curtains were never closed and audiences enjoyed watching the shadowy figures of the stage hands while the set, which was built on the principle of a jackknife, expanded or contracted.

Several critics felt the play oversentimentalized a shoddy situation in the final scene when Gittel realizes that Jerry has no intention of marrying her and is planning to return to his wife. Jerry and Gittel are both outwardly calm, but Jerry appears to be less disturbed by the parting than Gittel. Perhaps dissenting critics might have been more content if the last act had retained the light tone and bawdy banter of the first two scenes, but if it had, the popular appeal of the play would have been weakened immeasurably, for although Gittel definitely did not exemplify the popular situation of the triumphant woman, she did arouse sympathy. Audiences may not have condoned her promiscuity but they could feel sorry for her. They were, however, more content that Jerry decided to return to his wife, for the mismatched affair of Jerry and Gittel could lead only to eventual unhappiness for Jerry and to heartbreak for Gittel.

Perhaps the most distinctive feature about the long run is that *Two for the Seesaw* is one of the few popular plays dealing with an immoral situation and with a decidedly unhappy but inevitable ending to achieve a two-year run that may be credited not to the obvious plot but to the excellent acting, the smooth flowing dialogue, and the dramatist's ability to get sympathy for a confused hero and an unconventional heroine.

Nine
Best Plays

At a writer's conference for college students in the early 1950s, a well-known editor, in discussing the importance of titles, said that those which avoided confusion and misquoting were brief, clear, and usually no longer than five syllables. As a typical illustration, he cited *Gone with the Wind.* Theater history has disproved the editor's statement almost completely, for in recent years several Broadway productions have had long titles such as *How to Succeed in Business without Really Trying, A Funny Thing Happened on the Way to the Forum,* and the champion long title, *Oh, Dad, Poor Dad, Mama's Hung You in the Closet and I'm Feeling So Sad.* Nor have the longer titles always been clear. Many people are bewildered by the significance of the title *Who's Afraid of Virginia Woolf?*

Even brief titles may be confusing when two plays with similar titles, each comprised of three one-word syllables, run concurrently. When Paddy Chayefsky's *The Tenth Man* opened in November, 1959, audiences knew the play dealt with Orthodox Jewry and religious superstitions. After Gore Vidal's *The Best Man* opened in March, 1960, however, the similarity in titles bewildered a great many ticket buyers. Vidal's play, a timely drama, was rumored to have thinly veiled characterizations of Presidents as well as composite characterizations of Presidential candidates. Very soon the stage comics and newspaper columnists were telling the joke about the lady who went to see *The Tenth Man* and, at the end of the first act, said to her husband, "Which one is supposed to be Nixon?" Apocryphal as the story may sound, it has some basis in truth. A little checking revealed several people who were confused by the two plays. A college professor, head of an English department, asked a New York colleague to get him tickets for the play about the Presidential election, and found, when he arrived at the theater, that he had tickets for *The Tenth Man*. On the other hand, a group of ladies who read ecstatic reviews of Chayefsky's drama were eager to see what they hoped would be a modern version of *The Dybbuk*. To their dismay, they found they had erroneously ordered tickets for *The Best Man*.

In addition to the titles, *The Best Man* and *The Tenth Man* have one other common denominator; both are included among the ten best plays for the same season. *The Tenth Man*, which had the longer run, is a more uneven drama. The story is a curious combination of modern psychology superimposed upon religious folklore, religious ceremonies and customs practiced by men who are not sincerely devout, and humorous dialogue injected into serious episodes. Chayefsky has taken a serious plot, one that could end only in unhappiness, and has foisted upon it a sentimental ending to intrigue audiences that want a play with a love story, regardless of how contrived it might be.

The setting is a shabby Orthodox Jewish synagogue converted from a storeroom. As the play opens, the men gather for the morning prayers but are not too hopeful that they will have ten men, the minimum number necessary to conduct Orthodox services. To meet their quorum, they telephone two brothers and ask them to come to the synagogue to say memorial prayers for their father. They bring in also a man from the street, Arthur Carey, a young lawyer disillusioned with both life and religion, Mr. Foresman, another member of the congregation, comes with his eighteen-year-old granddaughter, Evelyn, a schizophrenic, who he believes is possessed by an evil spirit, a dybbuk, which he insists must be exorcised. The play builds up to the third-act climax in which the sexton prepares for the exorcism, but the congregation still numbers only nine. When a policeman appears to inquire about the girl because her parents had reported that she had disappeared with her grandfather, he reveals that he is Jewish, and the quorum of ten is set. The exorcism rituals begin, but as they gain momentum, the young lawyer, not the girl, falls into a faint. Alper, one of the ten men, says, "I think what has happened is that we have exorcised the wrong dybbuk." As Arthur comes out of his trance, he declares that he is in love with Evelyn and that he will cure her through his love; and the young people leave together.

The ending is far from satisfactory, particularly to those audiences familiar with S. Ansky's drama, *The Dybbuk,* which played on Broadway in the 1920s. Ansky dramatized a story of religious folklore in a Chassidic community, basing his play on two folk stories he had written. The drama intrigued a number of New York theatergoers who saw it at the Neighborhood Playhouse, a theater equivalent to some of the current off-Broadway houses, and soon became a popular draw in the Yiddish theaters. Later, on Broadway, the Habima Players from Palestine presented their version and again in 1964 opened their season on Broadway with Ansky's drama. In the original legend the evil spirit could be driven from the body of the person whom it had enslaved, but the victim, although saved from the dybbuk, would die.

Although there is no direct statement to prove that Chayefsky has written a modern version of the folk tale or even the drama, several critics have compared *The Tenth Man* and *The Dybbuk.* The setting for both plays is a synagogue. The evil spirit in both plays victimizes a heroine. Chayefsky, however, has sacrificed fantasy for reality by endowing the modern play with psychiatry and with a love story and by making the hero possessed of a different type of dybbuk. As a result, the play offers neither realism nor fantasy. Those who are familiar with the old story find the new ending unbelievable and unsatisfactory. Those who know nothing of the legend or of the Orthodox customs revealed in the play may follow the psychological discussions and the explanations of Evelyn's schizophrenic outbursts but are probably confused by the customs and stories upon which the modern psychological explanations are superimposed. In one out-of-town production, a non-Jewish critic suggested that it would be very helpful in understanding the play if the program contained a glossary of terms or explanations of religious customs.

Yet in spite of objections the play did prosper. Nor is it difficult to understand why *The Tenth Man* enjoyed a prosperous run in New York. A large segment of New York audiences was familiar with *The Dybbuk* or with Ansky's stories. Critics wrote favorable reviews, particularly of Tyrone Guthrie's direction and staging, commenting especially on Guthrie's perception and detailed accuracy in staging rites and rituals in a faith which, they said, must have been unfamiliar to him. Although the cast had no starring roles, at least two actors would have interested Jewish audiences in the New York area; Jacob Ben Ami, a well-known favorite in the Yiddish theater, and Risa Schwartz, daughter of Maurice Schwartz, an actor as well known as Ben Ami in the Yiddish theater. The play achieved much of its popularity, not for its serious theme or the implications of lack of faith and dissatisfaction with life, but for its inserted, and, incidentally, much publicized humor, for the advertisements referred to *The Tenth Man* as a comedy, even to the point of saying "many laughs." For example, in the midst of Zitorsky and Schissel's heated discussion about their daughters-in-law, Zitorsky says, "My daughter-in-law, may she grow rich and prosperous and buy a hotel with a thousand rooms and be found dead in every one of them." To which Schissel replies, "My daughter-in-law, may she invest heavily in General Motors, and the whole thing go bankrupt." Similar gags are inserted in discussions of cemeteries, subways, and even the cabalistic rites.

The long run does not indicate that all audiences left the theater contented or that all critics were ecstatic in their reviews. More than one critic objected to the ending, to the overuse of sentimentality, and to Chayefsky's inability to blend his fantasy and folklore with realistic overtones. One critic, in a private interview, said he thought the play really belonged in the Yiddish Art Theater, but he also admitted that Yiddish Art Theater audiences, unfamiliar with modern interpretations of Freud, would not accept Chayefsky's tampering with the old story or his final scene which left audiences wondering whether the girl would ever really be cured or whether the young man would lapse back into his disillusionment. Very devout Orthodox audiences would not accept the Rabbi's telephone conversation in which he discusses the modernization of religion and the use of gimmicks to attract people to the synagogue. His speech, rather, is a realistic indictment better understood by Broadway theater audiences and symbolizes the minimization of faith in all the men who are attending the services, including himself. For Broadway audiences, too, many of the customs depicted on stage, such as the wearing of phylactery and prayer shawls during services, helped the initial box office impetus. The publicized humor in the play and also the jokes that sprang up concerning the similarity of the title to *The Best Man* kept *The Tenth Man* in front of the public for a second season to give the production a total run of 623 performances.

Although Gore Vidal's *The Best Man* had a shorter run of 520 performances, it was a more completely satisfying drama than *The Tenth Man* but a play more dependent upon current headlines to sustain interest. The timeliness of the plot, which dealt with an oncoming Presidential election, and the fact that *The Best Man* opened in March, 1960, when party nominations were beginning to shape up, gave the play decided audience interest. As the run continued and as the contest for the Presidency settled into the Nixon-Kennedy debates, the play had still greater impact. Since Vidal had lived in Washington with his grandfather, Senator Thomas P. Gore of Oklahoma, his familiarity with Washington politics and politicians enabled him to give the play an air of authenticity which further intrigued audiences.

In some ways, *The Best Man* was, for the 1960s, what *State of the Union* was for the 1940s. Lindsay and Crouse's hero was rumored to be a thinly disguised but composite characterization of several key figures including the Presidential nominee, Wendell Willkie. Vidal's drama also included composite characterizations. The ex-President, Arthur Hockstader, resembled Harry Truman in many respects, but to a number of people he also represented Dwight Eisenhower.

The play deals primarily with the struggle between two men for the Presidential nomination, with each man threatening to do a polite form of blackmail. William Russell has been Secretary of State and now is running for the Presidency. He epitomizes suaveness, wisdom, and ethical principles in political life. In private life, however, he has not been so successful. His wife is on the verge of divorcing him, but she appears with him at the political convention and, in public, acts as if her marriage were a happy one. Joseph Cantwell, his opponent, is a self-made man seeking the Presidency to further his own ambitions. Russell is concerned about what happens to the country; Cantwell cares only what happens to him.

When Cantwell threatens to publicize the fact that Russell has had a mental breakdown, Russell, in retaliation threatens to expose an old army scandal concerning homosexuals which involved Cantwell. Although Russell's desire to fight fairly makes him prefer not to debase himself by employing Cantwell's tactics, he is ready, if necessary, to fight Cantwell with his own brand of publicity. Most of the play deals with the sparring for the party nomination until the last episode when the nomination seems to be stalemated. To defeat Cantwell, Russell throws his support to a dark horse, Governor John Merwin, who wins. Russell and his wife are reconciled, even though he says he regrets he cannot give her the opportunity to live in the White House. To make the title convincing, Russell tells the reporters he thinks Governor Merwin will make a fine candidate and, "I am, of course, happy the best man won."

The Best Man, like *State of the Union,* keeps political dissension within one party. Although Vidal has based some of his incidents on truth and has used topical references to news items and political figures, the play sustains interest on its own merit even if the audience cannot associate characters or incidents with Kennedy, Stevenson, Truman, Eisenhower, Nixon, or other figures prominent in the headlines in 1960. In this respect the play parallels *The Man Who Came to Dinner,* which amused audiences unfamiliar with Alexander Woollcott, Harpo Marx, or Noel Coward. On the other hand, part of the audience's enjoyment of *The Best Man* came from speculations about which characters represented prominent political figures.

Timeliness or political intrigue do not always give drama popular appeal, nor does bad politics, as one critic suggested, always make good theater. The same season *The Best Man* appeared, Lawrence and Lee's *The Gang's All Here,* an exposé of the Harding administration, failed. *The Best Man,* however, did make good theater because it avoided the usual pitfalls of topicality, kept interest in the plot rather than in the timely references, and built suspense through vivid characterizations. By making Russell and Cantwell both lose the nomination, Vidal avoided a conventional, sentimental ending like the unbelievable conclusion in *The Tenth Man;* and, by showing that neither Russell nor Cantwell was a proper Presidential candidate, Vidal contented the audience with ultimate victory of a dark horse.

Vidal also used the popular dramatic technique of contrast to excellent advantage. In the preface to the published play, Vidal says he first imagined what would happen if he contrasted a man whose public life was above reproach but whose private life was "immoral" with a second man whose private life was above reproach but whose public life was "immoral." Vidal decided to use mental instability for the man whose private life was not exemplary. Instead of elaborating on psychological discussions or explanations as Chayefsky had done in *The Tenth Man,* Vidal merely tainted Russell with the story of an earlier breakdown, which was sufficient to keep audiences interested without more detailed analyses. Vidal selected a charge of homosexuality against Cantwell, since Russell, in keeping with his desire to fight fairly, would not readily consent to exposing such information. The contrast, as developed, provided the major suspense, for Russell's knowledge of Cantwell's past but his unwillingness to capitalize on the information pointed out one of the major differences in the two candidates. Since the audience knew the truth about both Cantwell and Russell, the suspense was heightened by the uncertainty as to whether Russell would stoop to Cantwell's tactics, or if he would use some other method to prevent Cantwell's being nominated. Russell's final strategic move in acceding to Governor Merwin, therefore, lost him the nomination but won him the audience approval for stopping an unworthy opponent.

In his preface, Vidal also said he felt the cast for *The Best Man* was unusual in that he thought all the actors "were fine and I have no regrets, only admiration." The critics and public agreed with his appraisal. Melvyn Douglas gave Russell urbanity and finesse and made audiences understand Russell's strength as well as his political weakness. It is incidental to note that Douglas had also given an excellent performance earlier that same season in the unsuccessful play about politics, *The Gang's All Here.* Frank Lovejoy gave Cantwell the craftiness and wily underhandedness to convince audiences that he would not be their choice for the Presidency. Lee Tracy, as the ex-President, had not appeared in a long-running play for over thirty years, but critics still remembered him in *Broadway* and again praised his vigorous performance in *The Best Man.*

All through the 1960 political campaign, the Nixon–Kennedy TV debates, and the first few months of the Kennedy administration, *The Best Man* drew excellent houses. When the Presidential campaign and election were no longer headline news and public interest began to wane, box office receipts dropped and the play closed in July, 1961.

Unlike *The Best Man,* most popular plays do not depend upon current headlines for audience appeal. Two murder melodrama:, *Witness for the Prosecution* and *Dial M for Murder,* although set in contemporary times, have no connection with current headlines. The popular interest is in the solution of the crime rather than in the era of the play. Both these melodramas were listed among the ten best plays of their seasons, and the Critics' Circle cited *Witness for the Prosecution* as the best foreign play of the year. Newspaper reviews called *Witness for the Prosecution* by Agatha Christie, produced in 1954, "literate," "well contrived," and "tidy."

The cleverly developed, tightly woven plot keeps the audience guessing, for instead of giving the audience clues which will help unravel the mystery, Miss Christie deliberately keeps the audience uninformed as she unfolds the story of Leonard Vole, who comes to the Temple Chambers of Sir Wilfrid Robarts to explain his possible implication in the murder of Miss Emily French. Vole admits he had visited Miss French the night of the murder but that he had walked home before 9:30. Sir Wilfrid suggests the police may have a case against him if they can determine a motive for the murder. Leonard volunteers the information that the police could say he was after Miss French's money. He then asks if his wife's testimony that he was home at the time of the murder would be sufficient evidence to prove his innocence, but Sir Wilfrid reminds him that no one saw him walking home and that a wife's testimony unsupported by other evidence might not convince a jury. To complicate matters, Sir Wilfrid tells Leonard the police know Miss French's will has named him as sole heir. Leonard seems astonished at the news. When Leonard leaves, Sir Wilfrid and his associates think Leonard is either very naïve or extremely clever, and that if he is innocent, he is not aware of the danger of his position. Both men are surprised to learn that Mrs. Romaine Vole is waiting in the outer office. She appears to be extremely calm, and is almost condescending in her replies. She admits she is a foreigner and that she is not Leonard's wife. He had helped her to get out of the Russian zone and she had married him in Berlin, but she had not told him her husband was still alive. When Sir Wilfrid questions her, her answers are, "Is that what Leonard told you?" or "That is what Leonard wants me to say, is it not?" Before she leaves, Romaine recites in a monotone the evidence she will state about Leonard's actions on the night of the murder. The baffled barristers are suspicious of Romaine but they feel certain that Leonard is very much in love with her.

Six weeks later Leonard is on trial for the murder of Miss French. Sir Wilfrid and the prosecuting attorney build up and tear down evidence with the case hanging in the balance until Romaine is called to the stand, not as Mrs. Vole but as Mrs. Heilger because, as she explains, her husband is still alive and her marriage to Leonard is not valid. She testifies that Leonard did not return home until after ten, that he had blood on his sleeve, and that he admitted killing Miss French. On the basis of Romaine's testimony, the prosecuting attorney builds up sufficient circumstantial evidence to convict Leonard.

When the third act opens in Sir Wilfrid's chambers, the audience is as confused as Sir Wilfrid, who obviously knows someone is lying, but he can find no clue to prove Leonard's innocence or Romaine's deception. An overly made-up woman who speaks with a cockney accent comes to the office and offers to sell letters which she says will help Leonard. She tells Sir Wilfrid her motive is revenge because Romaine had taken away the man in her life and the man had slashed her face. Then she pushes aside her unkempt hair to reveal a deep scar on her cheek. As soon as the bargain is struck and the woman turns over the letters, Sir Wilfrid and his associate become engrossed in reading and do not notice that the woman quickly slips out before they can get her name and address. They are elated, nevertheless, for the letters give them the evidence they need. In the final scene, Sir Wilfrid recalls Romaine to the stand, produces the letters, and succeeds in breaking down her reserve as he reads a letter Romaine has written to her "Beloved Max" in which she says that she will lie about Leonard, have him convicted, and thus clear the way for her to be with Max. The trial is soon over and Leonard is declared "not guilty." Sir Wilfrid tells Romaine he cleared Leonard in spite of her, but, to his surprise, Romaine reveals she had disguised herself as the cockney woman, had delivered the letters in which she had written false evidence, and, by convicting herself had cleared Leonard. Sir Wilfrid, amazed at her courage, says he understands her motives, for Romaine has known that Leonard was innocent. Romaine says, "But you do not understand at all. I knew he was *guilty.*"

It was at this point that Miss Christie ended her short story "Witness for the Prosecution," but for the play she added a final twist which she preferred not to reveal to people who had not seen the stage production. In fact, when Kronenberger selected *Witness for the Prosecution* as one of the *Best Plays,* he ended his synopsis before the final episode, stating that Miss Christie has "requested that the outcome should not be published at this time." The last trick withheld from the non-theatergoing public exposed Leonard's duplicity which led to the vengeful Romaine's killing him.

Witness for the Prosecution completely violates Lamb's theory of naturalizing the audience. At no point before the denouement does Miss Christie reveal the true story, and yet the mystery is sufficiently intriguing to make audiences try to piece the clues together, to speculate just who did kill Miss French, and to try to understand Romaine's motives. These reactions might not be sufficiently appealing to make a long run, but Miss Christie has used Sir Wilfrid to mirror the audience's perplexity, for the spectators share Sir Wilfrid's dilemmas, his meager knowledge of the case, and his inability to handle Romaine. Audience sympathy, therefore, is with Sir Wilfrid whose logic in finding and sorting evidence as well as his desire to win the case influences the audience's attempt to unravel the mystery. The unexpected turns in each scene keep building tension, and the play gains in momentum, never lapsing from steadily mounting suspense.

Although there were no stars in the cast, at least three performers gave outstanding performances that pleased critics. Gene Lyons, as Leonard, with his air of bafflement, completely fooled audiences into believing he was innocent. Francis L. Sullivan, familiar to

American audiences through his numerous appearances in English motion pictures, made Sir Wilfrid convincing by his dignity and his bewilderment. Patricia Jessel, however, gave a dazzling performance as Romaine. So convincing was she that audiences were completely deceived by her disguise and cockney accent. Even the more seasoned theatergoers who scanned the program to find the name of the actress who played the cockney woman were baffled by the apparent omission in the program's cast of characters.

Witness for the Prosecution is one of the few plays in which the villain almost gets away with murder. Whether the play would have retained its popular appeal by following the short story and letting Leonard go free is a matter of speculation, but, by the trick ending, Miss Christie has her villain win the case but lose his life. The trick turns of the plot, the excellent performances, and the tightness of the story up to the final curtain when the villain is finally exposed had enough audience interest to give *Witness for the Prosecution* a run of 645 performances.

Dial M for Murder, Frederick Knott's melodrama, produced in 1952, is almost the antithesis of *Witness for the Prosecution* in its method of building suspense. Both plays deal with faithless husbands, both involve a murder, and both complicate the solution of the crime by conflicting evidence. The plot development, however, is totally different. Just as *Witness for the Prosecution* keeps the audience in the dark even up to the last few minutes of the play, *Dial M for Murder* reverses the situation by almost overinforming the audience. A murder is planned on stage. The audience knows who instigates the plan, sees the plot fail and the assassin get killed, and then anticipates how the police will solve the crime. In *Witness for the Prosecution,* the audience plods along with the lawyer trying to follow clues as he gets them; in *Dial M for Murder,* the audience knows the answers but waits for the police to catch up with the facts.

The story concerns Tony Wendice, an ex-champion tennis player, who has married Margot for her money. Margot and Max Halliday, a mystery writer, have fallen in love, and when Tony finds a letter Max has written to Margot, he sends her anonymous blackmail letters. At the same time, he shrewdly maneuvers to have her murdered. His motive is still money, for Margot has named Tony sole beneficiary in her will. He next traps Captain Lesgate who has a prison record and who, Tony knows, is responsible for the death of a Miss Wallace. Under pressure, Lesgate agrees to murder Margot. Tony then carefully plots the murder step by step, but the plot fails because Margot, in self-defense, grabs a pair of scissors, jabs them into Lesgate's back, and kills him. Tony skillfully maneuvers the evidence, including hiding Max's letter in Lesgate's pocket, to make the killing appear to be intentional murder. Margot is tried and found guilty.

Max's experience as a mystery writer helps him figure out what he thinks is a good story Tony can tell the police and thus free Margot, but, in reality, Max has solved the crime. Tony, of course, says the police would never believe such a ridiculous story; and when Max tries to repeat his idea to Inspector Hubbard, he fails to impress the officer. In the last act, the police bring Margot back to her apartment, find she knows nothing about missing keys or the key found in Lesgate's pocket, and are now certain she is innocent. Then, by clever strategy, they trap Tony into supplying the evidence they need to convict him and free Margot.

The evidence concerning the keys is carefully but meticulously emphasized in each act. When Tony explains the murder plot, he impresses upon Lesgate that there are only two keys to the apartment and that he will hide Margot's key under the rug outside the apartment. Lesgate is to replace the key after he has killed Margot. In the next act, the dramatist again emphasizes the importance of the key by having Tony ask Margot for her key, claiming he has misplaced his own. Margot says she prefers to keep her key because she might go out, but when she leaves the room for a few minutes, Tony quickly removes the key from her purse. In the next scene, when Tony returns and finds Lesgate's body, he again maneuvers to get Margot out of the room long enough to take the key out of Lesgate's pocket and replace it in Margot's purse. Thus, when the police find the key, Tony's distortion of the evidence makes it logical for the police to assume Margot must have opened the door to let Lesgate in.

During the last scene, Inspector Hubbard reveals that he checked the key found in Margot's purse and discovered it was Lesgate's own house key. Instead of waiting to return Margot's key after the murder, Lesgate had opened the door and then had placed the key back under the rug before entering the apartment. Inspector Hubbard, therefore, knowing Tony has his own key in his coat pocket, walks off with Tony's coat after directing Tony to go to police headquarters to pick up Margot's personal effects. Inspector Hubbard explains, after Tony leaves, that the only key Tony will find is Lesgate's, and that Margot's key will be under the carpet. If Tony tries to use the key in Margot's purse, finds it does not work, then looks under the rug to see if Lesgate, by error, had replaced the key before going in, the police will have the evidence they need.

In the last few minutes of the play, there is no dialogue. The audience hears Tony return, try the key in the lock, and then walk away. There is a pause, and the audience hears Tony return. Again there is a moment of silence as Tony presumably looks under the rug and discovers the key. When Tony opens the door, he looks at the key, and then at the rug, and the police quickly move in and surround him. The suspense is intensified not only because the audience wants to clear Margot but also because it knows what the police hope to find, and, therefore, waits expectantly for Tony to betray himself.

The scene in which Tony traps Lesgate is equally suspenseful, for the audience gets the information bit by bit and watches with growing suspicion Tony's craftiness as he shrewdly manipulates the conversation until he forces the powerless Lesgate to accept his proposition. Tony has inveigled Lesgate into coming to the apartment to sell him a car, but instead of using his own name, Tony has called himself a Mr. "Fisher." When Lesgate arrives, he recognizes Tony, but not before Tony has identified his visitor as a Mr. Swann whom he had known at Cambridge. Tony casually remarks that he remembers when Lesgate was treasurer of the College Ball and some of the money connected with the affair was stolen. Then slowly and carefully, Tony begins baiting Lesgate. He talks about his own marriage, admits he married Margot for her money, and reveals that he knows she and Max are in love. When Margot destroyed all of Max's letters except one, Tony says, he became curious, stole the letter, and began blackmailing Margot. Tony then changes the topic of conversation and tells Lesgate he saw him in a pub and remembered that Swann had been court-martialed during the war and had served a prison term. Lesgate, apprehensive of Tony's next move, tries to leave, but Tony warns Lesgate he has been checking up on him, knows how often he has changed his name, how many times he has moved owing money to landladies, that he is trying to sell a car for three hundred pounds more than the real owner suspects, and that he is responsible for the death of Miss Wallace from an overdose of cocaine which he obtained for her.

Tony's deliberate, strategic revelation of incriminating evidence and Lesgate's increasing fears not only build up tension but also make Lesgate's agreeing to commit the murder for one thousand pounds convincing. Even when the audience knows all the facts, the action is far from static. Suspense keeps mounting, first as Tony plots the murder, then as the plan fails, then as Tony maneuvers the evidence to convict Margot, and finally as Inspector Hubbard reveals he has uncovered the plot and must trap Tony. Max's theory of what could have happened, even though he is merely creating an alibi, adds further suspense, for the audience cannot help speculating why Max could surmise what happened and the police could not. Inspector Hubbard, in fact, seems almost too casual and unconcerned until he interrupts Max's insistence upon explaining his theory by saying, "Shut up! If you want to save Mrs. Wendice, keep quiet and let me handle this." From that point on, the audience knows the Inspector has found the solution to the crime. All subsequent action proves this but does not diminish the suspense, for the audience hopes the police will trap Tony without further interference from Max, particularly when Inspector Hubbard says, "May the saints protect us from the gifted amateur."

Excellent newspaper reviews indicated *Dial M for Murder* would have box office success. Critics praised the sound plot construction, the dialogue, and the acting. Maurice Evans, who starred as Tony, gave the role the proper combination of craftiness and villainy, and made audiences believe Tony could outsmart even the police, at least for more than half the play. Gusti Huber as Margot, Richard Derr as Max, and John Williams as Inspector Hubbard also intrigued critics and audiences.

With its total of 552 performances, *Dial M for Murder* was the third longest running play produced in the season of 1952–1953, exceeded only by *The Fifth Season* and *The Seven Year Itch*. It was by far the most literate play of the three and demanded more of its audience, for the complexities of the plot and the strategy of the police in contrast with Tony's scheming required the audience constantly to be alerted to clues, not only in solving the murder but in trying to find what misstep Tony would make. Louis Kronenberger has called *Dial M for Murder* "murder without mystery," which aptly summarizes the plot; but the dramatist's use of the technique of naturalizing the audience also makes the play suspense without mystery.

Tony's villainy is not half as frightening as the schoolboys' brutality in *Tea and Sympathy,* a play perhaps even more melodramatic than *Dial M for Murder* because the hero is persecuted relentlessly. The phenomenal popular success of Robert Anderson's *Tea and Sympathy,* produced in 1953, is not due to its frank references to homosexuality. In other long-runing plays dealing with perversion, such as *A Streetcar Named Desire,* which referred to a homosexual, the dramatist asked audiences, either directly or indirectly, to be tolerant of the abnormal character. *Tea and Sympathy,* however, by presenting an innocent victim who suffers from malicious gossip, gains audience sympathy for the persecuted hero who must prove his normality.

The setting is a boys' school in New England. The Headmaster, Bill Reynolds, has been married for a year to Laura, a former actress, but their marriage is not a happy one. Tom Lee, a sensitive seventeen-year-old boy, goes swimming with one of his teachers, Mr. Harris. Several boys from the school see them lying on the beach in the nude, jump to conclusions, and spread the story that both Tom and Mr. Harris are homosexuals. Harris is fired, and school gossip keeps mounting against Tom. Actions and appearances that seemed perfectly normal before the episode are now distorted to indicate that Tom is a pervert, including the fact that his nickname is "Grace," although he got the name as a joke because he went into ecstasies over a motion picture starring Grace Moore. Tom's father arrives, hears the story from Mr. Reynolds, and orders Tom to withdraw from a production of *The School for Scandal* in which he is scheduled to play Lady Teazle. Tom, who is in love with Mrs. Reynolds, is unable to complete the telephone call to the dramatic coach in her presence. Mrs. Reynolds tries to ease the situation by taking over the phone conversation and explaining to the director that Mr. Lee feels Tom has too much schoolwork to continue with the part.

When the boys' insinuations become outright insults, Tom, in desperation, makes a date with Ellie Martin, a waitress known for her promiscuity. He attemps to have sexual relations with her, is unable to do so, and tries to kill himself. Ellie stops him, calls the police and circulates the story around town. Mr. Reynolds is then ready to expel Tom. Laura Reynolds, knowing Tom is in love with her, insists that the boy is normal but Reynolds remains adamant. Finally, goaded by her own unhappiness, Laura accuses her husband of being sadistic because he sees in Tom what he fears in himself. Reynolds, stunned by the accusation, says, "I hope you will be gone when I come back from dinner."

In the last scene, Laura goes to Tom's room, talks to him for a few minutes, and tries to assure him that he is more of a man than he suspects. She tells him she is leaving Mr. Reynolds, starts to walk out, and, in a last-minute decision, bolts the bedroom door, comes over to the bed, and begins to unbutton her blouse. She sits on the bed, takes Tom's hand, and says, "Years from now . . . when you talk about this . . . and you will . . . be kind." And the curtain falls.

Tea and Sympathy and *The Children's Hour* are alike in presenting the effects of malicious gossip. *The Children's Hour,* however, stirred up dissenters who felt the play would have been more gripping if Martha had not admitted she might have an unnatural affection for Karen. *Tea and Sympathy* avoids this controversy. Anderson emphasizes the reasons why Tom might be falsely accused but never leaves any doubt in the minds of the spectators that Tom's accusers are completely unjustified. Instead, Anderson shows that Tom is naïve about perversion, is intensely in love with an older woman, but, at the same time, is a boy caught in a web of circumstantial evidence that can easily be misinterpreted. His allegedly awkward walk, his odd manner of playing tennis, even though he plays a championship game, his love for music and poetry, his refusal to wear a crew haircut, and his shyness with girls are all grist for the mill of those who condemn him. Even Tom's roommate, who knows there is no truth in the accusations, feels he must move. If Tom had been susceptible to perversion, if he had realized the implications of the accusations in the first act, the play would have been less vigorous. By keeping Tom innocent, however, the play becomes compelling drama, for the audience, sharing with Laura the belief that Tom is a normal boy being per-

Tea and Sympathy, Deborah Kerr and John Kerr

secuted, sees the net drawn tighter and the brutality of the gossip grow deeper.

To emphasize the situation, Anderson does contrive to make Bill Reynolds persecute Tom to cover up his own frailty. Without this twist of plot, audiences might not have been sympathetic to Laura's final decision to help Tom prove himself. Anderson builds up the plausibility of the final scene by having Laura admit Tom reminds her of her first husband, who, she says, had been killed in the war doing what was cited as an act of "conspicuous bravery," but which she felt he did because he thought other men had labeled him a coward. In a sense, by her accusation of Bill, Laura sees in Bill what could happen to Tom. At the end of the second act, when Laura overhears Tom making a date with Ellie Martin, she knows what he intends to do. She tries to prevent his going, is tender and affectionate, and insists that she must teach him to dance. Tom impulsively throws his arms around her and kisses her passionately, but when Tom tries to kiss her again, Laura says, "No—" and Tom rushes out. The next day Laura admits to Bill she was sorry she had sent Tom away because she knew he would try to prove his manliness with Ellie Martin and, she concludes, "Last night, I wished he had proved it with me." By contrasting Tom's love scene with Laura and Bill's cool indifference, Anderson convinces the audience Laura really believes Tom is far more manly than Bill.

The popular appeal of *Tea and Sympathy* depended as much upon expert performances as it did upon well-constructed dialogue and situations. To win audience sympathy, Tom had to be presented as a sensitive but not effeminate young man. John Kerr conveyed Tom's sensitivity counterbalanced by his ignorance of the situation and his inability to overcome the mounting shame and ridicule.

Laura also required an expert performer to epitomize the charm an older woman could have for a young man. The wrong performer could easily have made the last episode a seduction scene, but Deborah Kerr—and Joan Fontaine, who replaced her—made audiences understand rather than disapprove of the final scene. By referring to Laura as a former actress, Anderson tailored the role to fit Miss Kerr, but he gave no indication in the dialogue why so talented an actress would give up her career for an obviously unhappy marriage. Little is said, too, about her stage experience other than a casual reference to summer stock companies or to chorus girls. Nor does Anderson indicate at the end of the play that Laura will return to the stage. The few casual remarks about the theater, however, were in keeping with Miss Kerr's effective performance as Laura. She did not rely solely on her remarkable beauty to convey the charm Laura would have for young Tom. Her voice, her stage presence, her compassion as well as her anger created a woman whose motives audiences understood. It was Miss Kerr who made the final scene impressive, effective theater.

The characterization of Bill Reynolds is, perhaps, the key to the audience's acceptance of Laura's decision, for Bill must appear to be the athletic headmaster who enjoys taking camping trips with the boys. Yet, in the last act, when he says that Laura had been married to a "pitiable boy" whom she had wanted to mother, and that she tried to mother Bill and now wanted to mother Tom, Laura's accusation that Bill fears his own susceptibility to perversion comes as a surprise but not as a shock to the audience. Leif Erickson gave a convincing portrayal of Bill's strength as well as his weakness without sacrificing any of the outward manliness of the headmaster. Elia Kazan's expert direction enhanced the excellent performances to gain maximum audience reaction to the increasing maliciousness of Tom's tormentors and to the emotional climax.

Not all theatergoers approved of Laura; some were unmoved by Tom's predicament; but almost all were impressed by the performances and the thought-provoking plot. Audiences who kept the play running for 712 performances came to see Deborah Kerr, Joan Fontaine, and later Mary Fickett portray a woman whose story was fictional.

On the other hand, audiences came to see Anne Bancroft, Ralph Bellamy, Paul Muni, and Paul Scofield in plays which were definitely biographical. *The Miracle Worker* told the story of Annie Sullivan's struggle to teach Helen Keller; *Sunrise at Campobello,* Franklin D. Roosevelt's efforts to conquer the crippling effects of polio; *Inherit the Wind,* a fictionalized account of the Scopes trial with Clarence Darrow and William Jennings Bryan as the attorneys; and *A Man for All Seasons,* Sir Thomas More's refusal to yield to the demands of King Henry VIII.

The Miracle Worker by William Gibson, produced in 1959, was not included among the ten best plays of the season in the Kronen-berger volume, but it did receive the Antoinette Perry Award as the best play of 1959. The omission from the *Best Plays* does not signify that Kronenberger disliked the drama; on the contrary, he said the superb acting and direction made the play's crucial scenes "unforgettable drama." Today Helen Keller is a symbol, an in-spiration to the deaf, dumb, and blind throughout the world. *The Miracle Worker,* therefore, comes almost as a shock to audiences unfamiliar with the story of Helen Keller's childhood, for it depicts her almost as an animal, a pitiful child allowed to run wild. And yet, even in her willfulness, she wins audience sympathy. When she snatches buttons from her aunt's blouse, she is not being malicious. Ensuing action reveals she wants them sewn on the face of her doll so that it may have eyes. Similarly, when Helen clutches the lips of people near her, she is expressing her own desire to talk. Audiences understand Helen's actions, and hope, along with Annie Sullivan, that some miracle can be worked. The fact that Helen Keller even-tually did learn to make adjustments, that the title *The Miracle Worker* indicates Annie Sullivan did succeed, makes the intensity of Helen's struggles more bearable.

The story begins when Helen Keller is stricken with an illness which leaves her blind and deaf. At the age of six, Helen is unkempt and undisciplined. The Keller family, realizing she must be trained, send to the Perkins Institute for a teacher, and Annie Sullivan, an Irish girl from Boston, accepts the position. From then on the play resolves into a battle between pupil and teacher. Annie has brought Helen a doll and begins her training by spelling D-O-L-L into Helen's hand. Helen quickly spells the word back. Annie realizes she has taught Helen only to imitate finger gestures; but she is well aware that Helen is bright. When Annie tries to force Helen to spell the word again if she wants the doll, the willful child, accus-tomed to having her own way, fights, tries to hit Annie, and eventu-ally rushes out of the room and locks Annie in. The next day, Annie refuses to allow Helen to eat with her fingers or to grab food from anyone else's plate. She forces a spoon into Helen's hand, but Helen quickly throws it on the floor. Annie orders the family out of the room and then takes a handful of spoons. As fast as she puts a spoon in Helen's hand, Helen throws it on the floor. Before long, the two are brawling on the chairs, then on the floor, making a shambles of the room until Annie forces Helen to use the spoon. Later, Annie reports to the family that Helen had even folded the napkin. Mrs. Keller, delighted with the news, tells Annie that Helen had been a bright child and had started to talk when she was six months old by saying "wa-wa" for water.

Interference from the family, however, hampers Annie's teaching, and she finally insists she must be given two weeks alone with Helen. The Kellers finally consent to Annie's using the small house adjacent to their home. In those two weeks, Annie still does not teach Helen to communicate, but she does teach her to make a more presentable appearance, to eat properly, and to spell words into Annie's hand. At the end of the trial period, Annie brings Helen back to the dinner table. As soon as Helen senses that her family is with her, she again resorts to eating with her fingers, snatching food from plates, and fighting with Annie even to the point of emptying the water pitcher on Annie. The Keller family is stunned as Annie clutches the child and the water pitcher, drags Helen outside, and says she will force Helen to refill the pitcher. As she makes Helen work the pump and feel the water running on her hand, Annie keeps spelling the word into Helen's hand. Suddenly Helen drops the pitcher, which shatters, but she stands motionless as if in deep thought until she begins to associate the liquid with her first word, and then says, "Wa-wa." She puts her hand into the water, reaches for Annie's hand, and spells the word. She does it again, and then, in mounting excitement, pats the ground and holds up her hand to Annie who immediately spells "ground." Helen follows the same procedure as she touches the pump and the step on the porch. Meanwhile, Annie, who is frantically spelling words into Helen's hand, calls for Mrs. Keller. When Helen touches her, Annie quickly spells the word mother. She spells papa for Mr. Keller and assures him, "She knows." Helen breaks away from her family, finds Annie, touches her, and holds out her hand. Annie spells the word teacher. Helen thinks for a moment, stumbles about until she finds her mother, and then hits the pocket that contains the keys for the small house where she has spent the past two weeks with Annie. When Mrs. Keller gives her the keys, Helen spells a word into her mother's hand. In surprise, Mrs. Keller says, "Teacher," and then realizes that Helen has communicated with her for the first time. Annie, responding to Helen's tugging, takes her hand

and they go back toward the dining room where the family is waiting.

William Gibson obtained the material for his play from the letters of Annie Sullivan and from Nella Braddy's *Anne Sullivan Macy*. In his characterization of Annie, Gibson included those qualities he found in her letters: her wit, her courage, her fear for her own eyesight, and her strong desire to improve her education. In real life, Annie was almost totally blind and underwent extremely painful operations which partially restored her sight.

Several critics called the play "uneven" because it contrasted scenes of physical violence with subdued moments when Annie heard voices from the past or reflected on her own unhappy childhood and memories of the orphanage or expressed fear for her own eyesight. These scenes, along with the episodes of quarrels within the Keller family, were far less effective than the battles between Annie and Helen, but they did serve a dual purpose by easing the tension of the fight scenes and by building up Annie's fears as well as her courage.

Other critics thought the play too documentary, but the vigorous brawls between Annie and Helen were far more dramatic than documentary. These fight scenes were probably among the most realistic battles seen on the New York stage in years. Neither Miss Bancroft nor Patty Duke appeared to be simulating the fight scenes, for their grappling and hitting seemed intensive and exhausting. *Variety* magazine reported that in the first month of the play, at least thirty-five chairs were broken. Audiences also thought the lengthy scenes devoted to Annie's simple method of hand communication were effective theatrical moments rather than documentary episodes. In fact, audiences became more intrigued as Annie explained that a mother may say a million words before a child responds with one, and that she was prepared to spell a million words into Helen's hand until she did communicate. When Mrs. Keller, fascinated by the idea, asked Annie to teach her the hand language, Annie said, "I'll teach you tomorrow. That makes only half a million each."

Aside from the biographical authenticity, *The Miracle Worker* appealed to audiences because it embodied the popular situation of the triumphant woman. The triumph, however, is doubly effective, for Helen learns to overcome her handicap, and Annie is victorious in teaching Helen to communicate. The vigor of the play was not due entirely to the facts of Helen Keller's life nor to Annie Sullivan's stubborn determination to train the child. Nor is it discrediting the Gibson drama to say that the play alone was not entirely responsible for the popular success. It was, rather, a combination of the story and the remarkable performances of Anne Bancroft and Patty Duke that made *The Miracle Worker* a long-running commercial hit.

The role of Annie Sullivan was a complete change for Anne Bancroft after her vivid performance as Gittel in *Two for the Seesaw*. As the strong-willed Irish girl, Miss Bancroft dominated the stage with her intensity, her vital animation, and her vibrant personality. She epitomized the strength of Annie Sullivan's character, not only in her battles with her own physical handicaps and her desire to improve her literacy but also in her battles to teach Helen to communicate. Never for a moment does the audience doubt that Annie feels compassion for the unfortunate child. As a result, the audience understands Annie's lack of outward signs of tenderness, her hardheadedness in dealing with Helen's tantrums, and her firm determination to allow nothing to interfere with her attempts to reach Helen's mind. Miss Bancroft made audiences understand Annie's determination as well as her efforts to conceal her sympathy for Helen.

In one scene, students from the Perkins Institute for the blind appeared on stage, and their performances were heartbreaking, for the audience knew these handicapped children were not play-acting their sightlessness. From a theatrical point of view, their presence on stage became doubly effective because it emphasized the authenticity of Patty Duke's performance as Helen. As she stumbled across the stage, thrashed her arms about, clutched frightened children, or fought vigorously with Annie, she imitated to perfection the wild, blank stare of the blind children. The role was indeed a difficult one because Helen spoke only the word "wa-wa" in the last scene. For the rest of the play, she depended entirely on gestures, body movements, and action to communicate. To insure audience reaction, Gibson had Annie speak to Helen as though she could hear when she spelled words, fought with her, or tried to force her to obey orders, which made Helen's actions much easier for audiences to understand. Patty Duke played the role so convincingly that audiences soon forgot Annie's dialogue was to keep them informed and watched Helen's movements and gestures. Playing opposite so strong a theatrical personality as Anne Bancroft, a lesser actress could easily have been overshadowed in spite of the importance of Helen's role. Patty Duke, however, particularly in the fighting scenes, was as impressive as Anne Bancroft. The two actresses balanced each other's performance and made their scenes together exciting theater.

At the end of the first season, Tresa Hughes replaced Miss Bancroft during a summer vacation, and after a long and exhaustive run in the play, Anne Bancroft and Patty Duke were replaced by Suzanne Pleshette as Annie and Karen Lee as Helen. Their excellent portrayals helped prolong the run until the play acquired a total of seven hundred performances.

Both *The Miracle Worker* and *Sunrise at Campobello* illustrate man's ability to overcome physical handicaps. In *The Miracle Worker,* Helen Keller conquers loss of sight and hearing; in *Sunrise at Campobello,* Franklin Delano Roosevelt conquers the crippling effects of polio. The basic difference is that Helen Keller unwittingly opposes Annie Sullivan's efforts to help; Franklin Delano Roosevelt struggles valiantly but alone to regain the ability to walk.

Sunrise at Campobello by Dore Schary, produced in 1958, interested audiences regardless of political affiliations. Even those rabid Republicans who disapproved of Roosevelt's policies were impressed by the dramatic vigor of the play and by the dramatic representation of Roosevelt, his wife, his mother, Al Smith, and Louis Howe. Although the play was biographical, it fascinated audiences as though it were fictionalized drama.

The play spans a three-year period from August 10, 1921, the day Roosevelt was stricken with polio, to June 26, 1924, the night he nominated Al Smith for the Presidency at the Democratic National Convention in New York. The first act begins at Campobello, Roosevelt's summer home in New Brunswick, Canada, and establishes the happy family life of the Roosevelts. The first scene ends as Roosevelt takes ill. The next scene establishes the seriousness of the illness and introduces an argument between Roosevelt's mother and Louis Howe, his political advisor. Mrs. Sara Roosevelt believes her son should retire to Hyde Park and spend the rest of his life in comparative ease writing or managing the estate. Howe, on the other hand, believes Roosevelt could achieve greatness. Mrs. Roosevelt calls Howe's plans "grandiose ideas," but Howe says Roosevelt needs those ideas, particularly during this illness. In the third scene, Howe and Miss Lehand, Roosevelt's secretary, have made all arrangements to move Roosevelt back to New York. They have tried to insure as much privacy as possible, for Roosevelt is still immobile, and there is uncertainty whether he will regain the use of his legs. Howe tells Miss Lehand the newspaper reporters will not see Roosevelt until he is comfortably settled on the train. Mrs. Sara Roosevelt expresses her disapproval of the manner in which her son is being "placed on exhibition," but Eleanor Roosevelt explains that her husband is a public figure and that it will be impossible to keep crowds away. When Roosevelt is brought downstairs and approves of the plan, all arguments cease. Roosevelt looks cheerful until he is left alone for a moment. Only then does he allow himself to show the strain he has undergone. When he drops his hat and tries to reach for it, he cannot move. Eleanor Roosevelt comes back, sees what has happened, and hands him the hat. Roosevelt perks up, puts the cigarette holder in his mouth, holds the dog on his lap, and smiles as he is carried off stage.

The second act begins not quite one year later. Roosevelt is still in a wheel chair. He confesses to Eleanor that he has a fear that someday he may be caught alone, perhaps in a fire, and be unable to move. In secret, therefore, he has practiced crawling so that he could get to a window or door. When Howe arrives, Roosevelt, for the benefit of Eleanor and Howe, eases himself out of the chair and proves that he can crawl out of the room. The strain, however, has been telling on Eleanor. When the children arrive and insist that she read a story, the youngest child asks, "Mommy, who is older— you or Granny?" In the midst of the story, Eleanor begins to cry. Miss Lehand hustles the children out of the room and sends Louis Howe in. Eleanor regains her composure, says she knows she has frightened the children, and adds, "I won't ever do that again."

The second scene, six months later, builds to the inevitable quarrel between Mrs. Roosevelt and her son. Roosevelt informs her that Louis Howe predicted he could be President of the United States, but Mrs. Roosevelt thinks it would be far better if her son were to conserve his strength and forget about ambition. Roosevelt, firmly determined to prove that he is making progress, waits until everyone has left the room and then tries getting out of the chair and using his crutches. He is halfway out when a crutch slips away and he falls to the floor. The defeat stuns him. At the same time, he is fearful that someone may have heard him fall. He makes a desperate effort, using all his strength, until he gets back into the chair. Even though the task has exhausted him, he again reaches for the crutches and stubbornly starts to push himself up again as the curtain falls.

Five months elapse between Acts II and III. In the interim, Roosevelt has actively supported Al Smith for the Presidential nomination. Louis Howe says Al Smith is coming to see Roosevelt because he probably intends to ask him to make the nominating speech at Madison Square Garden. When Al Smith arrives, he and Roosevelt talk about what should be included in a nominating speech. Finally, Smith asks Roosevelt to make the nomination. As soon as Smith leaves, Roosevelt tells Miss Lehand to get a blueprint of the platform so that he can estimate how many steps he will have to take. Louis Howe says it will be ten steps, and "they are liable to be the biggest steps you ever took in your life."

The second scene takes place in a small room at Madison Square Garden the night of the convention, June 26, 1924. The noise of the convention and the roaring crowd is in the background. Roosevelt adjusts his braces and prepares for his entrance to the convention hall. His mother, completely reconciled to his participation, arrives in time to give him her blessing and to caution him, "Franklin, speak out loudly and clearly."

The final scene on the platform is short, effective, and reaches an impressive, emotional climax. After a few preliminary announcements, the chairman calls for the representative from Connecticut, who yields to the speaker from New York. The chairman then recognizes Roosevelt. The rest of the scene is played without dialogue. Jimmy hands his father the crutches, and Roosevelt, very slowly, walks the ten steps as the applause grows. The crowd yells and the band blares "The Sidewalks of New York." Roosevelt gains assurance, smiles, holds the lectern with his left hand and waves with his right hand, a gesture that people would always associate with him. He continues to smile and wave at the crowd which cheers and applauds as the curtain falls.

In the preface to the text, Schary states that he had the last scene in mind first and that he built the entire play up to this climax. In doing so, he has made the concluding few moments unforgettable theater. Nothing in the preceding action detracts from the emotional appeal of the last scene. Schary intentionally avoids having Roosevelt say, "My friends," but captures the Roosevelt personality by including the hand-waving, the cigarette holder, and even the Scottish terrier.

Although the play deals with politics and the Roosevelt family, it handles both superficially. Schary presents the quarrels between Roosevelt and his mother skillfully by keeping both characters sympathetic and by making certain that audiences realize Mrs. Sara Roosevelt is concerned with her son's health and is not interfering because she objects to his political ambitions. Just as in *State of the Union*, political discussion is kept to a minimum. Roosevelt does refer to the prejudices against Al Smith, the platform of the Democratic party, and the policies to be included in the nominating speech, but this discussion, for the most part, is limited to one scene. Most of the play emphasizes Roosevelt's struggle to overcome his handicap, his courage in the face of physical defeat, and his strong determination to walk again.

The popular appeal is partly in the story, for it illustrates the ability of man to overcome obstacles. Schary also prepares the audience for the scene between Smith and Roosevelt by indicating that Howe and Roosevelt expect Al Smith to ask Roosevelt to nominate him. When Smith arrives, the audience shares with Roosevelt the cat-and-mouse game of drawing Smith out.

Excellent performances, particularly by Ralph Bellamy as Roosevelt, Mary Fickett as Eleanor, and Henry Jones as Louis Howe helped draw audiences to the theater. Mary Fickett conveyed Eleanor Roosevelt's strength and courage. If she had tried to imitate Mrs. Roosevelt's voice, she might have ridiculed the character and lost audience sympathy. Those radio listeners who heard Mrs. Roosevelt's first series of talks remember that her voice was rather high-pitched. Mrs. Roosevelt later learned to modulate her voice and acquire a more pleasant tone in keeping with her warm personality. Mary Fickett simulated the Roosevelt voice problem by raising her voice only once or twice during the play, but for the most part, she concentrated on representing Mrs. Roosevelt's personality. She was particularly effective in revealing Eleanor Roosevelt's anxiety over her husband's health, her children's welfare, and her own efforts to help her husband keep active in politics.

The principal appeal, however, was Ralph Bellamy's remarkable performance as Franklin Delano Roosevelt, for he captured the famous Roosevelt grin and even the magnetic voice. In the final scene, as he took the ten steps and the crowd cheered, he bore a marked resemblance to Roosevelt. He was equally convincing in depicting Roosevelt's strength as well as his desperation in moments of physical defeat. Audiences may have been more impressed by Bellamy's remarkable performance than by the play, for the road company without Ralph Bellamy failed to duplicate the New York success of 556 performances.

Strangely enough, critics did not call *Sunrise at Campobello* documentary, even though it was based on fact and used actual names of the characters involved. On the other hand, critics did refer to *Inherit the Wind,* which used fictitious names and fictionalized sequences, as journalistic because it was based on the famous Scopes "monkey trial," and included some of the speeches made during the trial. Jerome Lawrence and Robert E. Lee, who wrote *Inherit the Wind*, produced in 1955, stated in the preface that the play was derived from the Scopes trial but they had not written merely a journalistic representation. They felt that time had added new interpretations to the issues of the trial. For that reason they had changed names, some of the events, and even some of the speeches. Theatergoers familiar with the background of the play, however, have little trouble identifying Henry Drummond as Clarence Darrow who defended Scopes; Matthew Harrison Brady as William Jennings Bryan, the three-time loser in Presidential elections, who prosecuted Scopes; E. K. Hornbeck as H. L. Mencken, the newspaper reporter; and Berton Cates as John T. Scopes, who was tried for teaching Darwin's *Origin of Species* in the classroom.

In retrospect, the play draws curious parallels with more recent political investigations, witch hunts during the Communism scare, and arguments over school practices. Even at this writing, school districts throughout the country are facing the problem of parents instituting lawsuits to fight voluntary Bible reading in the classroom or organizations protesting against the abolishment of Bible reading. *Inherit the Wind* does not, as some critics inferred, deride religion, but it does point out the prejudices of backwoods communities which blindly follow such religious zealots as Brady and the Reverend Brown. *Inherit the Wind* impresses audiences not only as a journalistic representation of the Scopes trial but also as a propaganda drama disclosing the difficulties of dealing with prejudiced people such as the Hillsboro folk who condemned Berton Cates.

As the play opens, Cates has been arrested for teaching Darwin's *Origin of Species* in the town's public school. Matthew Harrison Brady arrives to act as prosecuting attorney and is welcomed by the townspeople with banners, picnic lunches, and speeches. Brady is surprised, however, to discover that the Baltimore *Herald* has sent a reporter, E. K. Hornbeck, to cover the case. He is even more astonished when he learns that Henry Drummond, one of the most famous lawyers in the country, has agreed to handle the defense.

Drummond soon finds the trial getting out of hand, for Brady has the sympathy of the townspeople and even the court. When Drummond calls in three noted scientists, the head of a department of zoology, a professor of geology and archaeology, and a philosopher and anthropologist, to testify, he finds that Brady will not agree to any testimony on the sciences but he will permit testimony on the Bible. In a strategic move, Drummond summons Brady, whom he calls the most eminent authority on the Bible, to testify. Although the procedure is highly irregular, Brady agrees to take the stand. Drummond moves cautiously at first, asking questions about the Bible, questions which lead only to confusion for Brady.

Finally, Drummond tricks Brady into admitting that since the sun was not created until the fourth day, the first day could have been any length of time from hours to years to centuries. As Drummond continues to confuse Brady, the spectators begin laughing. Brady finally breaks down into jibbering and mumbling. When he is left alone on stage with Mrs. Brady, he tells her that he cannot bear to hear people laugh at him.

The third act leads up to the verdict. A radio announcer setting up equipment explains that this will be the first time a verdict has been broadcast from a courtroom. The scene points out the basic differences between the two attorneys, for Drummond frightens the radio announcer by saying, "God," and the announcer hastily warns him not to say the word on the air. When Drummond asks, "Why the hell not?" the announcer is completely upset. Brady, on the other hand, approaches the microphone, asks which side of the microphone he should use, and then asks whether his voice would have sufficient projection for the radio apparatus.

The mayor arrives with a telegram and advises the judge that it would be better to handle Cates carefully, for newspapers all over the country are raising a fuss about the trial, and the politicians at the state capitol are afraid that a wrong decision could do nation-wide harm. When the jury brings in a verdict of "Guilty," the judge hesitates, and then explains that since there is no precedent for the case, he will fine Cates one hundred dollars. Brady immediately objects and demands stronger punishment, but Drummond says he will appeal the decision to the State Supreme Court. Brady then tries to hold up the proceedings by pulling out a thick sheaf of papers and asking for permission to read his remarks. The judge tells Brady he may read his remarks after the court is adjourned. When the people in the courtroom begin filing out, Brady is dis-tressed by the inattention of the crowd, and by the interference from the radio announcer who tells him that the program is over. Unable to suffer this defeat, Brady is again reduced to gibberish, and collapses. As he is carried off stage, he makes an inaugural speech as President of the United States. Very shortly, word comes that Brady has died.

Cates learns that the Baltimore *Herald* has paid his bond money, and Cates prepares to leave with Drummond. The play gives no definite indication of what ultimately will happen to Cates, but when Cates asks Drummond if he won or lost, Drummond says, "You won," because the trial helped abolish a bad law. At the final curtain, the audience knows that Drummond will continue to assist Cates.

The title, a quotation from the Book of Proverbs, "He that troubleth his own house shall inherit the wind," is used twice, first by Brady when he interrupts Reverend Brown's prayer meeting. The minister's religious zeal causes him to pray for the destruction of Cates and even the destruction of his own daughter because she is in love with Cates. Brady stops the minister, calms him, and then quotes the passage from Scripture. In the last act, Hornbeck says Brady's quotation was, in a sense, his own obituary, but before Hornbeck can find the exact words in the Bible, Drummond quietly quotes the passage. Hornbeck, suddenly realizing that Drummond is not an agnostic, accuses him of being more religious than Brady.

Instead of denying the statement, Drummond remains silent.

Lawrence and Lee have enhanced the audience appeal by building up the circus atmosphere of the trial with ice cream and hot-dog vendors, religious revival meetings, and picnic lunches. They have changed fact for fiction by having Bryan die at the end of the trial, and, perhaps to add popular appeal, have built up the love story of Cates and Rachel Brown. These innovations help dim the journalistic aspects of the play and heighten the emotional impact. Instead of emphasizing the propaganda, the dramatists have kept their philosophical theory of the importance of the trial in current times to a minimum, and have inferred rather than stated their objectives. Drummond does say, "The right to think is on trial," and the play does prove that such trials do jeopardize freedom of thought.

Lawrence and Lee contrast Drummond and Brady for maximum dramatic effect. They develop the characterization of Brady to indicate that he is handling the case not to win justice but to be back in the limelight, for the trial offers him an opportunity to make headlines and to keep in front of the public. Brady's reactions, unlike those of a three-time loser for the Presidency, appear to be those of a man seeking to gain a possible nomination. Drummond, on the other hand, is much shrewder than Brady, but his brilliance frightens the townspeople, and, at times, even Brady. Yet the dramatists make Drummond's fight for justice convincing, for he seems less interested in the notoriety than in the verdict.

Even the entrances of the two characters provide contrast. For Brady, the dramatists establish the circus atmosphere and the wild public ovations. The entire first scene, however, is a build-up for Drummond's effective entrance. The opening scene introduces Cates, the mayor, Reverend Brown, his daughter, E. K. Hornbeck, and Brady. The action establishes the prejudices of the townspeople and the audience's suspicion that Cates will not have a fair trial in such a community. When the news breaks that Drummond will handle the case, there is further preparation for Drummond's entrance. People refer to Drummond as "Cunning," "Infidel," "the Devil," and "a slouching hulk of a man whose head juts out like an animal's." Finally, everyone leaves the stage except a small girl and Hornbeck. Drummond enters slowly. The evening shadows accentuate a sinister profile, and the little girl screams, "It's the

Devil." Hornbeck walks over to Drummond and greets him "Hello, Devil. Welcome to Hell," and the scene ends.

Perhaps the best illustration of the play's tremendous hold upon audiences occurred one evening early in the run. At the first intermission, the audience buzzed with excitement. People in the balcony crowded over the railing pointing to a famous motion picture and television star and an unidentified woman who were in aisle seats. Women crowded the aisle, and there seemed to be every indication that the audience would never return to normality. As soon as the lights went up for the second act, however, the theater was hushed. All during the performance, the star and his new flame were apparently forgotten, but at the end of the act, new crowds swarmed down the aisle or leaned over the balcony. Yet once the curtain rose on the third act, the theater audience was again hushed.

The phenomenal appeal of *Inherit the Wind* is not diminished by its fictionalized development, for most audiences associate the characters with their real-life counterparts. The play held audience interest on its own merits, but the magnetic performances of Paul Muni as Drummond, Edward Begley as Brady, and Tony Randall as E. K. Hornbeck were equally important in establishing the long run. Muni's brilliant performance, his tenseness seething under his casual air, particularly during the explosive courtroom scene, intensified the emotional appeal of the play. The peculiar fascination of Muni's performance was not limited to his voice. He made every gesture, every bit of stage business dominate the scene. When he played cat-and-mouse with Brady, he entranced the audience. Brady had the more spectacular role, more opportunity to shout Biblical quotations, sway the Hillsboro townspeople, and bask in the adulation of the crowd. Muni won audience sympathy not because he was the underdog but because he made Drummond's wit and brilliant strategy overshadow Brady's expansive bombast. Muni held attention whether he shrugged his shoulders, grunted, snapped his bright suspenders, or merely stalked across the stage.

During the run of the play, an eye operation forced Muni to leave the cast. Rather than continue with a stand-by performer, the producer, fully aware of Muni's importance to the play, closed the show, signed Melvyn Douglas to replace Muni, and put the production back into rehearsal to give Douglas proper time to learn

A Man for All Seasons, Olga Bellin and Paul Scofield

the role. After Muni returned to the cast, Douglas, who had given an excellent performance, starred in the road company.

One newspaper reviewer suggested that the appeal of the play was doubtful, for he thought the drama might offend those who were deeply devout and that although the play did show that the right to think was helped by the trial, he wondered if many theatergoers would be interested enough in the events that brought about this freedom to see the play. The phenomenal record of 806 performances proved that *Inherit the Wind,* particularly with Paul Muni in the cast, did have strong interest for theatergoers.

Man's right to think, as defended in *Inherit the Wind,* is, in a sense, the basis for Robert Bolt's *A Man for All Seasons,* produced in 1961. Sir Thomas More, the hero, has no sixteenth-century Clarence Darrow to defend his cause, but Robert Bolt's eloquent drama presents its own brilliant plea for a man's right to hold to his own personal beliefs.

Ecstatic newspaper critics called *A Man for All Seasons* "eloquent," "a classic," and "touching." The Critics' Circle cited the drama as the best foreign play of the year. The historical aspects of the drama may, perhaps, have helped the popular appeal, for a great many theatergoers knew that Sir Thomas More was Lord Chancellor during the early reign of King Henry VIII. In spite of his loyalty to the King, More would not give his consent to Henry's divorce from Queen Catharine nor would he approve of Henry's plan to marry Anne Boleyn. When King Henry set himself up as head of the Church of England, More would not express his opinion, but, by maintaining a stubborn silence, indicated his disapproval.

Although the basic plot deals with Catholicism and the split between King Henry and the Vatican, the drama is neither religious nor controversial propaganda. Instead, it presents a highly literate portrayal of a noble man who adheres to his ideals. Robert Bolt, who states in the preface to the text that he is not a Catholic, avoids religious discussions to justify More's beliefs or to disapprove of King Henry's actions. More's religion is of secondary importance to the audience; the primary interest is the characterization of a hero who refuses to lie and thus causes his own death. As Bolt further explains in the preface, More had many reasons for enjoying life. He was wealthy, a distinguished scholar, and an important political figure. Yet his integrity prevented him from betraying his conscience and committing perjury to keep alive.

Almost of equal importance to More is the role of the Common Man who played multiple minor roles but whose principal function as narrator helped link the scenes and action into an integrated drama. The Common Man consistently addressed the audience, telling where scenes were located or identifying characters. He was more than a narrator, for he kept the audience informed as the action progressed, showing his own likes or dislikes as the characters appeared.

The drama sustains suspense through the web of circumstances which leads to More's death. The intrigue builds slowly but steadily. As the play opens, the Common Man introduces More, his wife, his daughter, Sir Richard Rich, and the Duke of Norfolk. When More gives Rich a silver cup, he admits it had been sent to him as a bribe, and, therefore, he has no intention of keeping it. The audience, however, because of the Common Man's contemptuous tone as he introduces Rich, suspects the lavish gift will be used in some way to bring about More's downfall. The scene shifts quickly to Wolsey's office where Wolsey tries to convince More that since Henry is without an heir, he should divorce Catharine. More, however, refuses to intercede for Henry or to agree to Wolsey's suggestion that they could influence the Pope's decision. When More returns home, he does not discuss the details of the conference with his wife nor does he seem pleased when he says Norfolk has suggested that More will replace Wolsey as Chancellor.

In a brief passage between episodes, the Common Man announces that Wolsey, who has been charged with High Treason, has died on his way to the Tower, and More has become the Chancellor. When the lights come up and the audience sees Sir Richard Rich with Cromwell, it immediately suspects Rich will eventually aid Cromwell. A visit from the Spanish Ambassador adds further suspense, for Cromwell informs him that the King will ask More to agree to the divorce. The Ambassador is upset by the statement, but the Common Man, now playing the role of Cromwell's steward, has a few humorous moments as he assures the Ambassador that More does not discuss the divorce.

The scene shifts again to More's home where King Henry comes to ask for More's support but finds that he is unwilling to intercede for the King. Henry says he will not involve More in his future plans, but that he will have no opposition, that he wants no statements against him from More. Sir Thomas replies, "I am Your Grace's loyal minister."

In the next episode, Richard Rich pleads with More to employ him, but More refuses. The last scene of the first act takes place in a pub where Rich meets Cromwell. After a brief discussion, Cromwell indicates that More can be a stumbling block to his plans and that the only solution is to frighten More. The audience now knows definitely that Cromwell will persist in his cruelty until he has trapped More and that he will use the weakling, Sir Richard Rich, to carry out his plans.

In the second act, pressure mounts against More. He resigns as Lord Chancellor. He then is summoned by Cromwell to answer charges, but, in spite of all attempts to trick him into making an incriminating reply, he consistently gives noncontroversial answers. Finally, More is sent to prison. Despite the pleadings of his wife, his daughter, her husband, and the Duke of Norfolk, who berates him for his stubbornness, he refuses to change his attitude. His daughter suggests that if he says the words of the oath, he may still think otherwise in his heart, but More insists he cannot swear to the Act of Succession. At the trial, Sir Richard Rich distorts a statement More had once made, and then adds additional false testimony to provide sufficient evidence for Cromwell to order More to be beheaded.

Sir Thomas More and the Common Man dominate the play, but the other characters provide the proper background to develop More's conflict. King Henry appears in only one scene to impress the audience as the vigorous, handsome young king. Cromwell is properly villainous; the Spanish Ambassador is slyly suave as he attempts to encourage More to maintain his attitude. If any characters suffer, it is the More family, for Lady Alice More, although devoted to her husband, is not sympathetic to his cause. She berates rather than consoles him, for she does not believe he is justified in maintaining his stubborn silence and neglecting the welfare of his family. Sir Richard Rich begins as an ambitious young clerk and is immediately identified by the Common Man as a distasteful character, whom he introduces to the audience contemptuously as "Master Richard Rich." And when Rich leaves the stage at the end of the scene, the Common Man again expresses his dislike by telling the audience, "That one'll come to nothing." These remarks, however, are sufficient warning to prepare the audience for the last section of the play when Rich commits perjury to convict More.

The story of Sir Thomas More's life might not have had sufficient appeal to sustain a long run, but the heroic story was further enhanced by the physical production. *A Man for All Seasons* intrigued audiences with one set but multiple changes to give the effect of multiple scenes. And yet this feat was accomplished with a minimum of properties. A colorful drop, a different colored tablecloth, or a property or two changed the set instantly. As one of his many roles, the Common Man acted as stagehand, whipping off a cloth, doffing one hat and quickly donning another, or bustling with properties which he pulled out of a trunk as fast as he threw others back in.

The stage set, elegant in its simplicity, consisted primarily of a staircase that started backstage at the right and curved downstage to the left. An iron gate placed at the halfway landing became Sir Thomas More's prison cell. Downstage right, flanked by the curving staircase, a large table could signify Sir Thomas More's living room or the Court of Cromwell or a room in the prison merely by adding a new property and by removing another.

Were More portrayed solely as an epic hero, the play might not have been so popular, but Bolt emphasized not only More's integrity but also his wit. Bolt has included amusing lines which are not steeped in political intrigue or in church affairs. For example, when More returns home from his conference with Wolsey, he finds that William Roper is still there, even though it is three o'clock. As Roper and More's daughter come on stage, More says, "Good morning, William. It's a little early for breakfast." On one of his later visits to Cromwell, More, knowing that his family is having trouble obtaining proper food, says he will be back for dinner and adds, "I'll bring Cromwell to dinner . . . it'd serve him right," and his daughter says reprovingly, "Oh, father, don't be witty."

This interlacing of wit with the seriousness of the situation gives the play balance, for Bolt constantly provides comic relief through More's repartee or through the less subtle humor of the Common Man who makes asides about the characters or the situations. The complexities of his multiple roles are amusing in themselves and add to the comic relief. Even at the end of the play when More has been beheaded, the Common Man has the last lines as he comes to the front of the stage and addresses the audience. "It isn't difficult to keep alive, friends . . . just don't *make* trouble, or, if you must make trouble, make the sort that's expected."

Well-written literary drama in itself is not sufficient to insure a long run; brilliant acting cannot salvage a mediocre play; neither can a strong plot overshadow inferior performances. Stage settings and costumes in themselves are not sufficient to sustain audience interest for an entire evening, but when the physical properties, a superb cast, and a strong drama are all combined, they make not only excellent drama but also popular theater. *A Man for All Seasons* excelled in all these aspects. Audiences enjoyed the brilliant costumes, the physical production, the thought-provoking drama of Sir Thomas More, who remained true to his own convictions, and the excellent actors who interpreted the eloquent dialogue. As Sir Thomas More, Paul Scofield endowed the character with dignity, with keen intellect, and with quiet humor. The role, however, was not limited to one performer, for Emlyn Williams and later William Roderick proved capable in handling the many shadings of the characterization. All three actors underplayed rather than overemphasized the dialogue, and, by doing so, helped make the hero more human, more humble, and more appealing. George Rose, ideally cast as the Common Man, obtained laughs without overemphasizing lines. By doffing a hat or flipping a tablecloth, he made every gesture, in fact every word, count as he moved in and out of the play with dexterity, always maintaining his own individuality in spite of his numerous roles as narrator, stagehand, steward for More, steward for Cromwell, boatman, jailer, or headsman.

At the end of the first season, further box office impetus came from a multiplicity of prizes awarded to the play or the cast. In addition to the Critics' Circle Award, *A Man for All Seasons* won several prizes in the *Variety* Theater Critics' Poll and the Antoinette Perry Awards (Tony). Both Scofield and Rose won the *Variety* Poll for their performances. Scofield also received a Tony for the best male performance of the year. Robert Bolt, as author, and Roger L. Stevens and Robert Whitehead also received Perry Awards as producers. The *Variety* Poll designated Noel Williams as best director for *A Man for All Seasons*.

The popular success of *A Man for All Seasons,* however, surprised even its producers. One of the backers confided that he had invested in the show to enable the American public to enjoy a play which he considered a literary gem, and he was prepared to write off his investment as a tax loss. To his surprise, he found that even before the end of the first year's run, he not only regained his original investment, but also made a larger profit than he had ever realized on any other production. Toward the end of the run, the management did resort to the use of two-for-one tickets, but *A Man for All Seasons* was well established as a highly successful commercial venture before this practice was initiated. At the end of the second year on Broadway, *A Man for All Seasons* closed with a total run of 637 performances.

Nine
Prize Plays

Since 1950, the Critics' Circle Awards and Pulitzer Prizes for drama have helped prolong a number of runs on Broadway. Nine of the sixteen Critics' Circle Award plays in the years between 1950 and 1965 have run over five hundred performances. In this same period, seven of the thirteen Pulitzer Prize plays have run over five hundred performances. Two of these were musical comedies; the remaining five long-running Pulitzer plays also won the Critics' Circle Awards.

When the Critics' Circle and Pulitzer Committee choose different productions in the same season, the public does not always understand why or how the selections are made. In the 1949–1950 season, for example, the Critics' Circle selected Carson McCullers' *The Member of the Wedding,* but the Pulitzer Committee awarded its prize to *South Pacific.* Theater commentators who disapproved of the Pulitzer selection maintained that a musical comedy should not receive a drama award. Yet, that same season, several members of the Critics' Circle recommended that their award be given to Gian-Carlo Menotti's libretto for his opera *The Consul.*

Some observers believe the Critics' Circle considers not only the effectiveness of the drama but also its performers. If this statement is accurate, the critics undoubtedly chose *The Member of the Wedding* because the actors were excellent. Many critics, however, were skeptical about the play itself. They praised the natural dialogue, the remarkable acting, and the poetic tone of the drama, but they wrote with reservations, as though they doubted that audiences would support so poetic a drama. Some critics use *poetic* to designate plays with rhythmic cadence or dialogue written in verse form; others use this word when they condemn pseudoartistic or forced lyrical dialogue. *The Member of the Wedding* was called poetic, however, because the play dealt with emotions sharply etched in clear-cut characterizations, because the dialogue flowed naturally with subtle undertones that raised the realistic conversation above the level of commonplace chatter, and, finally, because the play emphasized characterization rather than plot.

The story concerns Frankie Addams, a twelve-year-old girl, whose mother is dead. Her father leaves Frankie in the care of Berenice, a Negress who is a combination cook and nursemaid. Berenice has been married four times, but her first husband, Ludie, she admits, is the only one she really loved. Frankie's only playmate is John Henry, her seven-year-old cousin, with whom she often grows short-tempered.

The girls' club which meets next door distresses Frankie, for she is not a member. Berenice explains that the girls are two years older; but when the club elects Mary Littlejohn, a girl about Frankie's age, to membership, Frankie is furious, for she had hoped to belong to the group. When Frankie's brother, Jarvis, who is in the army, comes home on leave to be married, Frankie decides that she will go along with Jarvis and Janice on their honeymoon. She feels that she now is always alone, but if she goes with them, she will belong to someone. Berenice laughs at the idea and reminds Frankie that when Noah took the animals on the ark, he took them by pairs.

After the wedding, when Jarvis and Janice are ready to leave, Frankie gets into the car with them, but her father drags her out and takes her back into the kitchen, followed by Jarvis and Janice who tell her she will visit them after they are settled. Later, Mr. Addams and Berenice discover that Frankie has run away and has taken her father's pistol.

Frankie returns at four o'clock the next morning to learn that

John Henry is critically ill. Before Berenice can explain, Honey Brown, Berenice's foster brother, appears and tells Berenice he had pulled a razor on a man and did not wait to find out whether he killed the man. He knows he must get away. Berenice warns him to avoid the white folks' section, for if they catch him, they will lynch him. After Honey Brown has left, Berenice tells Frankie that John Henry has meningitis.

The final scene occurs about three months later. Both John Henry and Honey Brown are dead. The Addams family is moving to another part of town, but Berenice is not going with them. When Berenice asks Frankie not to quarrel on this last afternoon together, Frankie says she will come to visit Berenice, but Berenice says she knows Frankie will not. Frankie is no longer a lonely, unwanted child, for she now has a friend in Mary Littlejohn, who will be riding in the moving van with her. Even Barney McKean, a boy whom she called nasty earlier in the play, now seems interested in Frankie. But just as Frankie's fear of loneliness is beginning to vanish, the same despair is crushing in on Berenice, who realizes that Frankie does not need her anymore, and that she does not understand what is happening to the young girl. The disconsolate Berenice, left alone on stage, picks up a doll, holds it as if it were a child, and begins to hum as the curtain falls.

Miss McCullers has developed her theme, the bitterness of loneliness, through characterization rather than plot. Frankie is fearful of being unwanted. She craves love and wants to be part of a group —any group. Sometimes Berenice understands Frankie's despair, for she, too, is unhappy. Berenice's loneliness is, in part, that of a woman hampered by her race, but she portrays also the loneliness of a woman who cannot cope with changing youth, who knows that the children she has raised will soon forget her, and who mourns for young John Henry and Honey Brown as if they had been her own children. John Henry, the third major character, is not a smart alecky seven-year-old but is a likable child who repeats statements, distorts them, and is amusing to the audience, but not to Frankie, whom he plagues.

With so thin a plot and with the emphasis upon characterization, *The Member of the Wedding* needed excellent actors to hold audience interest. Even more important, the role of Frankie required an experienced actress, rather than a child, for children often outgrow their roles if the play runs more than one season. Julie Harris not only looked the part but also aroused sympathy for Frankie, because, as she played the role, Frankie's ridiculous chatter, petty quarrels, and desperate cries to be wanted were heartbreaking. Eight-year-old Brandon de Wilde gave a remarkable performance as John Henry, and intrigued audiences with his ability to deliver lines, to arouse sympathy, and to make John Henry amusing rather than precocious. Fortunately, de Wilde did not outgrow his role during the run of the show.

Ethel Waters, however, dominated the play, for she endowed the role of Berenice with her own warm personality. New Yorkers who remembered her vivid performance as Hagar in the intense, gripping drama *Mamba's Daughters* were prepared for her matriarchal portrayal in *The Member of the Wedding*. Even audiences accustomed to seeing Miss Waters in musical reviews recognized her ability to arouse compassion as early as 1933 when she appeared in Irving Berlin's *As Thousands Cheer,* a review based on newspaper headlines, with emphasis throughout the show on humor. For one number, the words "Unknown Negro Lynched" were flashed on the screen, and the curtains opened to reveal a dismal shack with Miss Waters center stage in a rocking chair. Very slowly she began singing "Supper Time," and through the lyrics and the richness of her voice, she projected the heartbreak of the woman who waits for her husband, knowing he will never come home. The song was so completely different from anything else in the show that several columnists suggested it be cut because Miss Waters' effective performance stunned audiences and made the scene that followed less effective. Miss Waters created this same spellbinding effect upon audiences in *The Member of the Wedding,* particularly in the second act when she sang "His Eye Is on the Sparrow" and when she reflected on the deaths of Honey Boy, Ludie, or John Henry.

Both Miss Waters and Miss Harris deserved all the glowing praise they received. According to reports, the first-night audience gave both actresses a tremendous ovation. Such demonstrations usually result in word-of-mouth advertising effective enough to influence box office receipts.

The excellent acting, however, was not the sole reason for the long run. Miss McCullers' theme of loneliness had an emotional appeal. Anyone who understood Frankie's fear of loneliness or her desire to be part of a group would share her unhappiness. For those theatergoers who had experienced Frankie's misery but who had found security in companionship, the play was nostalgic and bitter-sweet. For those who wanted escape or vicarious pleasure in drama but who still shared Frankie's loneliness or Berenice's heartaches, the play was poignant and exhausting.

In 1950, the story of loneliness enhanced by the superb acting enabled *The Member of the Wedding* to run 501 performances. Today, the public's changing attitude toward segregation and civil rights could react against the drama. Some audiences might object to the characterization of Honey Boy Brown, who smokes reefers, kills a man, and tries to escape from his pursuers. Other audiences might object to Mr. Addams using the word "nigger," although Miss McCullers emphasizes the use of the word by making young John Henry, who obviously knows nothing of race problems, keep asking Berenice what it means.

Lillian Hellman's references to Negroes in *Toys in the Attic,* pro-duced in 1960, are, perhaps, more controversial than those of Miss McCullers in *The Member of the Wedding,* for Miss Hellman has included an interracial marriage and an affair between a white woman and a Negro, but she has developed both situations so deftly that audiences are quizzical rather than incredulous about these relationships. *Toys in the Attic,* Miss Hellman's second prize-winning play, received the Critics' Circle Award in 1960. The Pulitzer Committee, just as it had done the year *The Member of the Wedding* was produced, again awarded its prize to a musical comedy, *Fiorello!* Opposition to the Pulitzer selection of a musical was not so rabid as it had been in other years, for the Critics' Circle also chose *Fiorello!* as the best musical of the year.

Miss Hellman's play opened in February, 1960, at a time when the theatrical season had slumped. Almost two months had gone by with a single hit show, for only two of the eleven plays produced during January and February had run over ten performances. Many of the critics wrote enthusiastic reviews for *Toys in the Attic,* call-ing it "vivid" and "vigorous."

The scene is the Berniers' home in New Orleans. Thirty-four-year-old Julian Berniers, an easygoing drifter, has been supported by his two doting spinster sisters, Anna and Carrie. Julian, to the

dismay of his sisters, had married a peculiar, immature young heir-
ess, Lily Prine, whose mother gave Julian ten thousand dollars for
a wedding gift. As the play opens, the Berniers sisters know Julian
and Lily have returned to New Orleans from Chicago and think he
has probably lost his money. Julian brings Lily home and then
showers Anna and Carrie with expensive gifts including two steam-
ship tickets for Europe, a trip Anna and Carrie have always planned
to take. Julian opens a large envelope filled with money and admits
that he has been involved in a real-estate deal and that half the
cash is for his partner, whom he does not identify. Instead of being
happy, Anna and Carrie are miserable, for their happiness has
always depended upon Julian's need for them.

Mrs. Albertine Prine, Lily's mother, is having an affair with a
Negro, Henry, whom Carrie calls Mrs. Prine's "fancy man," and
who poses sometimes as her chauffeur, other times as her butler.
Lily confesses to her mother that she had been happier after Julian
had spent their wedding money and they were poor.

Bit by bit the audience learns the details of the business deal.
Julian has had an affair with a Mrs. Warkins, whose husband believes she is white. Julian, however, has known that she is part
colored and is Henry's cousin. To escape from her husband, who
has treated her brutally, Mrs. Warkins has helped Julian buy land
which Mr. Warkins wanted. Julian has then resold the property to
Mr. Warkins for a high profit, and Mrs. Warkins plans to use her
share of the money to escape from her husband.

Carrie overhears Mrs. Prine and Henry discussing the business
deal; and after they leave, she begins railing at Anna until Anna
finally accuses Carrie of being vindictive because she has always
had an incestuous desire for her brother. Carrie, infuriated, quarrels with Anna, who decides she will go alone on the trip.

In the last act, Carrie, still vehement, goads Lily into confiding
that Julian had told her of another woman in his life and had said
the woman's husband had treated her brutally. Carrie tells Lily
that the woman is Mrs. Warkins and that Julian is on his way
to meet her. In desperation, Lily calls Mr. Warkins and tells him
that his wife is related to Henry, that she is meeting Julian, and,
prompted by Carrie, where they are meeting. She then begs Mr.
Warkins to ask his wife to give Julian up.

Mr. Warkins sends two hoodlums to slash Julian and Mrs. Warkins and steal the money. Julian returns home bloody and badly beaten. Mrs. Warkins, he says, has probably been disfigured for life. Julian cannot understand how Mr. Warkins learned about their meeting place nor can he go to the police, for he is certain they will not believe he had so large a sum of money.

Mrs. Prine warns Lily not to tell Julian anything; but as she leaves, Mrs. Prine tells Carrie and Anna that when Julian does learn the truth, she will take her daughter home. As the play ends, Anna decides not to go on the trip, Carrie seems to regain some of her cheerfulness as she begins fussing over Julian; and the audience suspects that both sisters will again find some degree of happiness in taking care of their brother. Henry says good-bye to Mrs. Prine because Lily, who has always objected to him, will refuse to come home so long as he is there.

In one or two episodes, Miss Hellman arouses suspense by foreshadowing events, particularly in the third act when Carrie maneuvers Lily into calling Mr. Warkins. The audience suspects Carrie hopes Julian will be closer to her again when he discovers what Lily has done. The fact that Julian, at the final curtain, still has not learned of Lily's phone call or of Carrie's duplicity, does not lessen the suspense.

Miss Hellman keeps the audience better informed than any character on stage, but she does not always present the facts clearly. She provides clues and bits of information as if she were helping the spectators build a jigsaw puzzle, linking the pieces together but not filling quite all the gaps. She blocks in enough of the central picture at the final curtain to reveal what the ultimate outcome will be when all the pieces fit into place. The audience knows, for example, that Julian will eventually learn the truth about Lily, but it does not know what will happen to the Berniers or whether Warkins' influence will force Julian to leave town. These conjectures, however, are border jigsaw pieces that do not distort the picture.

The suspense, therefore, arises from looking for missing pieces and patching bits together. The audience may be surprised or shocked at some of the disclosures, but this reaction is counterbalanced by a realization that another piece has fit into the puzzle. When Anna accuses Carrie of lusting for Julian, for example, the audience may be shocked; but Anna's accusation clarifies Carrie's action and offsets some of the moral qualms of the audience. In the last act, Lily admits to Carrie that she has often wondered why Julian married her. Carrie tells Lily that Anna had needed an operation, and Julian had paid the bills, and then had married Lily, confirming Lily's suspicion that Julian had married her for her money. The audience may doubt this explanation, for it knows Julian had used at least part of the dowry to buy a factory in Chicago, but the statement fills in several gaps in the puzzle and provides a deeper insight into the characterization of Carrie.

Unsavory as the play may be, dealing with miscegenation and incestuous love, Miss Hellman's vigorous dialogue and action hold audience interest, as do her characterizations, although she draws them unevenly. Julian emerges clearly, as do Anna and Carrie, but Mrs. Prine remains shadowy. Her relationship with Henry and her treatment of Lily are not always convincing. Lily, too, is somewhat enigmatic. The play does not make clear whether Lily, as one critic has suggested, is mentally disturbed because her mother is having an affair with Henry, or whether, as another critic has indicated, she is merely immature and extremely emotional. Her conversation is often incoherent; but, as the action continues, the audience learns to piece the jumbled incoherencies into a unified whole. Lily's actions are for the most part understandable with the exception of one episode. Lily becomes involved with a morphine addict, trades her diamond ring for a knife which the addict calls a knife of truth, and then slashes her hand. Miss Hellman, by sheer force, makes even this episode seem plausible, if somewhat unrealistic. Henry is perhaps the most shadowy and yet the most complex character. He is almost too worldly, too dignified to be content to live in New Orleans or to be self-effacing when he poses as Albertine's chauffeur. In climactic scenes, however, Miss Hellman emphasizes Henry's importance to the plot. His knowledge of the Negro quarters enables him to recover Lily's ring. When Mrs. Warkins is in danger, it is Henry whom Julian asks to help her. And it is Henry who tells Albertine that he must leave her home when Lily returns.

In sharp contrast to the characterizations, Miss Hellman clearly defines the universal theme that man enjoys dreaming of the unattainable; but, once the goal is within reach, he finds it less desirable. In *Toys in the Attic,* the unattainable includes an unwillingness to risk security for adventure. Anna and Carrie have always talked of their trip to Europe, but once Julian makes that dream possible, they are afraid to go. In fact, they have no desire to go. Many essayists, poets, novelists, and other dramatists have used this theme. Even in popular songs lyricists have said that after we get what we want we don't want it. Many theatergoers react in the same way, for they make every effort to buy tickets for plays that are sellouts. If they discover that tickets are available anywhere in the theater, their desire to see the play often wanes. Miss Hellman's theme in *Toys in the Attic* is not too remote a variation of this reaction.

The excellent cast undoubtedly helped *Toys in the Attic* achieve a long run of 556 performances. Jason Robards, Jr., who had impressed critics and audiences a few seasons earlier in Eugene O'Neill's *Long Day's Journey into Night,* again won recognition for his performance as Julian, as did Anne Revere and Maureen Stapleton in the roles of Anna and Carrie. Irene Worth intrigued audiences with her cool aloofness as Albertine. The importance of the role is probably best illustrated by the fact that Constance Bennett starred as Albertine in the road company. Several drama columnists, instead of playing down the shock angle or sordidness, emphasized the shocking aspects, such as the ghastliness of Julian's make-up in the third act when he returns home bleeding. One columnist, in referring to the episode, said Julian's entrance made some women ill. This type of news story probably helped draw thrill seekers to the play.

Toys in the Attic and Lorraine Hansberry's *A Raisin in the Sun* have one basic plot similarity—business deals that result in a loss of money. Mr. Warkins hires hoodlums to rob Julian of his fortune; Walter Lee Younger in *A Raisin in the Sun* enters into a business deal with a shiftless character who absconds with the Youngers' insurance money. Both plays also involve dreams that come true, but the treatment of the theme differs. Miss Hellman's characters are more content when their dreams are unattainable; Miss Hansberry's characters are discontented until their dreams become reality. Miss Hansberry has taken her title from a poem by Langston Hughes that asks if a deferred dream could dry up like a raisin in the sun. Miss Hansberry's dreamers are a mother who aspires to move to a better neighborhood, a daughter who plans to attend medical school, a son whose greatest desire is to make money quickly, and a daughter-in-law who wishes for a happy family life with her husband and son.

In its treatment of Negroes, Miss Hansberry's play differs completely from *The Member of the Wedding* and *Toys in the Attic*. *A Raisin in the Sun*, produced in 1959, anticipated the current movement for civil rights for Negroes and predicted some of the problems that would arise in integrating communities.

The production opened out of town to excellent notices, and the management, unable to obtain an available theater on Broadway, kept the play on tour until the theater shortage in New York became less acute. When *A Raisin in the Sun* opened in March, 1959, the critics called it "honest," "a moving experience," and "the best new play of the season." Several drama commentators made a point to explain that the production was Negro in authorship, direction, and cast, except for one minor role. The fact that *A Raisin in the Sun* was the first play written by a Negro to be presented on Broadway and, more important, to win the Critics' Circle Award, would not have caused the long run of more than fifteen months. The Pulitzer Committee's selection of Archibald MacLeish's *J.B.* as its prize play for the season does not discredit *A Raisin in the Sun*, which outran *J.B.* and enjoyed popularity on its own merit because it combined excellent acting and a strong plot.

Although the basic story deals with the Negro housing problem, it also presents the universal problems of a mother who desires to raise her children properly in a good environment, to give them a good education, and to buy her own home. When the play opens, Mr. Younger has died, and Mrs. Lena Younger is waiting to receive his insurance money, with which she plans to buy a home and to send her daughter, Beneatha, to medical school. Since the scene is laid in Chicago, Miss Hansberry is not concerned with the problems of integrated schools or with the difficulty Beneatha might encounter in applying for admission to a medical school. The major objections Mrs. Younger meets are from the community where she intends to live, and from her son, Walter, a chauffeur, who would like to invest the money in a liquor store or in any business where he could make money quickly. Walter's wife, Ruth, who works as a maid, would prefer to have a home where she could raise their son, Travis, properly; but she realizes that if Walter had the opportunity to invest at least part of the money, he might be more con-

A Raisin in the Sun, Ruby Dee, Sidney Poitier and Diana Sands

tent, and their married life would be happier. Lena Younger, however, is determined to buy a house. She plans to go back to work
and believes that if they all contribute, they can meet the payments.

In the scene that takes place the next morning, the audience
realizes that Walter still hopes to get his hands on the money, for
he calls a friend to tell him the check has not yet arrived. Ruth tells
Lena, when they are alone, that she is pregnant; but Lena soon
surmises that Ruth has gone to a midwife who performs abortions.
When the check arrives and Mrs. Younger still refuses to give
Walter the money, he begins talking wildly about dreams until
Lena forces him to listen while she explains that Ruth is planning
to get rid of their child. Even though Ruth admits she has given
the abortionist a deposit, Lena cannot make Walter say he wants
the child.

Later that same day Lena tells her family she has made a down
payment on a house in Clybourne Park. Ruth says there are no
Negroes living in that area, and Mrs. Younger says there will be
now.

A few weeks later, the Youngers are preparing to move, but Lena
is worried. The people for whom Walter drives have called to tell
her that he has not come to work for several days and that if he
does not report the next day, they will hire a new man. Lena learns
that Walter has been borrowing cars, driving to night spots, and,
at other times, walking over on Chicago's South Side. Very much
upset by Walter's moodiness, she admits she has paid $3,500 down
on the house and gives him the remaining $6,500 but instructs him
to deposit $3,000 for Beneatha's tuition. The rest of the money
is his to manage.

One week later, the family is excited, for it is moving day. Walter
and Ruth are much happier together now, and even Walter and
Beneatha, who have quarreled constantly, are getting along well.
Lena has not yet returned from work when Mr. Lindner, a middle-
aged white man, calls and asks to see Mrs. Younger. Representing
a committee of neighbors, he explains that, perhaps, the Youngers
would be happier living in a Negro section and that the group he
represents is prepared to buy back the house and give the Youngers
a profit on the sale. Walter sends Mr. Lindner away, but Lindner
leaves his card in case Walter should change his mind. Shortly after
Lena returns, one of the men with whom Walter had planned to

go into business arrives to break the news that Willie, the third man, has run off with all the money. The Youngers soon learn that Walter had given the entire $6,500 to Willie.

In desperation Walter calls Mr. Lindner and asks him to return. Lena, unable to stop Walter, says that her family were slaves and sharecroppers but that no one had ever sunk to the level of taking that kind of money. Walter, nonetheless, is determined to sell the house to Mr. Lindner. Ruth wants to send her son, Travis, out when Mr. Lindner arrives, but Lena insists that the boy stay and that Walter explain to him what he is doing. Walter looks at Travis, sees the boy grinning at him, puts his arm around his son, and begins talking hesitantly. As he continues, he gains confidence. He tells Mr. Lindner that everyone in the family works, that Beneatha is going to medical school, that they will move into the house, and that they will try to be good neighbors. When Mr. Lindner leaves, the family is jubilant. Lena will work, as will Ruth, as long as she can; Walter will not neglect his work, and Beneatha will get her chance to attend medical school. Lena and Ruth are proud of Walter, prouder than they have ever been because he has, in their eyes, developed a new sense of dignity. Perhaps, as some critics have suggested, the change comes too quickly and the play might have been more realistic if Walter had sold the house to Mr. Lindner and then repented. The present ending, nevertheless, is plausible, and it does give the play a vigorous last act.

If audiences and critics had felt that *A Raisin in the Sun* was purely propaganda, the play would have merited consideration as a plea for civil rights, but propaganda alone is not sufficient motivation to keep lines at the box office. Furthermore, if Miss Hansberry had downgraded only the whites and pointed out only the exemplary qualities of the Negroes, the play might not have run more than a few months. Instead, Miss Hansberry has interlaced criticism of both races. When the Youngers approve of Beneatha's dating George Murchison because his family is wealthy, Beneatha says his folks would never consent to his marrying her and then adds that the wealthy Negro families are often more snobbish than the whites. Miss Hansberry does point out the need for better living conditions for Negroes, but she does not present it militantly. Her thesis is much more effective because she lets Lena make the observation that houses built for Negroes seem to cost twice as much as other houses. By making Walter the fall guy for another Negro, by having him lose his money in one fast deal, Miss Hansberry shows that Walter has yet a great deal to learn. In sharp contrast she presents Mrs. Younger as a proud woman determined to have a decent home and thus gives the entire family stature and makes the audience realize that people such as Mrs. Younger will fight courageously for equal rights.

The humor is much broader and more universal when Miss Hansberry forgets about race and color and concentrates on human foibles, such as Beneatha's flippancies, characteristic of girls her age, as she flits from hobby to hobby, from photography to horseback riding, to play acting, and to guitar lessons. Equally amusing is the scene between George and Beneatha when they return from the theater, because George wants to make love but Beneatha wants to talk. In the second act, while George is waiting for Beneatha, Walter begins goading him about his jacket, sweater, slacks, and white shoes. Walter's ridicule is a humorous criticism, not of any one race, but of all college students who become impressed with their own importance and who conform rigidly to standard patterns in dress.

The excellent cast undoubtedly helped make the play popular. Sidney Poitier's reputation as a motion picture actor also proved to have drawing power. Nor would it be discrediting to Poitier's splendid performance as Walter, which impressed both audiences and critics, to note that Claudia MacNeil, as Lena, dominated the play. When Ossie Davis replaced Mr. Poitier at the end of the season, the management quickly elevated Miss MacNeil to stardom, for she endowed the role of Lena with dignity and with strength of character. Ruby Dee and Diana Sands, with their convincing portrayals of Ruth and Beneatha, also helped *A Raisin in the Sun* to keep running for 530 performances.

One reader, looking over the notes assembled for this volume, said he might well prefer the Younger family as next-door neighbors to Martha and George, the inebriated couple in *Who's Afraid of Virginia Woolf?* The Youngers, he thought, would be quieter, less apt to give drunken parties at all hours of the night, and would use less profanity.

The profanity or, as some critics referred to it, "earthy language," as well as the immorality in Edward Albee's *Who's Afraid of Vir-*

ginia Woolf?, produced in 1962, aroused controversy among critics and audiences. In the Critics' Circle, for example, Albee's drama received the majority of votes and the award as the best play of 1962 although some of the critics thought the entire theatrical season was, in general, a poor one. Many theatergoers anticipated that the Pulitzer Committee would also award its prize to the same play, but the Pulitzer trustees overruled the advisory committee's recommendation of *Who's Afraid of Virginia Woolf?* and offered no prize for the season. In the aftermath, two members of the committee, John Mason Brown and John Gassner, both resigned.

Albee's drama runs over three hours, but rather than cut the script to conform to a more conventional time limit, the producer started the evening performances at 8:00 instead of the customary 8:40 or 8:50 curtain. One drama professor, asked to comment on the unusual length, said, "Shakespeare covered more ideas in *Macbeth* in less time."

The entire three acts span a period from 2 A.M. to dawn in a play that is serious but far from sober, for the two couples involved in the plot drink almost continuously. The fact that three of the four characters stay on their feet in spite of the vast quantity of liquor consumed seems almost incredible. Although the play is a combination of reality and fancy, Mr. Albee does not clarify which episodes are real and which are fanciful. Even without lucid explanations, the play maintains a semi-clarity that permits audiences to recognize the following basic truths. George, a college professor, is six years younger than his wife, Martha, daughter of the college president. After George had married Martha, he became acting head of the history department during the World War II years, but Martha's father decided George was not competent in the position. George is now an associate professor of history. George and Martha, unable to have children, have created an imaginary son and have used this child as a means of baiting and of taunting each other. They have kept the pretense of the son, however, to themselves.

As the curtain rises on the first act, George and Martha return from a party given by her father; and, because her father has asked her to be hospitable to Nick, a biology professor and a new member of the faculty, Martha has invited him and his wife to stop for a drink on their way home from the party. Nick and Honey arrive after two in the morning. Nick is self-satisfied, self-assured. Honey is shallow and annoyingly cute. As the four continue drinking, George and Martha snap at each other. George has cautioned Martha not to discuss their imaginary son; but Martha, to anger George, begins talking about the boy. As the night wears on, Nick admits to George, when they are alone, that he married Honey because he thought she was pregnant, nor does he deny George's accusation that he married Honey because she was wealthy. Later, Honey tells George she does not want to have children and that she has used every ruse to avoid having any, even to feigning illness.

Martha makes advances to Nick, and George finds them in a passionate embrace but steps out of the room before Martha sees him. When he does re-enter, Martha begins quarreling with George, but he says that if she wishes to have an affair with Nick, she need not go through the sham of having a fight. Martha is infuriated and soon has little difficulty inducing Nick to go upstairs with her. George, unable to control his anger, hurls a book at the door chimes. The sound wakens Honey from a drunken sleep, and she asks who rang the bell. George says triumphantly that he will have his revenge because a Western Union messenger has rung the bell and has delivered a telegram stating their son was dead.

In the last act George tells Martha and Nick that he has received the telegram. In the ensuing accusations and denials between George and Martha, Nick realizes the son has been a figment of their imagination. Nick and Honey leave very much subdued, and George and Martha know they must face a future of despair and frustration.

These facts are interlaced with events which George and Martha discuss as though they had actually happened, but the audience is never quite certain whether it is hearing fact or fancy. Martha, for example, talks about her first marriage to a gardener who worked at the school she attended and adds that her father and the school officials arranged to have the marriage annulled. This story may be as fictional as George's statement that Martha once took part in a seven-day dance contest. George relates the case history of a boy who accidentally shot his mother, killed his father in a car wreck, and finally ended in a mental institution. Later, George asserts he was the boy. Martha, however, says George has really told the plot of a novel he had written, but her father had refused to allow him to publish it. The audience assumes George's story

Who's Afraid of Virginia Woolf?, Uta Hagen, Arthur Hill, Melinda Dillon and George Grizzard

may be as imaginary as the son he created. George's resentment of Martha's ridiculing the book, nevertheless, is real.

The symbolism in the play is equally confusing. Some critics have suggested that the theme of the play is sterility because the names George and Martha could refer to George and Martha Washington, who were childless. Other critics have extended the theme to mean spiritual sterility.

The title, too, has puzzled audiences. The words and rhythm are similar to the song, "Who's Afraid of the Big, Bad Wolf?" but George and Martha sing their parody to a different melody (because of copyright problems). The title may, as some observers believe, signify George and Martha's scoffing at the enemy that would destroy them. The enemy might even be George and Martha themselves when they rail at each other, revealing their innermost secrets to strangers. A dowager president of a woman's club asked a librarian to help her find all comments about the title because one of the club members had suggested that since the name Virginia appeared in the title, the reference might have been to a female wolf. According to stories heard on Broadway, Albee originally intended to call the play *The Exorcism*. One night when he was in a bar, he saw the words "Who's Afraid of Virginia Woolf?" written on a washroom wall. In some versions, it is the wall of a telephone booth, but in both reports, Albee is reported to have been intrigued with the line and decided to use it as his title. If the story is true, Albee must be enjoying all the consternation he has aroused.

Out of the maze of truth, fiction, and bewilderment of the entire play, from the title down to the final curtain, there emerges the story of four people whom Albee characterizes mercilessly. As a result, the audience feels no compassion for Martha, promiscuous and vulgar, who humiliates her husband before guests; for George, less promiscuous, perhaps, but equally blasphemous and vulgar, who married Martha because she was the college president's daughter; for Honey, the shallow wife, who lived with Nick, then tricked him into marrying her, and now refuses to have children; or for Nick, arrogant and smug, who takes advantage of Martha's advances while Honey lies in a drunken stupor on the bathroom floor. At the end of the play, when George has killed their imaginary son and he and Martha must face grim reality alone, the audience is moved, at best, not to sympathy, but to pity. Perhaps the reaction of one middle-aged matron after a matinee performance is characteristic of audience reaction. As the final curtain came down, she said to her companion, "If they are like this when they're drunk, Heaven help them when they're sober."

The words "morbid fascination" would be more logical than "popular appeal" in explaining the long run of *Who's Afraid of Virginia Woolf?* Some theatergoers attended the play because it was reputed to be shocking. Others insisted they were disgusted with the story and with the characters but were interested enough to see all three acts. Still others found the play an exhausting experience as they watched the characters blurting out truths and not always talking coherently. Most audiences, instead of taking offense, accepted the lapses into profanity and the repetitious dialogue as being characteristic of inebriates. Since the play was a constant topic of argument, many theatergoers felt compelled to see *Who's Afraid of Virginia Woolf?* to discover whether they agreed with the approving or dissenting viewpoints.

Even more important to the long run were the excellent critical reviews that helped make the play a sellout during the first season. Critics hailed the vigor of the well-drawn characterizations, the excellent cast, and the naturalistic dialogue. Several reviewers even heralded Albee as a worthy successor to Eugene O'Neill. One columnist stated that the management had intended to cut the script but decided against making changes when the critics acclaimed the production and the lines of ticket buyers formed at the box office.

At the end of the season the numerous prizes awarded to the play, the author, the cast, the director, and the producers helped sustain continued audience interest. In addition to the Critics' Circle Award, the following list of citations reveals that almost everyone connected with the production received some form of recognition:

CATEGORY	WINNER	SOURCE OF AWARD
Best Author	Edward Albee	Tony
Most Promising Playwright Broadway Debut	Edward Albee	*Saturday Review* Drama Critics' Poll *Variety* Drama Critics' Poll

CATEGORY	WINNER	SOURCE OF AWARD
Best Male Performance in Leading Role	Arthur Hill (George)	Tony *Saturday Review* *Variety* *Best Plays* editor, Henry Hewes
Best Female Performance in Leading Role	Uta Hagen (Martha)	Tony *Saturday Review* *Variety*
Best Director, Straight Play	Alan Schneider	Tony *Saturday Review* *Variety* Outer Circle
Best Broadway Debut	Melinda Dillon (Honey)	*Saturday Review* *Variety*
Drama Producers	Richard Barr and Clinton Wilder	Tony

George Grizzard (Nick) and William Ritman (scene designer) were runners-up in both the *Saturday Review* Drama Critics' and *Variety* Drama Critics' Polls. The entire cast of *Who's Afraid of Virginia Woolf?*, as a group, received the Outer Circle Award for outstanding ensemble acting. All these citations and nominations were well earned, for the actors without exception gave excellent performances in the long, exhausting roles. The management, aware of the heavy strain upon the actors, had two separate New York casts: Arthur Hill, Uta Hagen, Melinda Dillon, and George Grizzard appeared in the evening performances; Sheppard Strudwick, Kate Reid, Avra Petrides, and Bill Berger played the matinees.

Although audiences were interested in seeing the prize-winning actors, they were equally interested in seeing the play because the drama continued doing profitable business when the cast began to change as early as April, 1963. Before the end of the run, both New York casts, with the exception of Bill Berger, had changed at least twice. After box office receipts began to drop, the management used two-for-one tickets to prolong the run and finally closed the production in May, 1964, with a total of 664 performances and an estimated profit of more than $700,000.

At least one character, Big Daddy, in Tennessee Williams' *Cat on a Hot Tin Roof*, could surpass Martha and George in crudity, and a second character, Brick, could match them in drinking. Albee and Williams have both written naturalistic dramas, but Albee's play is clouded with symbolism; Williams' plot is obviously lucid. By clashing fancy with reality, Albee often obscures his theme. He ends with a strong, realistic final scene, nevertheless, that permits the audience to speculate on the grim future. Williams, on the other hand, keeps more than one theme running throughout the play. Yet, at the final curtain, he fails to unify the strands of plot sufficiently to give the audience more than a hazy ray of hope.

Among the five plays produced since 1950 which have won both the Pulitzer and Critics' Circle Prizes, *Cat on a Hot Tin Roof* is by far the most controversial. Audiences were shocked by the earthy dialogue, particularly in an off-color story told by Big Daddy which was cut after the play opened in New York, although the printed text still retains the passage. Many theatergoers anticipated that Williams' drama, produced in 1955, would win the Critics' Circle Award that year, but they were surprised that it also received the Pulitzer Prize. Skeptics thought the Pulitzer trustees might object to the homosexuality in the play just as they had objected to Lillian Hellman's *The Children's Hour* in 1935. The Pulitzer Committee, apparently, had not considered the references to homosexuality in Williams' *A Streetcar Named Desire* when it awarded its prize to the play in 1948, for the character involved never appeared on stage. Brick, the potential homosexual in *Cat on a Hot Tin Roof,* however, is one of the three major characters who dominate the action.

The unpleasant plot deals with perversion, greed, and falsehood, or, as Williams prefers to call it, mendacity. Big Daddy Pollitt, a wealthy Southern plantation owner, does not know he is dying of cancer. His favorite son, Brick, a former athlete, refuses to sleep with his wife, Maggie, because she accused Skipper, Brick's teammate and closest college friend, of having a homosexual desire for her husband. Skipper had then telephoned Brick, who refused to listen and hung up on him. Within a short time, Skipper drank himself to death.

As the play opens, Brick knows Maggie's accusation was true, but he is obsessed with guilt over Skipper and is following his example in trying to drink himself to death. Maggie dominates the first act as she pleads, cajoles, and entreats Brick in a series of accusations and revelations about both their relationships with

Skipper. Big Daddy would prefer to entrust his estate to Brick and Maggie if they had a child, for his other son, Gooper, and his wife, Mae, have five children, all of whom Big Daddy dislikes. Big Daddy observes, however, that something must be radically wrong when his favorite son is drinking too much and Maggie is still childless.

Big Daddy dominates the second act. He is loud and vulgar. His comments about his wife, Big Mama, are worse than Brick's sullen, silent hatred of Maggie. He is completely fooled by the false report that he is cured. In the climactic scene which closes the act, Big Daddy forces Brick to talk about himself and Skipper, and although Brick admits under Big Daddy's insistent prodding that Skipper had confessed how he felt about Brick when he made the phone call, Big Daddy tells Brick he is responsible for Skipper's death because he refused to face the truth about himself and Skipper. In retaliation, Brick tells Big Daddy that he won't be around for any more birthdays. Brick hedges when Big Daddy asks him if the doctors found he was cancerous, and Big Daddy, aware that Brick is the only one who has told him the truth, begins calling everyone liars as the curtain comes down.

In the last act, Gooper and Mae plan to take over the plantation. Big Mama would prefer to have Brick manage the estate, but the arguments among the family members stop when Big Daddy reappears. Maggie, equally determined to win her battle, lies brazenly by telling Big Daddy she is pregnant, and Big Daddy, aware of Gooper's plotting to take over the estate, says he will talk to the attorney in the morning. When Big Daddy leaves, Gooper and Mae insist that Maggie has lied, for they have listened at the walls, have heard Maggie pleading with Brick, and know that he is not sleeping with her. Suddenly Brick speaks up, defends Maggie, does not deny her announcement, and forces Gooper and Mae out. When they are left alone, Maggie smashes the liquor bottles, tells Brick she will get him more when they make her lie to Big Daddy come true, and then she will get drunk with him. As Maggie is wheedling Brick into acquiescence, the curtain falls.

To analyze Williams' plays closely often leads to bewilderment. In *Cat on a Hot Tin Roof,* for example, is Maggie trying to make her lie come true because she wants to win back her husband's affection, or is she also eager to grab the largest part of the inheritance? In the theater, audiences may be sympathetic to Maggie, but as they reflect over the drama, they may question Maggie's motives and suspect her possible avarice. Instead of being a play about a husband, a wife, and their problems, the plot becomes a loosely knit series of stories without sufficient emphasis to enable the audience to determine whether the play is really about Brick and Maggie, about Brick and Skipper, about Big Daddy, or about the whole Pollitt family. At the conclusion, Williams does not draw the problems together but allows them to branch out so that nothing is resolved. That Big Daddy will die is a certainty. But whether Maggie will make her lie come true, whether she will win Brick back completely, whether Gooper and Mae will still fight for control of the estate, are all questions which remain unanswered. As a result, the play is not a complete drama of one man, one marriage, or one family but is a combination of all three linked tenuously by the thread of mendacity.

The inconclusiveness of the play has caused several critics to question the third act as it was presented in New York, for in the printed text Williams included the third act he originally wrote and obviously preferred. In the preface, Williams explained that he had rewritten the final act to satisfy Elia Kazan, the director. Williams stated that by including both versions he made it possible for the reader to judge which third act seemed preferable. That Kazan's influence definitely made the third act superior becomes obvious not in the reading but in the playing. In London, for example, where the production did not have Kazan's direction or the revised third act, the play failed to sustain audience interest. One critic, in fact, who had thought Kazan was wrong in requiring the revisions, admitted after seeing the play that Kazan's direction was essential to make the play effective.

In Williams' original third act, Big Daddy did not appear. Big Mama, who was not so colorful a character, dominated the action. Maggie, therefore, told her brazen lie to Big Mama, and then, without any assistance from Brick, denied the accustations made by Gooper and Mae. Although the act ended with Maggie still trying to make the lie come true, the general tone at the final curtain was pessimistic.

In the revised version, Big Daddy's reappearance revitalizes the morbid action. When Maggie tells her lie to Big Daddy, his belief that she is telling the truth makes the play more theatrical, perhaps, but also more effective. By having Brick, rather than Maggie, defend the lie, the entire scene creates some degree of hope for both Brick and Maggie. Maggie's final speech in the revised version, moreover, includes her telling Brick that there is nothing more determined than a cat on a hot tin roof, a statement which definitely epitomizes Maggie's characterization.

The revisions Kazan required do not detract from Williams' power to write vigorous dialogue, to write intensely emotional scenes, and to create vivid characterizations which hold audience interest. *Cat on a Hot Tin Roof* has all these qualities in varying degrees. The climax between Brick and Big Daddy, when played properly, has so much driving force that the last act is almost a letdown. Williams' indebtedness to Kazan for helping make the play a popular success, therefore, cannot be denied, for the original third act is even weaker without the reappearance of Big Daddy. The revisions give Big Daddy the opportunity to dominate the action for the short time he is on stage, and to help make Maggie's possible victory seem more plausible.

Williams' ability to depict mentally unhealthy people or people obsessed with guilt or shame makes his characters more theatrical but also more forceful when their behavior is abnormal. These characterizations, however, require superb actors to make the characters believable, if not sympathetic. Audiences, for the most part, although interested in or perhaps even enthralled by the characters in *Cat on a Hot Tin Roof,* are often dispassionate rather than sympathetic to their problems.

In New York, *Cat on a Hot Tin Roof* enjoyed a long run because Barbara Bel Geddes as Maggie, Burl Ives as Big Daddy, Ben Gazzara as Brick, and Mildred Dunnock as Big Mama intrigued audiences with their vivid, compelling acting. These roles, when played by less skillful actors, can, unfortunately, become dull or perhaps make audiences laugh at the wrong lines. A production performed by amateurs or by an incompetent professional cast may often be a long evening of boredom. The reviews of the play on tour and in London show only too clearly that not all actors can sustain the dramatic force and drive of the play. In Chicago, for example, the reception by both critics and audiences was unfavorable. One or two of the Chicago critics objected to Kazan's direction; other critics thought the cast, with the exception of Thomas Gomez as Big

Daddy, was inferior to the play. The reception in London, where critics praised only Kim Stanley's performance as Maggie, was equally unfavorable, but the fault must also be credited to the fact that London saw the original third act.

The New York success, however, is undeniable. Even with cast replacements, the play continued to draw audiences for a total of 694 performances, a run of approximately eighteen months, but a six months' shorter run than Williams' *A Streetcar Named Desire.* The fact that no play Williams has written since *Cat on a Hot Tin Roof* has reached the five-hundred-performance mark may indicate the importance of Kazan's direction to long runs, for *Cat on a Hot Tin Roof* was the last Williams play directed by Kazan.

In *Cat on a Hot Tin Roof,* Big Daddy cows his family into submission and tolerates his wife. Similarly, in *Look Homeward, Angel,* adapted by Ketti Frings from Thomas Wolfe's autobiographical novel, Eliza Gant browbeats her children and deigns to overlook her husband's animosity. Family quarrels over money, land grabbing, and deception appear in both plays, but the dialogue, the characterizations, and the plots are almost totally different.

Look Homeward, Angel, produced in 1957, and winner of both the Critics' Circle Award and Pulitzer Prize in 1958, delighted those critics who had doubted that Wolfe's lengthy novel could be condensed into a taut drama. Miss Frings integrated the characterization of Eugene Gant (Thomas Wolfe) into a play that emphasized the roles of the mother and father as well as the arguments which included the older brother and sister. As the curtain rose on the first act, Miss Frings projected the autobiographical aspect by having the audience hear Eugene's voice reading several sentences he had written about his brother Ben, but as the action began, the play became the story of the entire family.

The principal characters in the drama are Eliza Gant, who runs a boardinghouse; her husband, W. O. Gant, a dealer in tombstones and marble monuments; her son Ben, who wants to be a flyer in the Canadian Army but cannot pass the physical examination; her daughter, Helen Gant Barton, who resents her domineering mother; and Eugene, a seventeen-year-old adolescent who unwillingly performs menial household duties. The motley assortment of roomers includes Mrs. Marie "Fatty" Pert, who has an affair with Ben; Laura Brown, who has an affair with Eugene and then returns to

Richmond to marry her fiancé; an ex-dancing master; a cloying spinster; an unpleasant older woman and her brash son. With the exception of Mrs. Pert and Miss Brown, the boarders are minor characters who provide atmosphere or comic relief, for the plot deals mainly with the sequences that lead to Eugene's leaving home: Ben's denouncement of his mother; Mr. Gant's refusal to sell his prize monument, the Carrara Angel; Mrs. Gant's attempt to sell the marble yard; Ben's death; Eugene's love affair with Laura; Eugene's rebellion against his mother's domination; and Eugene's tearful farewell to his mother.

The exposition in the first scene reveals Eliza's penny-pinching to build up security and her plan to sell her husband's marble yard to raise cash to buy a more desirable piece of real estate; Ben's relationship with Mrs. Pert as well as his concern over Eugene's future; and Mr. Gant's coming home drunk. Once these facts have been established, the audience is prepared for the family disagreements that become increasingly depressing to Eugene. Miss Frings builds each episode until it culminates in a tense, emotional outburst. The drama, therefore, becomes a series of climaxes, each widening the chasm that inevitably separates Eugene from his family, and each followed by action that arouses the audience's sympathy for one or more of the characters involved.

The first climax occurs after Gant has told Eliza he will not sell his marble yard and has also added that his first wife really understood him and his desire to carve a perfect angel. Although Eliza is furious, she does not give vent to her anger until she sees Ben and Mrs. Pert together on the porch. She begins railing at Mrs. Pert. Eugene is unable to stop her, but Ben retaliates by upbraiding Eliza for abusing her family. Eliza becomes even more incensed and slaps Ben. Without a word of reproach, Ben walks off with Mrs. Pert. At the end of the act, nevertheless, audience sympathy is built up for Eliza when she comes out of the house, sees no one, and calls plaintively for Ben.

Eliza's second emotional outburst occurs in the marble yard. Mr. Gant refuses to sell his beautiful Carrara Angel to Madam Elizabeth, the town's most prosperous madam, who wants to buy a tombstone for one of her young girls who has died. Later in the scene the audience is surprised when Eliza produces the deed for the sale of the property and Mr. Gant agrees to sign it. He takes

Look Homeward, Angel, Jo Van Fleet and Anthony Perkins

316 Look Homeward, Angel

the check from Eliza, says he bought the land with money from his first wife's estate, and now plans to leave town and take Eugene with him. Becoming infuriated again, Eliza takes the check out of his pocket and tears it up. In this scene, the audience sympathy is definitely not with Eliza.

The third emotional climax comes in the second act. Ben, who collapsed in the marble yard, is dying. When he asks for Mrs. Pert, she sits at his bedside and sings to him. Suddenly Mrs. Pert calls for Eliza, who rushes in. Not until Ben loses consciousness does Eliza take her place at his bedside. As she holds Ben's hand, he turns to her and dies. Eugene tries to persuade Eliza to leave, but Eliza shakes her head and refuses to let go of Ben's hand. Again the audience's sympathy is with Eliza in her grief.

The last act builds to two emotional climaxes. Eliza is ready to stop Eugene from marrying Laura, but she discovers that Laura has no intention of marrying Eugene. In fact, Laura, hoping to avoid saying good-bye, gives Eliza a letter for him. When Eliza tells Eugene that Laura has gone back to Richmond, he accuses Eliza of sending her away. After he reads the letter, Eliza tries to cajole him, but Eugene is in no mood for her humor. He upbraids Eliza for treating him as a drudge and for making his life miserable. Furthermore, he is determined to leave home immediately, go to Chapel Hill, and enter college as soon as possible. Shaken by Eugene's rebellion, Eliza suddenly loses her sense of reason. In a rage, she picks up a porch rocker, smashes it, and says she would like to destroy the house. Mr. Gant gleefully helps break up the furniture while Eliza kicks out panels on the veranda and drives the boarders out of the house. Suddenly reaction sets in. Eliza is horrified by what she has done. Then, by sending her daughter after the boarders to apologize and to persuade them to return, she loses any audience sympathy she might have won.

When Eugene is ready to leave, Eliza promises to deposit money in the Chapel Hill Bank. Eugene, although asserting his independence, still shows traces of the adolescent as he embraces Eliza and they bid each other a tearful, sentimental good-bye. This final episode parallels reconciliation scenes in other long-running plays when parents realize that their children still have deep affection for them. The basic difference is that audiences have more compassion for the parents, like Willy Loman in *Death of a Salesman,* for example, than they do for Eliza Gant.

Yet it was Eliza who helped *Look Homeward, Angel* achieve its long run, for audiences could not be impassive to her. She horrified some women, particularly in her moments of fury; she annoyed others in her bludgeoning attempts to be humorous; but even those women who disapproved of her could pity the mother whose dying son preferred to have Mrs. Pert near him, the wife whose husband indulged in periodic drunken sprees, or the second wife who endured jibes about the first wife. Mr. Gant, although colorful, could not overshadow Eliza in his drunken rages, in his moments of frustration, or in his futile attempt to outwit her in the real-estate deal. Miss Frings made Eliza a complex character, a combination of greed, hard-headedness, shrewishness, and infrequently, tenderness. Eugene remained the pivotal but not the most vivid character in the play. Audiences, aware that Eugene would become a famous writer, were less interested in him than in Laura, Ben, Mr. Gant, and, above all, Eliza.

Several critics, although admitting the play had merit, did not agree with the majority who called *Look Homeward, Angel* the best play of the season. These dissenters thought the characters who provided the comic relief were overdrawn and that the play at times became maudlin. Most audiences, nevertheless, enjoyed the humor and the theatricality in the emotional climaxes. Audiences laughed, for example, at Madam Elizabeth's references to Mr. Gant's former patronage of her establishment, and at her insistence on buying the Carrara Angel for a tombstone. The scene, however, carried undertones that raised it above the level of a bowdlerized burlesque skit, for it revealed Gant's artistic frustrations, his unwillingness to degrade his best work by selling it to the madam, and Eugene's ingenuity in pacifying the madam and convincing her to buy another of Mr. Gant's statues. Despite the sentimentality, the emotional climaxes, aided by the counterbalancing comic relief, became doubly effective. In Ben's death scene, most women shared Eliza's grief; most men understood Eugene's sorrow. Some audiences were sympathetic to Laura's involvement with Eugene; others disapproved of both Laura and Mrs. Pert. The emotional tenseness and the vivid characterizations held audience interest, and, as a result, the drama had popular appeal because it aroused this variety of audience reactions.

Jo Mielziner's stage setting further enhanced audience interest. Reversing one wall of the house to disclose various rooms, including Ben's, Mr. Gant's, and Laura's, eliminated stage waits for set changes and enabled the simultaneous action on the porch, in front of the house, and in the bedroom to have the fluidity of a motion picture. Not only the excellent reviews but also the good press releases and publicity attracted the reading public to the theater, for several magazines carried stories about Wolfe's life. Two or three magazines carried interviews with members of Wolfe's family and included their reactions to their stage counterparts.

Compelling performances by Jo Van Fleet as Eliza, Hugh Griffiths as W. O. Gant, and Tony Perkins as Eugene were also responsible for the popular success of the drama. Miss Van Fleet emphasized the complexities in the difficult role of Eliza. She made audiences understand her ruthless drive for financial security, her problems as the second wife who lives in the shadow of the first wife, and the paradox of her affection and mistreatment of her children. Tony Perkins admirably portrayed the gangling, sensitive Eugene who became mature in his love affair with Laura. At the end of the first season, after replacements for Miss Van Fleet, Mr. Griffiths, and Mr. Perkins entered the cast, box office receipts began to drop, but the play had sufficient appeal to continue its profitable run and did not close until it had reached a total of 564 performances.

Just as the biographical aspect of *Look Homeward, Angel* may have appealed to some audiences, many were intrigued by the authenticity of the 1955 play *The Diary of Anne Frank,* a story of a young girl who recorded the events of her life while she and her family tried to avoid capture by the Nazis, although *Look Homeward, Angel* and *The Diary of Anne Frank* were both adapted from widely read books, their theatrical appeal was not limited to audiences familiar with the original sources. Both plays profited from skillful adaptations, emphasis upon characterization, and excellent casts. Frances Hackett and Albert Goodrich, who adapted *The Diary of Anne Frank* from *Anne Frank, the Diary of a Young Girl,* did not convert the book into pure propaganda. Instead, they created an emotionally tense drama that became a stimulating experience in the theater. The play, which received both the Pulitzer Prize and Critics' Circle Award in 1956, proved to be popular with the critics, who wrote ecstatic reviews, and equally popular with the public whose word-of-mouth advertising helped form long lines at the box office.

The play opens in 1945. The setting is the top floor of a building in Amsterdam where eight Jews had hidden during the German occupation. Mr. Frank, the only survivor, enters with Miep Gies, his former stenographer, who gives him the diary Anne had started to write three years earlier and which she left behind when the Nazis discovered the hiding place and took the victims to concentration camps. As Mr. Frank begins reading, the lights dim, and the ensuing action dramatizes incidents Anne had recorded about the eight people who lived in the attic: Mr. and Mrs. Frank and their daughters, Margot, aged eighteen, and Anne, thirteen; Mr. and Mrs. Van Daan and their son, Peter, aged sixteen; and Mr. Dussell, a dentist. The two remaining characters, Mr. Kraler and Miep, had brought provisions and kept the eight informed on what was happening in the occupation area.

During the course of the play as the victims wait in hiding, they learn to be deathly still during the hours when the lower floors of the building are occupied, and to regulate their eating and sleeping habits to conform with the necessary silence. Money becomes scarce; food becomes increasingly difficult to obtain; and the claustrophobia that develops becomes almost unbearable. The victims are fearful when they hear a night prowler in the building; they are hopeful when Miep brings news of D day. Finally, the enemy, having been informed of their hiding place by the prowler, begins hammering on the door. The curtains close and the audience hears the crash as the enemy breaks into the attic. The epilogue is again 1945. Mr. Frank puts aside the diary, and tells Miep he had learned of the deaths of all the others except Anne, but only the day before he had learned that Anne had died at Belsen.

The play, which might easily have overemphasized the terror of the victims as they waited for what they feared would happen, blends sentiment, fear, and the enjoyment of being alive to make the characters react rationally, not hysterically, to impending danger. The family feuds emerge as normal quarrels which arise when people are huddled together waiting for the inevitable. Although the eight victims hope for freedom, they are resigned when the Nazis arrive, for what they feared most has become a reality.

If all the characters had been saintly, or at least without normal faults, the play would not have had the same emotional appeal. Even Mrs. Frank, who is probably the most resigned of the characters, has her moment of hysteria when she discovers Mr. Van Daan is raiding the icebox. Anne, far from angelic, is mischievous and often rude but is, nevertheless, an appealing child, particularly when she falls in love with Peter. Mrs. Van Daan's weakness is her love for material possessions; and even in moments of desperation, she tries to salvage what she cherishes most. When Mr. Van Daan gives her fur coat to Miep and tells her to sell it to raise money for food and cigarettes, and also to start paying off a blackmailer, the audience understands Mrs. Van Daan's despair over losing the last status symbol of her former wealth.

Some theatrical critics have said that the presentation of Nazi cruelty and the appeal to Jewish audiences caused *The Diary of Anne Frank* to run almost three seasons on Broadway. In 1960, Millard Lampell's dramatization of John Hersey's *The Wall* dealt with the same plot, the hustling of Jews to concentration camps and to ultimate death. The play, in fact, dealt even more frankly with Nazi purges and the terrors of those victims who went into hiding. If the appeal to Jewish audiences and the preachment and propaganda against Nazis were valid reasons for box office successes in New York, *The Wall* should have drawn capacity houses. Although the play was an artistic triumph, it failed as a commercial venture, for it lacked the broad, sympathetic appeal of *The Diary of Anne Frank*. Some New Yorkers thought *The Wall* too disturbing, too shocking to be an evening's entertainment. One college professor who had been in a concentration camp said, "I lived that play. It reminded me too vividly of the things I wanted to forget"; but when he was asked how he felt about *The Diary of Anne Frank,* he said, "During the play I kept calm because Mr. Frank tried to keep all the people in the attic calm, and I reacted the way they did."

The theory that man fears the danger he knows exists but cannot see, if applied to *The Diary of Anne Frank,* explains the drama's emotional impact upon audiences. The conflict is between the eight victims in hiding and their Nazi pursuers, but the enemy remains unseen. The drama achieves heightened suspense by revealing only the anguish and anxiety of the pursued as they wait, huddled together, knowing that the Nazis are on the outside and may strike at any moment. As a result, the audience shares the fears, the hopes, and the desperation of the victims. *The Wall* does not arouse this same rapport with audiences because it is broad in scope and deals with many people; *The Diary of Anne Frank* is intimate and emphasizes characterization. The audience learns the strengths and the weaknesses of the eight victims and is sympathetic when the characters reveal their frailties. The popularity of the diary in book form was based, in part, on the retelling of events by a young girl, and the same appeal carries over into the play which retains the simplicity, the blending of young emotions, and the problems of adults revealed in the book. With the exception of the opening and closing scenes, the play is Anne's story.

The original New York cast also helped make the play a long-running hit. Joseph Schildkraut dominated most of the scenes with his excellent interpretation of the patient, wise, and humble father. Audiences responded to his leadership just as the characters in the play did. Susan Strasberg made Anne wholesome, sometimes mischievous or petulant, but always appealing. Lou Jacobi effectively portrayed Mr. Van Daan, the wealthy man who could not pay his way to freedom. Equally effective were Gusti Huber as the quiet, reserved Mrs. Frank; Eva Rubinstein as Margot; Jack Gilford as Mr. Dussel; and Dennie Moore as Mrs. Van Daan. Most of the major roles, with the exception of Schildkraut's, had cast replacements long before the end of the run, but the play continued to profitable business and finally closed with a total of 717 performances.

The popularity of *The Diary of Anne Frank* was not limited to New York audiences. In other cities in the United States and in European countries, the play attracted audiences, for it was effective and emotionally sound drama and engendered sympathy for the victims hopelessly trapped in their attic. The drama was extremely effective in Germany, even though played by a non-Jewish cast. Critics who saw both the New York and German productions reported that the impact upon spectators in Germany was greater than in New York; for the stunned audiences, at the end of the play, did not applaud and left the theater silently.

In the role of narrator, Anne read selections from the diary to bridge gaps between scenes. These transitional passages in which the audience heard Anne's voice were less interesting than the action on stage. The narrator, Sakini, in *The Teahouse of the August Moon,* produced in 1953, was more effective, for he provided transitions by stepping in front of the curtain and speaking directly to the audience, and was just as delightful in his role of narrator as he was in the play itself.

In direct contrast to *The Diary of Anne Frank,* which deals with World War II realistically, *The Teahouse of the August Moon* by John Patrick deals satirically with the war and with the United States occupation of Okinawa. The drama, based on a novel by Vern Sneider, lampoons American officers, the Pentagon, geisha girls, and the Oriental custom of "saving face." The leading character, Captain Fisby, a young idealist, is sent to Tobiki to develop a rehabilitation program which includes building a schoolhouse modeled after the Pentagon. His interpreter, Sakini, an impish rogue, outwits Fisby from the very start by arranging to take natives as passengers on the journey from headquarters to the village of Tobiki and delays Fisby's scheduled arrival by more than a week.

Sakini gradually becomes aware of Fisby's sincerity and, in spite of his cunning, is sufficiently impressed to cooperate with Fisby, although he still strategically maneuvers the young captain into giving the natives their own way. The villagers bring Fisby an assortment of welcoming gifts including hand-painted lacquerware, a cricket cage for good luck, and Lotus Blossom, a geisha girl whom Fisby belatedly discovers has been a source of trouble in other military quarters. Fisby's problems multiply when the villagers, impressed by Lotus Blossom and guided by Sakini, trick him into building a teahouse for Lotus Blossom instead of a schoolhouse.

Colonel Purdy, Fisby's superior officer, hearing disturbing reports from Tobiki, sends Captain MacLean, a psychiatrist, to investigate Fisby's actions. MacLean is startled to see that Fisby has discarded his uniform and is wearing a makeshift native outfit consisting of his own bathrobe, straw slippers, and straw hat; but when Fisby begins talking about his agricultural program, MacLean, a frustrated farmer, soon becomes enchanted with the idea of staying on and conducting a series of experiments. Fisby hopes to convert Tobiki into a thriving village by having the people sell their artwork and weaving as souvenirs. His plans fail because the American

The Teahouse of the August Moon, Mariko Niki, David Wayne and
John Forsythe

occupation troops prefer to buy machine-made products at lower prices. When Fisby learns that the villagers make sweet-potato brandy, he puts through a phone call to another military base and announces that he has brandy for sale, which he calls Batata, the Haitian word for sweet potato. Tobiki becomes a prosperous village.

The thriving community soon has a beautiful teahouse aptly called The Teahouse of the August Moon, and Lotus Blossom presides over the opening festivities. At the height of the celebration, Colonel Purdy arrives to check on Fisby and MacLean and is horrified to see both officers dressed in bathrobes leading the men in a song fest. Purdy orders the teahouse and all the stills in the village destroyed.

To his dismay, Purdy later gets word that American senators, impressed by news reports, are coming to Tobiki to see the prosperous community, and in desperation, Purdy pleads with Sakini and Fisby to do what they can to restore the village to its former state. The cunning Sakini then reveals that the stills and teahouse have not been destroyed. Within minutes, the natives put the teahouse together again; Lotus Blossom begins dancing; Fisby, MacLean, and Purdy enter the teahouse; and, as they sit down to enjoy the comforts of the establishment, Sakini announces that the play has ended.

The swiftness of the ending epitomizes the appeal of the play, for it follows an old maxim in show business, "Always leave them wanting more." The play closes with the audience wishing it could see what happens when the senators arrive, how Colonel Purdy succumbs to the spell of Lotus Blossom and the teahouse, and how Sakini maneuvers another strategic plan.

John Patrick has condensed several episodes and eliminated time spans to keep the action within the limits of a three-act play. The novel dealt with two geisha girls, but Patrick has used only Lotus Blossom. The condensation is most evident when Captain MacLean succumbs almost too quickly to the spell of Tobiki and the opportunity to become an experimental farmer. The trip from headquarters to Tobiki also is cut to one short narrative passage by Sakini.

Recent political developments have somewhat dimmed the satire, for when Eisenhower visited Okinawa in 1960 and the natives greeted him with "Yankee, go home," his reception was far different from the delightful one given Captain Fisby. Army officers who had been in Okinawa, however, maintain that the vocal demonstrators constituted only a small part of the population. Furthermore, to evaluate the popular appeal of the play in 1953 in the light of subsequent political developments is similar to being a Monday morning quarterback who explains how the football coach erred in the big game on Saturday. The undercurrents of discontent may be inherent in the basic plot, but the glib charm of the novel, and particularly of the play, glosses over incidents that, under analysis, could reveal growing dissension. Americans enjoy laughing at their own foibles, but the Oriental may not appreciate this type of humor. One of the more amusing episodes, for example, is a fight staged in the teahouse. The loser, who is thrown out of the ring, is declared the winner. Fisby asks Sakini why the judges have given the wrong decision, and Sakini explains that the judges are all related to the loser, that everyone knows who really won the fight, and that the decision saves face for the loser. The whole idea is contrary to the American spirit of sportsmanship, but the incident is amusing, particularly to army men who had served in the Orient and who insist that the episode is an excellent satire on face-saving tactics.

Although *The Teahouse of the August Moon* received both the Pulitzer Prize and Critics' Circle Award in 1954, it did not receive unqualified praise from all critics. Most newspaper reviews indicated the critic's delight with the production, the acting, and the plot, but one or two dissenters, who admitted the comedy provided a delightful evening's entertainment, thought *The Teahouse of the August Moon* lacked depth. Yet this lack of depth gives the play its charm, for the satire is frothy rather than bitter, and the humor ranges from the outright gag to pure whimsey. The few serious moments are offset by hilarity. For example, when the villagers bring presents to Fisby, he asks Sakini if there is any special method of electing officers. Sakini tells him to decide who brought him the best gifts and to select his officers on that basis, but Fisby insists that this is not the democratic way. Sakini then asks him to define democracy and Fisby explains that democracy means he can write to the President and express his views if he disagrees with him. This definition puzzles the natives, who understand that he might write such a letter but they would like to know if he actually sends it. The more raucous gag is typified in the scene where MacLean and Fisby are offered a sample of Tobiki brandy but both decline to take the first drink. They decide to test it first on a goat, which Fisby has named Lady Astor, and the animal laps up the liquor with no ill effects. Lady Astor, in fact, gets one of the biggest laughs in the show.

Even the episodes which might have become bawdy emerge as wholesome amusement. Fisby, for example, thinks, as do all the American characters in the play, that geisha girls are prostitutes, and he is horrified when Sakini says they have an organization, pay dues, and have very specific duties. When Sakini explains that they are merely hostesses in teahouses and that their sole duties are to provide musical entertainment and to listen to the troubles of their patrons, Fisby apologizes for having misunderstood the situation. Then, when the villagers plead with him to build the teahouse, he agrees and the entire sequence becomes a delightful, innocent story rather than a superimposed whitewash of a burlesque skit. The misunderstanding about geisha girls, however, reoccurs when Fisby tries to explain his relationship with Lotus Blossom to Colonel Purdy, who misinterprets every statement Fisby makes.

Among the gifts Fisby receives is a cricket cage for good luck, but Sakini tells him he must catch his own cricket. At the end of the second act, when Fisby is exultant because he knows the native brandy is a product American troops will buy, he suddenly swoops down, grabs something on the floor, and announces he has caught his cricket. Good omens always bring good luck in children's stories, and the audience, familiar with this fairy-tale tradition, expects the play to end happily even though the situation appears to be dismal in the last act.

The popular appeal of the play in the 1950s was enhanced by the foreign locale which intrigued audiences who had heard returning soldiers tell romantic tales of the Far East and the loveliness of Oriental women. The drama had the same mysterious appeal for audiences that stories of the Far West had for Eastern readers in the nineteenth century. Audience interest in long-running plays dealing with the Orient, produced later in the decade, such as *The World of Suzie Wong* and *A Majority of One,* may well have been whetted by *The Teahouse of the August Moon,* the first long-running drama on Broadway dealing with American troops in the Orient.

Unlike most war plays, however, John Patrick's drama had no salty language, and no love story. Audiences did not take too seriously Lotus Blossom's protestation of love for Fisby. When Fisby said such a marriage was out of the question, Lotus Blossom immediately asked him to select a proper mate for her, and the audience already knew that Lotus Blossom had decided to marry the young man who had won the boxing match but who had been declared the loser.

A great deal of the charm is supplied by Sakini, whose comments between scenes not only help explain the play but also add touches of humor. In the last act, Sakini steps in front of the curtain and the audience hears the sound of chopping and crashing, presumably the sergeant's following of Colonel Purdy's orders to destroy all the stills, Sakini shakes his head despondently, says, "No comment," walks off stage, and gets a bigger laugh than he does in his longer speeches. Sakini's manner of calling Captain Fisby "Boss" is reminiscent of Don Marquis' *Archy and Mehitabel* stories, and Sakini's affectionate tone when he says, "Boss," is infectious.

Excellent actors in the three major roles also helped make the play popular. David Wayne gave a superb performance of Sakini, who had the wisdom of an old man and the disarming innocence of a child; John Forsythe made Captain Fisby a likable young officer who would appeal to the natives; and Paul Ford regaled audiences as the blundering, blustering Colonel Purdy. During the long run, Burgess Meredith and Eli Wallach also gave effective performances as Sakini, as did Scott McKay and John Beal in the role of Captain Fisby.

The setting by Peter· Larkin further enhanced the play. Instead of one curtain, Larkin used four bamboo panels that could be raised individually or in combinations to reveal part or all of the stage. With the exception of the scene revealing the teahouse, Larkin obtained a maximum of effect with a minimum of scenery. The simple elegance of the bamboo fit the play perfectly.

The motion picture version illustrates even more sharply the appeal of the stage play, for the Hollywood production, although beautifully photographed, depended too much upon visualization and minimized the audience's opportunity to exercise its imagination. As a result the motion picture by overemphasis failed to capture the fairy-tale lightness of the plot, the stage suggestion of opulence rather than detailed richness, the impish qualities of Sakini, the innocence of Fisby, and the cunning gracefulness of Lotus Blossom. Although the play dealt with war, politics, and army bungling, the stage production resembled a child's story told for adults with little or no realism, no profanity, no serious complexities, and no sex plot. Instead it blended fantasy, laughter, the exotic Orient, and delightful characterizations portrayed with disarming affability to keep audiences enchanted for 1,027 performances.

Rebuilding a teahouse within three minutes in *The Teahouse of the August Moon* is stage fantasy, but building *The Subject Was Roses,* produced in 1964, from a potential failure to a decided hit is reality. Frank D. Gilroy's log, *About Those Roses or How Not to Do a Play and Succeed* records his setbacks and disappointments before his play went into production and during rehearsal up to the opening night. The list of actors who turned down the play would read like a sample listing of "Who's Who in Show Business." Gilroy could now write a sequel showing how his drama, which loomed as a financial failure during its first few months on Broadway, developed into a long-running play. *The Subject Was Roses,* more than any other prize play produced since 1950, also reflects the influence of prize awards at the box office, for the preceding four plays— *Cat on a Hot Tin Roof, Look Homeward, Angel, The Diary of Anne Frank,* and *The Teahouse of the August Moon*—were all established hits before prizes were announced.

The Subject Was Roses opened inauspiciously May 25, 1964, with a low advance sale, but received generally favorable reviews. Walter Kerr, for example, prophetically stated he regretted the play had come too late to be considered for a prize. Howard Taubman called the play "honest." One critic, who liked the production, doubted whether it would have sufficient appeal to be a hit. Certainly the receipts for the first month substantiated this pessimism, for the play operated at a loss, even though the *Variety* Poll designated Mr. Gilroy as the most promising playwright to make a Broadway debut. Both Gilroy and Jack Albertson, who plays the father, have publicly expressed their thanks to the many people active in show business who paid for advertisements calling the public's attention to the show. *The Subject Was Roses* had to its advantage a production cost of less than forty thousand dollars and could operate on lower receipts than those needed for the average Broad-

The Subject Was Roses, Martin Sheen and Jack Albertson

way production. For several months the show teetered, and then it began making a profit. In September, the play moved from the Royale Theater to the Winthrop Ames, formerly the Little Theater, with a smaller seating capacity. Receipts during the first year fluctuated from week to week until the Critics' Circle awarded its prize in the spring of 1965 and the box office sales increased. The subsequent Pulitzer Prize and Tony Award for the best play of the year further bolstered receipts, which more than doubled from the weeks before prizes had been announced.

The relatively simple plot concerns three characters, John Cleary, his wife Nettie, and their son Timmy, who has just returned from the Army. The time is 1946, and the entire action spans a period of forty-eight hours. As the play begins, the Clearys appear to be affable, but Nettie's tenseness and John's belligerence soon reveal that husband and wife are estranged and that each is striving for Timmy's affection. Timmy realizes that in the past he had sided with his mother against his father. Later he blames his mother for their unhappiness, but, after watching both parents, he knows that neither is wholly to blame.

Timmy accuses Nettie of goading John and says they must both stop ganging up on him. Nettie makes no comment but takes her collection of coins, leaves the house, and does not return until late that night. Timmy and John are both upset, and, in their concern over Nettie, get into an argument. Timmy infuriates John who loses his temper and hits him. When Nettie returns, she refuses to explain where she has been other than to state that for once she has felt free. This withholding of information is contrary to the theory that audiences must understand all details if a play is to be successful. Gilroy does imply, however, that where Nettie has been is not so important as the fact that she admits she wanted to stay away but couldn't.

Timmy decides that if he is to have a happy life of his own, he must leave home. Nettie understands, admits to John that she will miss him, but refuses to comply with John's suggestion that she ask Timmy to stay. John tries to talk to Timmy, makes every effort to keep from saying the wrong thing, but loses control of his temper. Timmy says he had never heard John say he loved his son, but he also is aware that he has never told his father how he felt about him, and then says frankly and unashamedly, "I love you, Pop." John breaks down, takes his son into his arms, and little more is said. After this reconciliation, audiences may have expected Timmy to stay, but John, realizing that Timmy would be leaving soon anyway, tells Timmy he must go, knowing full well, however, that the bond of affection between father and son is strong. The ending may be disappointing, but Gilroy, by having Timmy force both parents to face the truth about themselves, enables the audience to presume that John and Nettie might possibly reach some type of compromise after Timmy has gone.

Several critics have called the characters, the plot, and the dialogue commonplace, for the Clearys are average people living unhappy lives. The dialogue, which lacks theatricality, represents everyday conversation characteristic of the people who are speaking. Gilroy makes no attempt to soar into poetic phrasing, but he also resorts to very few vulgar or earthy lines even when the Clearys give vent to their pent-up emotions.

One or two references to Catholicism and John's anger at Timmy's unwillingness to attend Mass preclude any idea of divorce and make the problem of adjustment between Nettie and John understandable to those familiar with the doctrines of the Church. By underwriting, Gilroy does not limit the problem to any one religious denomination and thus gains wider audience interest.

The play's appeal is proportionate to the identification audiences can make between themselves and the characters. Unhappily married men whose wives have prevented them from taking business gambles that would have been profitable sympathize with John, for Nettie objected to his accepting a position that later proved to be very lucrative. Children who have heard their parents quarrel day after day understand Timmy's unhappiness. Wives who feel they have married the wrong man understand Nettie's discontent.

None of the characters is blameless. Nettie's insistence upon living near her mother as well as her making plans without consulting her husband and son irritate the men in the audience as much as John and Timmy are irritated. For example, when Timmy suggests to John that they go to a baseball game, Nettie says to John, "Why don't you?" The audience thinks she is sincere, but Nettie knows John is leaving to keep a business appointment. John, however, returns and says he is grateful his son has come home safe and unharmed, that he can keep the appointment at any time, and will take Timmy to the game after all. Nettie then becomes upset and admits she has made other arrangements for Timmy that afternoon. Almost every man in the audience resents, as do Timmy and John, her maneuvering to get her own way without being entirely honest about her plans. Women would sympathize with Nettie who knows her husband has been unfaithful, but most men would understand why John has been driven to infidelity. Timmy drinks too much and oversteps his filial rights when he reprimands his parents, but he is not an insolent young rebel. He loves Nettie and John, but he also knows he cannot be happy so long as he lives with them.

The title refers to Nettie's love for roses which leads to one of the minor emotional climaxes. Timmy has bought Nettie red roses but says they came from John. Her husband's supposed thoughtfulness seems to soften Nettie but, during one of their arguments, John tells her he had nothing to do with the flowers.

With the emphasis upon characterization rather than plot, Gilroy needed superior performers to make the play convincing, and he found them in Jack Albertson, who received a Tony for his excellent performance as the hotheaded but likable Irishman, John Cleary; Irene Dailey, who portrayed the unhappy Nettie; and Martin Sheen, who proved to be an ideal choice for Timmy. In June, 1965, Martha Scott replaced Irene Dailey. By September 1, 1965, *The Subject Was Roses* had run 532 performances, making it one of the few plays produced since 1950 which survived public lethargy to become one of the ninety-nine longest-running plays on Broadway.

To predict which plays now running on Broadway will exceed the five-hundred-performance mark is mere guesswork, for cast changes, economic conditions, the arrival of new hit plays, or change in public taste may shorten runs of successful productions. At press time, *Luv* by Murray Schisgal and *The Odd Couple* by Neil Simon appear likely to run through at least one more full season. Several plays that have passed the five-hundred mark, such as *Barefoot in the Park,* may go beyond one thousand performances. With the exception of *The Subject Was Roses,* however, Broadway plays have become too costly for managements to operate at a loss for more than a very short time. For that reason, even if prices remain unchanged and present economic conditions prevail, the possibility of any production breaking the longevity record established by *Life with Father* seems very unlikely.

THE LONG RUNS

As of September 1, 1965, the following plays had run 500 or more consecutive performances:

PLAY	NO. OF PERFORM- ANCES	YEAR PRO- DUCED	AUTHORS
Life with Father	3,224	1939	Howard Lindsay and Russel Crouse, after stories by Clarence Day
Tobacco Road	3,182	1933	Jack Kirkland, after novel by Erskine Caldwell
Abie's Irish Rose	2,327	1922	Anne Nichols
Harvey	1,775	1944	Mary Coyle Chase
Born Yesterday	1,642	1946	Garson Kanin
Mary, Mary	1,572	1961	Jean Kerr
The Voice of the Turtle	1,557	1943	John Van Druten
Arsenic and Old Lace	1,444	1941	Joseph Kesselring
Angel Street	1,295	1941	Patrick Hamilton
Lightnin'	1,291	1918	Winchell Smith and Frank Bacon

PLAY	NO. OF PERFORM- ANCES	YEAR PRO- DUCED	AUTHORS
Mister Roberts	1,157	1948	Thomas Heggen and Joshua Logan
The Seven Year Itch	1,141	1952	George Axelrod
The Teahouse of the August Moon	1,027	1953	John Patrick, after novel by Vern Sneider
Never Too Late	1,007	1962	Sumner Arthur Long
Anna Lucasta	957	1944	Philip Yordan
Kiss and Tell	957	1943	F. Hugh Herbert
The Moon Is Blue	924	1951	F. Hugh Herbert
The Bat	867	1920	Mary Roberts Rinehart and Avery Hopwood
My Sister Eileen	865	1940	Joseph A. Fields and Jerome Chodorov, after stories by Ruth McKenney
White Cargo	864	1923	Leon Gordon
A Streetcar Named Desire	855	1947	Tennessee Williams
You Can't Take It with You	837	1936	George S. Kaufman and Moss Hart
Three Men on a Horse	835	1938	George Abbott and John Cecil Holm
Inherit the Wind	806	1955	Jerome Lawrence and Robert E. Lee
No Time for Sergeants	796	1955	Ira Levin, after novel by Mac Hyman
The Ladder	789	1926	J. Frank Davis
Barefoot in the Park **	777	1963	Neil Simon
State of the Union	765	1945	Howard Lindsay and Russel Crouse
The First Year	760	1920	Frank Craven
Two for the Seesaw	750	1958	William Gibson
Death of a Salesman	742	1949	Arthur Miller
The Man Who Came to Dinner	739	1939	Moss Hart and George S. Kaufman
Claudia	722	1941	Rose Franken
The Gold Diggers	720	1919	Avery Hopwood

** Still running on September 1, 1965.

PLAY	NO. OF PERFORM-ANCES	YEAR PRO-DUCED	AUTHORS
The Diary of Anne Frank	717	1955	Frances Goodrich and Albert Hackett, after *Anne Frank: The Diary of a Young Girl*
I Remember Mama	714	1944	John Van Druten, after stories by Kathryn Forbes
Tea and Sympathy	712	1953	Robert Anderson
Junior Miss	710	1941	Jerome Chodorov and Joseph A. Fields, after stories by Sally Benson
Seventh Heaven	704	1922	Austin Strong
The Miracle Worker	702	1959	William Gibson
Cat on a Hot Tin Roof	694	1955	Tennessee Williams
The Children's Hour	691	1934	Lillian Hellman
Dead End	687	1935	Sidney Kingsley
The Lion and the Mouse	686	1905	Charles Klein
Dear Ruth	683	1944	Norman Krasna
East Is West	680	1918	Samuel Shipman and John B. Hymer
Come Blow Your Horn	677	1961	Neil Simon
The Doughgirls	676	1942	Joseph Fields
Boy Meets Girl	669	1935	Bella and Samuel Spewack
Who's Afraid of Virginia Woolf?	664	1962	Edward Albee
The Women	657	1936	Clare Boothe
Blithe Spirit	657	1942	Noel Coward
The Fifth Season	654	1953	Sylvia Regan
Rain	648	1922	John Colton and Clemence Randolph, after story by W. Somerset Maugham
Witness for the Prosecution	645	1954	Agatha Christie
Any Wednesday **	643	1964	Muriel Resnik
Janie	642	1942	Josephine Bentham and Herschel Williams

** Still running on September 1, 1965.

PLAY	NO. OF PERFORM- ANCES	YEAR PRO- DUCED	AUTHORS
The Green Pastures	640	1930	Marc Connelly, after stories by Roark Bradford
Auntie Mame	639	1956	Jerome Lawrence and Robert E. Lee, after novel by Patrick Dennis
A Man for All Seasons	637	1961	Robert Bolt
The Fourposter	632	1951	Jan de Hartog
The Music Master	627	1904	Charles Klein
The Tenth Man	623	1959	Paddy Chayefsky
Is Zat So?	618	1925	James Gleason and Richard Taber
Anniversary Waltz	615	1954	Jerome Chodorov and Joseph Fields
The Happy Time	614	1950	Samuel Taylor, after book by Robert Fontaine
Separate Rooms	613	1940	Joseph Carole and Alan Dinehart in collaboration with Alex Gottleib and Edmund Joseph
Affairs of State	610	1950	Louis Verneuil
Peg o' My Heart *	603	1912	J. Hartley Manners
Broadway	603	1926	Philip Dunning and George Abbott
Street Scene	601	1929	Elmer Rice
Kiki	600	1921	Adapted from French of André Picard by David Belasco
The Two Mrs. Carrolls	585	1943	Martin Vale
Detective Story	581	1949	Sidney Kingsley
Brother Rat	577	1936	John Monks, Jr., and Fred F. Finklehoffe
The Show-Off	571	1924	George Kelly
Happy Birthday	564	1946	Anita Loos; songs by Richard Rodgers and Oscar Hammerstein II and James Livingstone; incidental music by Robert Russell Bennett
Look Homeward, Angel	564	1957	Ketti Frings, after novel by Thomas Wolfe

* Also listed as 604 or 692 in several sources.

PLAY	NO. OF PERFORM- ANCES	YEAR PRO- DUCED	AUTHORS
The Glass Menagerie	561	1945	Tennessee Williams
Strictly Dishonorable	557	1929	Preston Sturges
A Majority of One	556	1959	Leonard Spigelgass
Sunrise at Campo- bello	556	1958	Dore Schary
Toys in the Attic	556	1960	Lillian Hellman
Dial M for Murder	552	1952	Frederick Knott
Within the Law	541	1912	Bayard Veiller
What a Life	538	1938	Clifford Goldsmith
A Raisin in the Sun	538	1959	Lorraine Hansberry
The Subject Was Roses **	532	1964	Frank D. Gilroy
The Solid Gold Cadillac	526	1953	Howard Teichman and George S. Kaufman
The Boomerang	522	1915	Victor Mapes and Winchell Smith
The Best Man	520	1960	Gore Vidal
Victoria Regina	517	1935	Laurence Housman
The World of Suzie Wong	508	1958	Paul Osborn, after novel by Richard Mason
Personal Appearance	501	1934	Lawrence Riley
The Member of the Wedding	501	1950	Carson McCullers
Bird in Hand	500	1929	John Drinkwater
Sailor, Beware!	500	1933	Kenyon Nicholson and Charles Robinson
Room Service	500	1937	John Murray and Allen Boretz
Tomorrow the World	500	1943	James Gow and Arnaud d'Usseau

** Still running on September 1, 1965.

SOURCE MATERIALS

Newspaper and magazine articles, personal interviews, printed texts of plays with the exception of *Kiki* by André Picard and *The Gold Diggers* by Avery Hopwood, which are available only in typed manuscript at the New York Public Library.

Best Plays series from 1894 to 1964, edited by G. P. Sherwood and John A. Chapman (1894–99), Burns Mantle and G. P. Sherwood (1899–1919), Burns Mantle (1919–20 to 1946–47), John A. Chapman (1947–48 to 1951–52), Louis Kronenberger (1952–53 to 1959–60), Henry Hewes (1960–64). New York: Dodd, Mead.

Best Plays of the Modern American Theatre, edited by John Gassner, covering plays from 1918 to 1961 (6 vols.). New York: Crown.

Blum, Daniel C., editor, *Theatre World* (1944–45 to 1962–63). New York: Crown.

Chapman, John A., *Theatre* (annual volumes from 1953). New York: Random House.

Nathan, George J., *The Theatre Book of the Year* (from 1942–43 to 1949–50). New York: Knopf.

New York Critics Review, N. Y. Critics Reviews Inc. (from 1940 on) includes reviews from New York *Times,* New York *Mirror,* New York *Journal-American,* New York *Daily News,* New York *Post,* New York *World-Telegram and Sun,* New York *Herald Tribune.*

Variety (from 1925).

The following books have also provided source material:

Atkinson, Brooks, *Broadway Scrapbook*. New York: Theatre Arts, 1947.

Bentley, Eric, *The Playwright as Thinker*. New York: Reynal and Hitchcock, 1946.

Block, Anita, *The Changing World in Plays and Theatre*. Boston: Little, Brown, 1939.

Blum, Daniel C., *Pictorial History of the American Theater 1860–1960*. Philadelphia: Chilton, 1960.

Bradford, Roark, *Ol' Man Adam an' His Chillun*. New York: Harper, 1928.

Brown, John Mason, *Broadway in Review*. New York: Norton, 1940.

————, *Seeing Things*. New York: Whittlesey House, 1946.

————, *Seeing More Things*. New York: Whittlesey House, 1948.

————, *Two on the Aisle*. New York: Norton, 1938.

Caldwell, Erskine, *Tobacco Road*. New York: Grosset & Dunlap, 1932.

Cartmell, Van H., and Cerf, Bennett, editors, *Famous Plays of Crime and Detection*. Philadelphia: Blakiston, 1946.

Cerf, Bennett, and Cartmell, Van H., editors, *Sixteen Famous American Plays*. Garden City: Garden City, 1942.

————, *S.R.O.* Garden City: Garden City, 1944.

Churchill, Allen, *The Great White Way*. New York: Dutton, 1962.

Clark, Barrett H., and Freedley, George, editors, *A History of Modern Drama*. New York: Appleton-Century, 1947.

Downer, Alan S., *Fifty Years of American Drama, 1900–1950*. Chicago: Regnery, 1951.

Forbes, Kathryn, *Mama's Bank Account*. New York: Harcourt, Brace, 1943.

Freedley, George, and Reeves, John A., editors, *A History of the Theater*. New York: Crown, 1947.

Gagey, Edmond M., *Revolution in American Drama*. New York: Columbia University Press, 1947.

Gassner, John, *Theater at the Crossroads*. New York: Holt, 1960.

————, *The Theater in Our Times*. New York: Crown, 1954.

Gaver, Jack, *Curtain Calls*. New York: Dodd, Mead, 1949.

Green, Abel, and Laurie, Joe, Jr., *Show Biz*. New York: Holt, 1951.

Gibson, William, *The Seesaw Log*. New York: Knopf, 1959.

Gilroy, Frank D., *About Those Roses*. New York: Random House, 1965.

Hammond, Percy, *But Is It Art?* Garden City: Doubleday, 1927.

Heggen, Thomas, *Mister Roberts*. Boston: Houghton, Mifflin, 1946.

Krutch, Joseph Wood, *The American Drama Since 1918*. New York: Random House, 1939.

Lamb, Charles, *The Works of Charles Lamb,* vol. 3. Boston: Crosby, Nichols, Lee, 1930.

Langner, Lawrence, *The Play's the Thing*. New York: Putnam, 1960.

Maugham, W. Somerset, *East and West*. Garden City: Garden City, 1934.

Morehouse, Ward, *Matinee Tomorrow*. New York: Whittlesey House, 1949.

Morosco, Helen M., and Dugger, Leonard Paul, *The Oracle of Broadway*. Caldwell, Idaho: Caxton Printers Ltd., 1944.

Moses, Montrose J., and Brown, John Mason, *The American Theater as Seen by Its Critics, 1752–1934*. New York: Norton, 1934.

————, *Representative American Dramas*. Boston: Little, Brown, 1941.

Nathan, George J., *Encyclopaedia of the Theater*. New York: Knopf, 1940.

————, *The Entertainment of a Nation*. New York: Knopf, 1940.

————, *The Morning after the First Night*. New York: Knopf, 1938.

————, *The Theatre of the Moment*. New York: Knopf, 1950.

Nicoll, Allardyce, *World Drama*. London: Harrap, 1949.

O'Hara, Frank Hurlbut, *Today in American Drama*. Chicago: University of Chicago Press, 1939.

Omanney, Katharine Anne, *The Stage and the School*. New York: Harper, 1939.

Quinn, Arthur Hobson, *A History of the American Drama*. New York: Crofts, 1945.

Skinner, Richard Dana, *Our Changing Theatre*. New York: Dial Press, 1931.

Sneider, Vern, *The Teahouse of the August Moon*. New York: Signet Books, 1956.

Sobel, Bernard, *The Theatre Handbook and Digest of Plays*. New York: Crown, 1946.

Tynan, Kenneth, *Curtains*. New York: Atheneum, 1961.

Woollcott, Alexander, *Long, Long Ago*. New York: Viking Press, 1943.

Young, Stark, *Immortal Shadows*. New York: Scribner, 1948.

Zolotow, Maurice, *No People Like Show People*. New York: Random House, 1951.

INDEX

THE AUTHOR AND HIS BOOK

ABE LAUFE, *born in Pittsburgh, Pennsylvania, in 1906, received his education at the University of Pittsburgh and Columbia University. He has a Ph.D. from the University of Pittsburgh. He served in the Special Services division of the United States Army from 1942 to 1945 and was given the Legion of Merit for service upon his discharge. After the war he worked for two years as an editor in New York before returning to the University of Pittsburgh to teach. Presently an Associate Professor of English at the Cathedral of Learning, he is known especially for his courses on American musicals and dramas. A popular lecturer on the American theater for many years in western Pennsylvania—and now in Ohio, Massachusetts and New York—Mr. Laufe presents his material in a unique fashion: he combines his many humorous and little-known stories with musical examples, which he plays on the piano. He is at present preparing a second book on the theater which dissects musical hits.*

ANATOMY OF A HIT *(Hawthorn, 1966) was composed by Harry Sweetman Typesetting Corp., of South Hackensack, New Jersey, was printed by Mahony & Roese, Inc., of New York City, and bound by The Book Press, of Brattleboro, Vermont. The text type is Times Roman, which was designed originally by Stanley Morison for* The Times *of London.*

A HAWTHORN BOOK